Praise for *Employment Relations in the Shadow of R*

'WERS 2011 is an agenda-setting analysis of co
relations and employment trends. It sets out in
crash recession on UK workplaces that should g.
making and industrial relations food for thought. From stagnant w..g
contracts, WERS 2011 will certainly help shape the trade union movement's bargaining
and campaign work in the years ahead.' **Frances O'Grady, TUC General Secretary**

'*Employment Relations in the Shadow of Recession: Findings from the 2011 Workplace Employment Relations Study* offers a major contribution to employment relations. Its unique coverage of the impact of the global financial crisis on employment relations and workplaces within the UK ensures that it will become a go-to text for all policy makers, researchers and students with an interest in employment relations.' **David G. Blanchflower, Bruce V. Rauner Professor of Economics, Dartmouth College, USA**

'WERS is the definitive source of data on employment relations and it is difficult now to imagine how our understanding might have developed without it. This book provides us with an update to 2011 as well as insights – some surprising – on how the recession has shaped employment relations. It will be required reading for all HR professionals, employee representatives, policy makers, commentators and researchers with an interest in the world of work.' **Mark Beatson, Chief Economist, Chartered Institute of Personnel and Development (CIPD), UK**

'With Britain in the grip of a prolonged recession, the findings of the 2011 Workplace Employment Relations Survey have been keenly awaited. This authoritative overview and analysis is replete with insights into the variegated effects on employment relations, the responses of employers to the challenges arising and the underlying trajectory of workplace relations. It is a 'must read' for the academic and professional employment relations community.' **Paul Marginson, Professor of Industrial Relations, University of Warwick, UK**

'The new WERS offers the same authoritative account of the state of employment relations as its predecessors. This book should be required reading for HR professionals and those concerned with the development of trade union strategy. Even though the labour market has performed relatively well during the recession, WERS reveals real concerns about the extent of employee involvement in decision making and trust in senior management that must be addressed if the economy is to return to sustainable growth.' **David Coats, Director of WorkMatters Consulting and a Fellow at the Smith Institute, UK**

'This book provides a fresh, timely and highly engaging account of the state of UK workplace employment relations in the second decade of the 21st century. It uses advanced statistical techniques to render transparent the complex relationships between context, organisational structures and the conduct of management, unions and employees in contemporary workplaces. Many entrenched assumptions and arguments about the direction and character of changes in work organisations and employment relations are scrutinized and challenged in light of the economic crisis and the onset of austerity measures. The book is essential reading for policy-makers, practitioners and students of work, employment and industrial relations.' **Peter Nolan, Professor of Work and Employment Futures, University of Leicester, UK**

EMPLOYMENT RELATIONS IN THE SHADOW OF RECESSION

Findings from the 2011 Workplace Employment Relations Study

Brigid van Wanrooy
Principal Researcher, Acas

Helen Bewley
Senior Research Fellow, National Institute of Economic and Social Research

Alex Bryson
Principal Research Fellow, National Institute of Economic and Social Research

John Forth
Principal Research Fellow, National Institute of Economic and Social Research

Stephanie Freeth
Senior Research Officer, Department for Business Innovation and Skills

Lucy Stokes
Senior Research Fellow, National Institute of Economic and Social Research

and

Stephen Wood
Professor of Management, University of Leicester

First published 2013 by
PALGRAVE MACMILLAN

Palgrave Macmillan in the UK is an imprint of Macmillan Publishers Limited, registered in England, company number 785998, of Houndmills, Basingstoke, Hampshire RG21 6XS.

Palgrave Macmillan in the US is a division of St Martin's Press LLC, 175 Fifth Avenue, New York, NY 10010.

Palgrave Macmillan is the global academic imprint of the above companies and has companies and representatives throughout the world.

Palgrave® and Macmillan® are registered trademarks in the United States, the United Kingdom, Europe and other countries.

ISBN 978–1–137–27577–6   hardback
ISBN 978–1–137–27576–9   paperback

This book is printed on paper suitable for recycling and made from fully managed and sustained forest sources. Logging, pulping and manufacturing processes are expected to conform to the environmental regulations of the country of origin.

A catalogue record for this book is available from the British Library.

A catalog record for this book is available from the Library of Congress.

Typeset by MPS Limited, Chennai, India.

Printed and bound by CPI Group (UK) Ltd, Croydon, CR0 4YY

Contents

List of Figures

List of Tables

List of Boxes

Foreword

This book draws on the evidence from the 2011 Workplace Employment Relations Study (WERS). The Study is the sixth in the series and I have been proud to have chaired the 2011 WERS Steering Committee throughout the project.

The three core objectives of the Study are:

i   To map British employment relations over time;
ii   To inform policy and practice and stimulate debate;
iii To provide a comprehensive and statistically reliable database for public use.

WERS is unique in its perspective. It offers depth in its coverage of issues and breadth in terms of its robust sample. In addition, it draws on multiple perspectives – managers, employees and employee representatives – all providing accounts of the employment relationship inside the workplace. The fact that the WERS series has mapped British employment relations over time adds considerably to its value and this is especially the case for the 2011 WERS where the effect of the broader context of the economic recession was one of the central themes explored.

Although WERS plays an important role in informing government policy, it is not a Government study. It is run by a Steering Committee that includes a wide range of sponsors. These 'guardians' help to ensure the rigour of the Study and its usefulness to the sponsors and, just as importantly, its relevance to British workplaces.

The key to WERS' endurance has been the ability to adapt over time. As workplaces have evolved, so too has WERS. The topics covered by the Study have changed, reflecting transformations in the employment relations landscape and management practices. One example of this is the introduction of the employee survey in 1998, to reflect the growing interest in the experience of working life; another has been the inclusion from 1998 onwards of smaller workplaces. The 2011 study has seen the inclusion of a special suite of questions addressing managers', employees' and representatives' perspectives on the recession. In addition, great effort was expended to streamline the study so that the separate panel and cross-section elements now form one combined study, in effect, expanding the scope and breadth of data collected from workplaces that participated in the previous study in 2004.

I welcome this book as a major contribution. And so should all observers of the world of work. However, in the time-honoured tradition of the WERS series, it represents the start and not the end of data exploration. I hope that it has whetted the appetites of all those that will want to explore the whole suite of six studies. Then we can see what has happened and also *'What works at work'*.

Bill Wells
Department for Business Innovation and Skills
Chair of the 2011 WERS Steering Committee

Acknowledgements

The WERS series as a whole is the result of the combined efforts of many individuals. The conduct of the 2011 WERS is no exception, involving many people and organisations. The 2011 study is jointly sponsored by the Department for Business, Innovation and Skills (BIS), the Advisory, Conciliation and Arbitration Service (Acas), the Economic and Social Research Council (ESRC), the National Institute of Economic and Social Research (NIESR) and the UK Commission for Employment and Skills (UKCES). NIESR's involvement is made possible through funding from the Nuffield Foundation, without which this book would have not been possible.

The Steering Committee that has guided and overseen the project and advised on the content of this book consists of representatives from the sponsoring organisations, as well as the Health and Safety Executive (HSE). The members of the Steering Committee over the course of the project were Bill Wells (Chair), Vivien Brighton, Bernard Carter, Stella Yarrow, Kelly Taylor and Sumit Rahman from BIS; Gill Dix (Acas); Peter Elias, Scott Court, Claire Feary, Joanna Lake and Stephen Wood (ESRC); Aoife Ni Launaigh and Richard Garrett (UKCES); Alex Bryson and John Forth (NIESR); and Beverly Bishop and Alison Higgins (HSE). The authors of this book comprise the WERS Research Team and come from the sponsoring organisations. Although not an official member of the research team, Gill Dix played a critical role in advising the team and contributing to their work. In addition to this, Mark McConaghy led the establishment and design of the 2011 WERS in his role as Project Leader until October 2010. Hülya Hooker was a member of the research team during the design phase and made a particularly valuable contribution during fieldwork.

Conducting the fieldwork for WERS – a study of significant scope and scale – was a challenge; nevertheless it was a challenge that was met by the National Centre for Social Research (NatCen). We would like to thank the many field interviewers across Britain who visited workplaces to carry out the survey, and the core team of researchers who led the testing of the instruments, and collection and processing of the data. Martin Wood provided committed leadership of the project from start to finish and was supported by a strong team of researchers including, Kavita Deepchand, Emma Drever, Nick Gilby, Zoë Lancaster, Yvette Prestage and Sarah Tipping. At key points in the project Tracy Anderson, William O'Connor, Rachel Craig and Stuart Reeve provided valuable input. The cognitive testing of the research instruments was carried out by Debbie Collins and Meera Balarajan.

Further expert advice was provided by Susan Purdon from Bryson Purdon Social Research and Chris Skinner from the London School of Economics on the sample design and weighting. Francis Green from the Institute of Education and Mark

Beatson from the Chartered Institute of Personnel and Development provided valuable comments on the draft manuscript.

One of the keys to the success of the WERS series is the involvement of the academic community, as well as industry partners. In particular, thanks goes to Nick Bacon, Willy Brown, Andy Charlwood, Alan Felstead, Kim Hoque, John Purcell, Richard Saundry and Keith Whitfield for their academic input. Further, the following organisations played an important role in contributing to the consultation exercise and endorsing the study during fieldwork: Alliance of Sector Skills Councils, British Chamber of Commerce, British Retail Consortium, the Chartered Institute of Personnel and Development, Confederation of British Industry, EEF the manufacturing organisation, Federation of Small Business, Involvement and Participation Association (IPA), Trade Unions Congress and The Work Foundation.

Most importantly, the 2011 WERS would not have occurred without the participation of the managers, employees and employee representatives at the workplaces that were surveyed – without the time they and their colleagues volunteered, the study would not exist and a book of this kind would not be possible.

The authors write in a personal capacity and their views do not necessarily reflect those of the sponsoring bodies.

Reporting Conventions

Unless otherwise stated the results presented in this publication exclude cases where the respondent did not provide an answer (that is, they refused to provide one or were unable to express a view). The level of missing cases never exceeds 10 per cent, unless otherwise stated.

SYMBOLS WITHIN TABLES

0	Represents less than 0.5 per cent, including none.
( )	The unweighted base is between 20 and 50 observations and should be treated with caution.
–	Not applicable/No estimate available.
_	An underlined figure indicates that the difference between the 2004 and 2011 estimates is statistically significant at the 5 per cent level.

1 Introduction

Reflecting on the evidence offered by the Workplace Employment Relations Study (WERS) series, Brown et al. (2009: 354) stated categorically that 'the workplace of the early twenty-first century has changed radically from that of a quarter century earlier'. They highlighted the 'collapse of collective bargaining' and the extent of decline in union membership as key elements of this change, suggesting that they reflected 'a fundamental shift in attitudes towards individualism and away from collectivism'. In their stead have come forms of communication between management and employees that are largely reliant upon employers for their existence and effectiveness. This core change in the nature of employment relations has unfolded against an ever-changing backdrop, including the rise of white-collar workers and the feminisation of the workforce, growth in the presence of trained human resource specialists at the workplace, and a revolution in technologies. Together they have created an employment landscape which, as Brown et al. (2009: 1) noted, would have been incomprehensible to the average employee in work in 1980.

This book takes the analysis presented in Brown et al. (2009) a stage further by exploring change in employment relations between 2004 and 2011. It draws on the findings from the 2011 WERS – the sixth in the series which began in 1980 – to develop a comprehensive and nationally representative portrait of employment relations within Britain's workplaces. The central aim of the book is to assess how employment relations changed between 2004, when the last survey was conducted, and 2011, a quite exceptional period for the British economy.

The beginning of the period was marked by a buoyant phase of economic growth. Employment levels had been growing for around a decade, wages were increasing and working hours were in decline (Fitzner, 2006). However, the financial crisis of 2008 precipitated a sustained contraction in output from which the economy has yet to recover. Employment levels have proved surprisingly resilient, but workers have felt the effects in other ways, not least through the reversal of previous wage gains (Levy, 2013). In short, the economic climate between 2008 and 2011 has been particularly challenging for Britain's workplaces and their employees.

This book examines how employment relations have evolved and how workplaces and employees have fared 'in the shadow of recession'. In difficult economic times the overall efficacy of markets often becomes the main focal point of enquiry and the challenges and opportunities in the workplace – including those relating to the employment relationship – are sometimes overlooked. Yet, the way that relations at work are managed affects a vast array of economic and social outcomes and is, indeed, an important element in determining the efficacy of the labour market. The employment relationship affects how people are paid and their working conditions, which in turn impacts upon their health, well-being, and home and social lives. It also affects how workplaces respond to economic and market challenges, how they innovate, their productivity and competitiveness, and ultimately whether they survive and prosper.

WERS links responses from workplace managers, employee representatives and individual employees in over 2,500 workplaces to provide an integrated picture of the state of employment relations in Britain in 2011. The study is particularly well placed to indicate how workplaces have responded to the economic downturn and how working practices have been affected. The primary analysis of the study began with the publication of 'first findings' around six months after fieldwork was completed (van Wanrooy et al., 2013). This volume represents a second, more substantial contribution.

THE ECONOMIC, LABOUR MARKET AND POLITICAL CONTEXT 2004–11

The purpose of this book is to quantify the extent of change in the employment relations landscape between 2004 and 2011 and to explore employees' experiences within this. To provide some background for this analysis, an overview is provided of the main changes to the economic, social, and political landscape over this period.

The Economy and the Labour Market

In discussing the economic context for the period 2004–11 it is appropriate to consider events within two distinct phases, separated by the onset of recession in mid-2008. Until 2008 the British economy had enjoyed almost 15 years of sustained economic growth. In the years leading up to the 2004 WERS, the economy was growing at around 3 per cent per year and it continued to grow at this rate for a further three years after the 2004 survey. Inflation rates were low and on target, the currency was strong and employment levels were rising. In 2008, three quarters of the working age population were in employment and the unemployment rate had been consistently below 6 per cent for around nine years.

Growth in employment and low levels of unemployment brought gains for many workers. Average real wages had been growing since the mid-1990s (Gregg and Wadsworth, 2011: 17). The increase in work intensification seen in the 1990s had halted (Green, 2011); perceptions of job security had increased among employees (Fitzner, 2006); the share of temporary jobs had fallen slightly; and job tenure was rising (Faggio et al., 2011).

Low wage workers continued to be aided by the National Minimum Wage, which had helped to arrest the widening of the earnings gap at the lower end of the distribution, although shifts in demand in favour of higher skilled workers meant that inequality in earnings continued to rise at the top (Machin, 2011). The gender gap in employment rates continued to close, while the gender wage gap also fell (Bovil, 2013). Net migration increased the diversity of the labour force, while rising employment rates among older people contributed to an ageing of the workforce. The proportion of all employees belonging to trade unions fell but at a considerably slower rate than had been seen in the previous two decades (Brownlie, 2012).

The second quarter of 2008, however, brought the beginning of a deep and protracted fall in output. The economy contracted more than at any time since the depression of the 1930s with five consecutive quarters of negative growth. After a rally in 2010, the economy stagnated again in 2012, and at the time of writing, output was not expected to return to its pre-recession level for some time. While the private sector bore the brunt of the downturn in the early stages, the consequent impact on public finances led the Chancellor of the Exchequer to announce substantial cuts to public expenditure beginning in 2010.

The impact of the recession on gross output had been much stronger than the impact on employment. Whereas the unemployment rate had averaged almost 8 per cent since the onset of recession, Gregg and Wadsworth (2011) estimated that a proportionate employment response to the fall in output would have led to the loss of an additional one million jobs. These divergent outcomes led to falling productivity and prompted a variety of explanations, including the potential importance of welfare to work policies, low interest rates, a fall in real wages and the relatively healthy levels of profitability among firms when recession began.

On wages, there were concerted attempts at moderation, for example, in the public sector where – despite the protests of trade unions – headline pay levels for all except the lowest paid workers were frozen in 2011–12 and 2012–13. More generally, the period since the onset of recession has seen a fall in real wages across the entire economy (Office for National Statistics, 2012a: 4). This is in marked contrast to the recession of the early 1990s, when wages continued to rise faster than prices. The number of part-time employees has also risen since the onset of recession (as it did during the 1990s) and there is some evidence of under-employment, for example, in relation to desired working hours and the mismatch between jobs, skills and qualifications (Bell and Blanchflower, 2013). The broad implication is that, within the workplace, there has been a greater level of accommodation to the changing environment than might have been expected. In some cases this has involved efforts to limit job cuts. However, in contrast to the 1980s, this has been done without a programme of state-funded short-time working (as was adopted in some other countries such as Germany) and without direct state subsidies, other than to specific parts of the finance sector.

Indeed the suggestions made early on during the recession were that – with the adjustments mentioned previously put to one side – the changes taking place have not involved a systematic transformation of work and employment practices within the workplace (Brown and Reilly, 2009; Incomes Data Services, 2009; Lambert, 2010). This has some echoes of the experience that has been documented in Ireland (Roche and Teague, 2013), where unemployment more than doubled, output fell 11 per cent between 2007 and 2009, and there were substantial reductions in average weekly earnings in real terms in both the public and private sectors. The main focus of Irish employers, in navigating the recession, was deemed to have been on the maintenance of pre-recession employment arrangements (op. cit. p.18). Throughout the period, employment relations were judged to have remained orderly and changes were typically small scale and defensive, with Roche and Teague not having identified comprehensive shifts either in favour of cost reduction or in favour of engendering high employee commitment. However, one of the effects of the recession in Ireland has been a notable increase in work pressure among employees (Russell and McGinnity, 2013).

An important feature of the 2011 WERS is that it will provide a unique insight into how the recession affected Britain's workplaces and employees. Official statistics on sectoral output and employment would lead one to expect a more extensive impact in manufacturing, construction and finance than in other parts of the private sector. In the public sector, one might expect a more extensive effect on central and local government, than in health where spending has been largely protected, or in education where employment levels have remained relatively stable. But WERS allows us to go beyond these broad sectoral patterns to understand which workplaces were most or least affected, what types of actions managers took in response, to what extent these actions were subject to consultation with employees, and how employees' experience of work changed as a result of the recession.

The Political Context

For a large part of 2004–11 New Labour were in government, having held three terms between 1997 and 2010, after which a Coalition of the Conservative and Liberal Democrats parties took office. The Labour governments' approach to labour law attempted to counterbalance the previous Conservative governments' focus on enhancing the flexibility and competitiveness of the economy with increasing fairness for individual workers (Davies and Freedland, 2007). Their legislative programme can be viewed in three phases that broadly correspond to their three parliamentary terms in office (1997–2001; 2001–05; 2005–10). The initial phase was dominated by the 'Fairness at Work' legislative programme that included the creation of a National Minimum Wage, a statutory trade union recognition procedure, rights to request flexible working, and expanding anti-discrimination laws. Such changes were largely framed in the continued expansion of individual employment rights. Following this was a period of bedding down the changes with some amendments to these laws: for example, provisions for unfair labour practices were included in the statutory union recognition procedure, and age was added to anti-discrimination legislation. By the Labour government's third term the emphasis was on a non-regulatory approach to further innovations which included, among other things, conducting reviews on topics such as dispute resolution, worker well-being and employee engagement, to influence debate as well as policy development (Gibbons, 2007; Black, 2008; MacLeod and Clarke, 2009).

In addition to these developments both the Labour and Coalition governments continued to comply with European Union Directives. Under the Labour government the Information and Consultation of Employees (ICE) Regulations 2004 was introduced which – after a phased implementation – gave employees in organisations with 50 or more workers the right to be informed and consulted over certain workplace changes. The Agency Workers Regulations 2010 came into force in 2011 under the Coalition government. Negotiated under the previous Labour government, it entitled agency workers to be treated equally with comparable permanent employees, with regards to basic employment conditions, after an agency worker has spent 12 weeks in a given job.

Both the Labour and Coalition governments have been concerned with 'better regulation'. This focus was first articulated by the Conservative government of the 1980s, not least through the establishment of the Deregulation Unit (renamed the Better Regulation Unit in 1997 when Labour entered office). The distinction in approach of the Coalition government is its emphasis on reducing the number of regulations by way of the 'Red Tape Challenge' that closely scrutinises regulation at the point of implementation (see BIS, 2011a). By the time the 2011 WERS field-work was completed in June 2012, the Coalition government had been in term for just over two years. In this time they had removed the default retirement age, changed the unfair dismissal qualifying period from one to two years and instituted the Agency Workers Regulations. However, other changes, such as reforms to the Employment Tribunal system and the extension of the right to request flexible working, were subject to ongoing consultation at the time the survey was conducted.

THE 2011 WORKPLACE EMPLOYMENT RELATIONS STUDY

The survey population for the 2011 WERS was all workplaces in Britain that had five or more employees. The survey covered the private and public sectors, and all industries except that of Agriculture, forestry and fishing, and Mining and quarry-ing. A workplace is defined in WERS as comprising 'the activities of a single employer at a single set of premises'; a branch of a high street bank, a factory, the head office of a large firm and a local council's town hall, for example, are all considered to be workplaces in their own right.

The overall population represented by the 2011 WERS comprised around 750,000 workplaces that together employed around 23.3 million employees. This population accounted for one third of all Britain's workplaces and around 90 per cent of all employees in 2011. Some of the key features of this population are indicated in Table 1.1 (workplaces) and Table 1.2 (employees), using data from WERS. There were some small changes between 2004 and 2011, reflecting changes in the broader economy and labour market. For the most part, however, the profile of these populations in 2011 was very similar to that at the time of the 2004 survey, with the exception that there has been a notable increase in employees' qualifications.

Fieldwork for the 2011 WERS was carried out between March 2011 and June 2012. Face-to-face interviews, which averaged 90 minutes in length, were conducted with the most senior manager with responsibility for employment relations, human resources or staff at the workplace. Prior to the interview a self-completion ques-tionnaire was given to the respondent to determine the profile of the workforce. After the interview, management respondents in the private sector and in trading public sector corporations were given a second self-completion questionnaire on the financial performance of the workplace.[1]

Where a management interview was conducted, face-to-face interviews were sought with one union and one non-union employee representative, where present.

Table 1.1 *Workplace size, industry sector and ownership, 2004 and 2011, column per cent*

	Percentage of workplaces		Percentage of employment	
	2004	**2011**	**2004**	**2011**
Workplace size				
5–9 employees	44	44	10	10
10–19 employees	25	26	11	11
20–49 employees	20	18	19	17
50–99 employees	6	6	13	14
100–499 employees	4	4	28	27
500 or more	1	1	20	21
Industry (SIC 2003)				
Manufacturing	11	10	15	11
Electricity, gas and water	(0)	0	(1)	0
Construction	6	5	4	3
Wholesale and retail trade	25	25	17	15
Hotels and restaurants	9	9	6	6
Transport and communications	4	5	6	7
Financial services	4	(2)	5	(4)
Other business services	16	18	14	17
Public administration	2	2	6	7
Education	5	6	9	11
Health and social work	11	12	13	14
Other community services	7	7	5	4
Sector of ownership				
Private sector	88	88	76	76
Public sector	12	12	24	24

Base: All workplaces with five or more employees.
Figures are based on responses from 2,295 (2004) and 2,680 (2011) workplace managers.

Union representative interviews were conducted with the most senior representative of the largest recognised union or, if there was no recognised union, with the most senior representative of the largest non-recognised union. Non-union representative interviews were conducted with the most senior non-union representative sitting on the workplace's Joint Consultative Committee (JCC) or, if there was no JCC, a stand-alone non-union representative who acted on behalf of employees at the workplace. Worker representative interviews lasted 30 minutes on average.

Finally, a self-completion questionnaire was distributed to 25 randomly selected employees at the workplace.[2] Workplace managers and employee representatives were asked to act primarily as informants about their workplace, and so the vast majority of the data collected in those interviews related to the features of the sampled workplace rather than to the particular characteristics of the individual respondent or their personal viewpoints. In contrast, the Survey of Employees focused primarily on employees' own characteristics, experiences and attitudes.

In 2011, the workplace sample consisted of (i) a cross-section of workplaces that were surveyed for the first time in 2011 (randomly selected from the

Table 1.2 *Characteristics of employees, 2004 and 2011, column per cent*

	2004	2011
Gender		
Male	51	49
Female	49	51
Age		
Less than 30 years	23	21
30–49 years	50	49
50 or more years	26	30
Ethnicity		
White	93	91
Mixed, Asian, Black, Other	7	9
Academic qualification		
None	17	15
Below A-levels	42	40
A-levels	15	13
Degree or higher	26	32
Occupation		
Managers and senior officials	12	15
Professionals	11	13
Associate professionals and technical	15	17
Administrative and secretarial	17	16
Skilled trades	8	6
Personal service	7	8
Sales and customer service	9	7
Process, plant and machine operatives	9	7
Elementary occupations	12	13

Base: All employees in workplaces with five or more employees.
Figures are based on responses from at least 22,345 (2004) and 21,835 (2011) employees.

Inter-Departmental Business Register or IDBR) and (ii) a panel of workplaces that had been surveyed in 2004 and met the criteria to be surveyed again in 2011. A design innovation of the 2011 WERS was that workplaces in the panel sample, in addition to the cross-section, were invited to participate in all four components of the study. The majority of panel workplaces therefore provided comparative data from workplace managers, employee representatives and employees in both 2004 and 2011 (although not necessarily from the same individuals). Accordingly, weights have been devised that enable the panel sample to be combined with the cross-section sample to form a sample that is cross-sectionally representative of all workplaces in 2011.

The basis of the analysis in the book is representative data from 2,680 workplaces in 2011 and 2,295 workplaces in 2004 (Table 1.3). These workplaces provided data for a total of 1,002 worker representatives (984 in 2004) and 21,981 employees (22,451 in 2004). Data is available for 989 panel workplaces. In these cases, survey responses from 2011 can be directly compared with survey responses collected from the same workplace in 2004 in order to assess the extent to which practices, behaviours and experiences have changed in workplaces that continued to operate through the intervening period.

Table 1.3 *Response for the 2004 and 2011 WERS instruments*

	Survey of Managers		Survey of Worker Representatives		Survey of Employees	
	Number	Response rate (%)	Number	Response rate (%)	Number	Response rate (%)
2004 Cross-section sample	2,295	64	984	77	22,451	61
2011 Cross-section sample (combining panel and refreshment)	2,680	46	1,002	64	21,981	54
2011 Refreshment sample	1,691	43	570	63	13,160	53
2011 Panel sample	989	52	432	66	8,821	56

Base: All workplaces with five or more employees.

The overall workplace response rate of 46 per cent in 2011 was lower than the 64 per cent achieved in 2004 and can be attributed to both the difficult economic climate and a general long-term decline in response to business and social surveys. Response rates were also lower in 2011 than in 2004 for the Survey of Worker Representatives and the Survey of Employees, although the differences were smaller in these cases. The response rates for WERS remain highly creditable, given the prevailing environment and the large scale, complexity and richness of the survey.

Weights that account for variations in the probability of selection and observable non-response biases have been devised to bring the profiles of the achieved samples of workplaces and employees into line with the profiles of the respective populations. The approach for detecting and adjusting for non-response biases was necessarily extended in 2011, in view of the lower response rate. In order to optimise the validity of the 2004–11 comparisons presented in this book, a revised set of 2004 weights has been derived using the same approach to non-response adjustment as was adopted for the 2011 data. Some of the 2004 estimates cited in this book will therefore differ from those previously published elsewhere, although the impact of the revised weights is generally very small. Further details about the survey methodology are provided in the Technical Appendix.

STRUCTURE AND CONTENT OF THE BOOK

This book adopts a similar approach to its immediate predecessor (Kersley et al., 2006) in that it seeks to examine change in employment relations between the current and previous survey, locating this in a broader socio-economic and political context. However, one noteworthy departure is that the recession provides a strong backdrop to the analysis, and the book then has a more consistent theme than has tended to be evident in previous books in the series (for example, Kersley et al.,

2006; Cully et al., 1999). Like its predecessor, the current volume also does not attempt to chart longer-term patterns, as in Millward et al. (2000) and Brown et al. (2009). Instead the analysis focuses on the comparison between 2004 and 2011, although the longer-term trajectory typically forms part of the broader narrative. The following provides an outline of the contents of the book.

Chapter 2 begins the assessment of what it means to be 'in the shadow of recession'. It examines how markets for products and services changed in the recession. It also considers managers' assessments of the direct impact of the recession on their workplaces and employees' reports of the impact of the recession on their jobs. The insights gained from managers and employees come from questions that were specially designed for the purpose in the 2011 survey. Subsequent chapters look at the broader changes in employment relations between 2004 and 2011, before the impact of the recession on workplaces and employees is subject to further examination in Chapter 9.

Chapter 3 examines change in the nature of employment between 2004 and 2011. It looks in particular at workplace closure, the characteristics of new workplaces and the extent to which employment levels changed in workplaces that continued to operate through the period. The chapter also outlines the ways in which labour is deployed, through the use of arrangements for numerical and functional flexibility, and whether this changed during the recession.

Chapter 4 then goes inside the workplace to look at the ways in which managers approach organisational change. The chapter investigates who has day-to-day responsibility for personnel and employment relations issues at the workplace and examines variations in these managers' attitudes towards consultation over workplace change. It also assesses the extent to which workers have mechanisms for articulating their views on workplace issues. The chapter then goes on to investigate the extent to which employees were involved in shaping changes at the workplace.

Chapter 5 turns to the determination of pay and conditions, including the role of unions in negotiating pay and conditions, the scope of the negotiations and the outcomes of the pay determination process. Other aspects of rewards and pay setting are also examined, including fringe benefits, performance pay and performance appraisals. The chapter concludes with the role of the recession in pay outcomes, most notably pay freezes.

Chapter 6 examines a variety of aspects of job quality in Britain. It considers a range of issues, including work intensity, job control, skill utilisation, safety and job security, and whether the recession has led to a deterioration in job quality. The chapter also considers the extent to which job quality is determined by the workplace in which an employee is located, rather than simply by their occupation.

Chapter 7 focuses on employees' well-being. It considers the role of job quality in determining levels of well-being for employees, before going on to examine how levels of well-being have changed between 2004 and 2011.

Chapter 8 explores the employment relations climate in British workplaces, and whether it has deteriorated since 2004. It uses a range of measures in order to assess whether levels of discontent in the workplace have changed over time. The chapter also examines the prevalence of procedures for resolving disputes in the workplace.

Chapter 9 returns to focus on the experiences of workplaces and employees in the recession. It goes beyond the descriptive analysis presented in Chapter 2 to examine in more detail which types of employees were affected by recession-induced changes at the workplace. It also uses the panel survey to identify particular employment relations practices that were associated with better or worse outcomes from the recession.

Chapter 10 concludes the book by drawing together some of the key themes underlying the book; in particular, it explores the role that both government policy and the recession has played in shaping employment relations in Britain post-2008.

Nature of the Analysis

The primary focus of the book is to provide a mapping of the 2011 results in comparison to those from 2004, where consistent measures apply. Analysis in the main publication of the 2004 WERS data (Kersley et al., 2006) concentrated on workplaces with ten or more employees to enable comparisons with the 1998 survey; however, this book includes all workplaces surveyed.[3]

The primary data sources used in the book are the Survey of Managers and the Survey of Employees. The Survey of Worker Representatives is used to a lesser extent. Most reporting on the Survey of Managers relates to the population of workplaces. These estimates are heavily influenced by the characteristics of small workplaces, which account for the majority of the workplace population (see Table 1.1). However, some estimates from the Survey of Managers have been weighted to reflect the distribution of employment, which is more concentrated in larger workplaces. Instances in which the data from the Survey of Managers have been weighted by employment are clearly marked.

The survey estimates presented in the book are based on weighted data so that one can extrapolate from the survey to the population from which it was drawn. Like other sample surveys, however, WERS is subject to sampling errors whereby the results computed from the sample provide only an estimate of the true figure within the population as a whole. It is possible to quantify the degree of error through the calculation of standard errors and confidence intervals. For ease of reading, these are not reported within the text, which reports estimates as if they were exact. However, the Technical Appendix to this book includes tables which allow the reader to approximate standard errors for various percentages, based on average design effects, for both the 2011 cross-section and 2004–11 panel estimates. Where differences or associations are highlighted in the text, these have all been tested and are statistically significant at the 5 per cent level. In tables that compare 2004 and 2011, an underline is used to identify estimates that differ to a statistically significant extent between the two years.

The analyses presented in this book are, in the main, cross-tabular in nature. However, multivariate analyses have been conducted on occasion to identify the independent association between two variables, while holding other variables constant.

2 In the Shadow of Recession

INTRODUCTION

Recessions are periods of sustained contractions in a nation's aggregate output. They originate in negative economic shocks which result in a reduction in consumer demand and a consequent decline in production and sales. The economic recession that began in 2008 has been the most severe downturn the British economy has experienced since the 1930s. It began with a worldwide financial crisis that hit the banking sector directly, but which subsequently impacted upon credit flows to the rest of the economy. Allied to this was a crisis in public finances, exacerbated by the costs of bank bailouts, increased public spending and falling tax revenues.

Some of the implications of the recession for aggregate output and employment were outlined in Chapter 1. But what did the recession look and feel like from a workplace perspective, and how did it affect workplaces and the employees working within them? At the time when the 2011 WERS fieldwork was conducted, between March 2011 and June 2012, the 2008 financial crisis was still fresh in the minds of managers and employees alike. There were no signs of a sustained recovery in the private sector and the Government had embarked on a programme of public sector austerity. The timing of fieldwork, therefore, presented a unique opportunity to examine how workplaces experienced and responded to this recessionary period.

This chapter embarks on the assessment of what it means for workplaces to be 'in the shadow of recession'. It begins by looking at the private sector, using managers' testimony to establish how markets for products and services changed in the recession. The second part of the chapter looks more broadly at the private and public sectors, and examines managers' assessments of the direct impact of the recession on their workplaces and jobs. The third and final part of the chapter again covers both the private and public sectors, and presents employees' reports of the impact of the recession on their terms and conditions of employment. The insights on the recession gained from managers and employees come from questions that were specially designed for this purpose in the 2011 survey.

The chapter therefore focuses explicitly on the impact of the recession on Britain's workplaces. Subsequent chapters take a broader look at the changes in employment relations between 2004 and 2011 (Chapters 3–8), but refer back to the survey items discussed here when seeking to evaluate what role, if any, the recession may have played in influencing employment relations over the period.

The impact of the recession on workplaces and employees is then subject to more detailed examination in Chapter 9.

Throughout the chapter, an important distinction is made between the effects of recession in the private and public sectors. There are at least four reasons for doing so. First, the public sector is not exposed to the market in the same way as the private sector. While a minority of state-owned workplaces do operate in market environments, and many others operate in increasingly marketised settings, there remains a fundamental distinction between the nature of much economic activity in the public and private sectors of the economy. Second, in some respects the public sector may be seen as one large employer. Although it is clearly differentiable along dimensions such as local authorities, health and education, many of which have considerable autonomy from central government, there remain opportunities for intervention by central government, not least through its control of resources. The same features are seen in multi-site organisations within the private sector, but the scale of the public sector sets it apart. Third, in stark contrast to the private sector, significant areas of the public sector remain heavily unionised and unions remain at the heart of setting pay and conditions, either through collective bargaining or Independent Pay Review Bodies. This is likely to have implications – which could be positive or negative – for public sector employers' ability to make rapid changes in response to the crisis. Fourth, the 'recession' took on a different form in the public sector. The period of public sector budget cuts associated with the curb on public finances began somewhat later than the downturn in demand that was experienced in the private sector. It also had particular ramifications, leading directly to the imposition of new terms and conditions on large numbers of employees across many parts of the public sector. For all these reasons there is merit in treating the public sector differently to the private sector in the analyses in this chapter.

There is, of course, also variation within both the public and private sectors. While data from the Office of National Statistics (ONS) and elsewhere has indicated how different parts of the economy were affected, WERS is the only data source able to uncover the experiences of individual workplaces. This proves to be important because the extent to which workplaces and employees were affected by the recession differs substantially within, as well as between, industries.

HOW DID THE RECESSION AFFECT PRIVATE SECTOR MARKETS?

The discussion of the workplace experience begins by considering how the recession affected the markets in which private sector workplaces were operating. Workplace managers were asked a range of questions about the market for their main product or service. A comparison between 2004 and 2011 in managers' perceptions of the market conditions they faced provides a unique insight into the way in which workplaces were affected by the recession.[1]

In fact, there was little change on most market measures. In both 2004 and 2011, around three fifths of private sector workplaces faced 'Many competitors' (six or more) in the market for their main good or service (62 per cent in 2004 and 60 per cent in 2011). Nearly four in ten operated in a market where the degree of competition was 'Very high' (39 per cent in 2004 and 35 per cent in 2011). Almost half (48 per cent in 2004 and 47 per cent in 2011) operated in a market that was primarily 'Local' (within one hour's drive) while around one in ten (11 per cent in either year) were operating in an 'International' market. The proportion that faced competition from overseas-based suppliers had not changed significantly either, standing at around one quarter (26 per cent in 2004 and 22 per cent in 2011). The UK market share of the company to which the workplace belonged also saw no substantive change on average. The percentage of workplaces with a market share of less than 5 per cent remained at around three fifths (57 per cent in 2004 and 59 per cent in 2011). At the other end of the spectrum, the percentage with a market share of over 50 per cent remained at around one in ten (11 per cent in 2011 and 10 per cent in 2004).[2]

However, there was one dimension on which there was considerable change: this related to the state of the market the workplace operated in. Managers were asked, 'Looking at this list, which of these statements best describes the current state of the market in which you operate … The market is: Growing; Mature; Declining; Turbulent.' The percentage of workplaces operating in a 'Growing' market fell from nearly one half (48 per cent) in 2004 to one third (32 per cent) in 2011, as shown in Figure 2.1. Some of this was due to an increase in the percentage operating in a 'Declining' market, but for the most part it was due to an increase in the percentage operating in a 'Turbulent' market – this rose twofold from 17 per cent in 2004 to 34 per cent in 2011.

Figure 2.1 relates to all workplaces surveyed in either 2004 or 2011, and so gives a snapshot of the market conditions facing those private sector workplaces

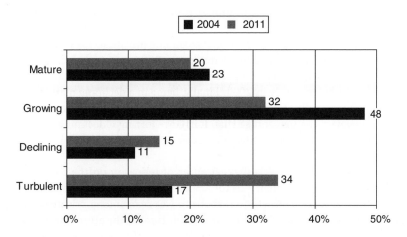

Figure 2.1 *State of the market for main product or service, 2004 and 2011, column per cent*

Base: All trading private sector workplaces with five or more employees. Figures are based on responses from 1,582 (2004) and 1,734 (2011) workplace managers.

Table 2.1 *Change in the state of the market for the main product or service, 2004–11, column per cent*

	Growing	**Turbulent**	**Declining**
Both 2004 and 2011	13	6	3
2011 only	<u>11</u>	<u>33</u>	<u>15</u>
2004 only	36	11	8
Neither 2004 nor 2011	40	50	75

Notes: An underline indicates that the difference between the figures in the row labelled '2011 only' is statistically significant from those in the row labelled '2004 only'.
Base: All private trading sector workplaces with five or more employees surveyed in 2004 and 2011. Figures are based on responses from 573 workplace managers.

that were in existence in either year. However, the broad patterns were equally apparent among the subset of workplaces that had been in operation throughout the period 2004–11, confirming that increasing turbulence was a tangible experience of workplaces that lived through the recessionary period.[3] The proportion of these workplaces operating in a 'Growing' market fell from 50 per cent in 2004 to 24 per cent in 2011, while the proportion operating in a 'Turbulent' market rose from 17 per cent in 2004 to 39 per cent in 2011. Going further, the first column of Table 2.1 shows that only 13 per cent of trading private sector workplaces reported that their market was growing in both 2004 and 2011. Another two in five (40 per cent) did not report a growing market in either year. The remainder had switched status, with over one third (36 per cent) stating that their market was growing only in 2004 (and not in 2011), while 11 per cent stated that it was growing only in 2011. The proportion of continuing workplaces in the trading private sector that stopped reporting growth therefore exceeded the proportion that began to report growth by 25 percentage points.

Conversely, the proportion of continuing workplaces that began reporting turbulence was some 22 percentage points higher than the proportion that stopped reporting turbulence. One third (33 per cent) of trading private sector workplaces in the panel were not facing a turbulent market in 2004, but were facing such market conditions by 2011. This compared with 11 per cent of workplaces who reported market turbulence only in 2004. Finally, being in a declining market was a less common event, only affecting one quarter (25 per cent) of workplaces at some point. However, the percentage that started reporting a declining market outweighed the percentage reporting the end of a declining market by seven percentage points.

This heterogeneity in workplaces' experiences of recession on their markets partly reflects the different industry sectors in which workplaces were operating. The greatest transition from growth to turbulence was seen among private sector workplaces in Construction, Wholesale and retail trade, Education and Other community services. These sectors were unique in that the proportion of panel workplaces reporting an end to growth over the period 2004–11 exceeded the proportion reporting growth for the first time, and the proportion reporting the onset of turbulence exceeded the proportion reporting that it had ended.[4]

These findings give a very clear impression of deteriorating market conditions characterised by an increase in market turbulence. However, they also indicate that experiences differed markedly across workplaces. Despite the prevailing conditions, around one third of all trading private sector workplaces reported that they were operating in a growing market in 2011 (Figure 2.1), and around one in ten of those workplaces that had continued to operate between 2004 and 2011 reported the onset of growth in their main market over this period (Table 2.1).

WERS does not collect equivalent information for public sector workplaces. The closest equivalent to the market conditions faced by a workplace in the private sector might be a measure of the change in resources allocated to individual workplaces in the public sector. While there is no workplace level indicator in WERS, the broad trend is well known, with expenditure on public services rising between 2004–05 and 2009–10, before the 2010 Spending Review signalled the onset of substantial cuts. Yet, as in the private sector, these changed conditions have not affected all parts of the public sector equally, with the NHS broadly protected, and spending on Education affected to a lesser extent than many areas of Local Government (Crawford et al., 2011).

Looking across the private and public sectors then, it is clear that market conditions have changed in notable ways between 2004 and 2011. Moreover, the changes have varied – sometimes considerably – between different workplaces. In order to further examine the role of recession and its impact on individual workplaces, we turn to survey questions which sought directly to establish how workplaces had been impacted by the economic downturn.

WHICH WORKPLACES WERE MOST AFFECTED BY THE RECESSION?

There are potentially a number of ways to measure the impact of recession on workplaces. Metrics might include profits, sales growth, employment levels and, in the extreme, workplace closure. Workplace closure and employment levels are both discussed in the next chapter. The advantage of designing surveys, however, is that one can obtain direct assessments of the impact of recession from respondents inside the workplace. These provide an overall impression of the effects of recession, potentially capturing aspects of the effect that might not be immediately apparent from looking at separate isolated measures of performance.

Workplace managers were asked, 'Can you tell me to what extent your workplace has been adversely affected by the recent recession?' There was considerable variation among the responses, ranging from one fifth (19 per cent) of workplaces saying they were affected 'A great deal' through to one tenth (11 per cent) saying they had suffered 'No adverse effect'. One quarter (24 per cent) were affected 'Quite a lot', another quarter (27 per cent) said they had been affected 'A moderate amount' and one sixth (18 per cent) had been affected 'Just a little'.

The degree to which workplaces were affected by the recession varied according to industry. To aid comparability with official statistics, managers' responses are weighted by the number of employees at the workplace in Figure 2.2 and reveal a cross-industry pattern that is broadly consistent with statistics on industry output and employment for the period since the onset of recession.[5] Both sets of data show that Manufacturing, Construction, Financial services and Public administration were among the hardest hit. However, a wide range of experiences *within* industry is also evident from the WERS responses. Each sector shown in Figure 2.2 – with the exception of Electricity, gas and water – had at least one third of its workforce in workplaces that were affected 'A great deal' or 'Quite a lot' and at least one sixth of its workforce in workplaces that experienced little or no effect from the recession.

The previous section described the changes in market conditions that were experienced at workplace level. These changes can be shown to be associated with the impact of recession. In Table 2.2 there is a strong association between the onset of market turbulence and the degree to which the workplace was adversely affected by the recession. Around two fifths (43 per cent) of the panel workplaces surveyed in 2004 and 2011 who were affected a great deal by the recession reported the onset of market turbulence between 2004 and 2011, compared with just 7 per cent of those for whom the recession had no effect. Similarly, those who were most affected by recession were more likely than those who were least affected to stop reporting that their market was growing.

In order to look in more detail at the types of workplaces that were most affected by the recession a multivariate analysis was conducted. The analysis used the panel of workplaces surveyed in both 2004 and 2011, and sought to identify whether

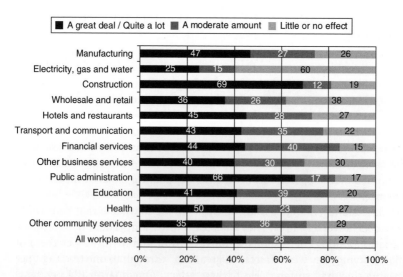

Figure 2.2 *Extent to which the workplace was adversely affected by the recession, weighted by employment, 2011, row per cent*

Base: All employment in workplaces with five or more employees. Figures are based on responses from 2,665 workplace managers.

Table 2.2 *Change in state of the market and adverse effect of the recession, 2004–11, column per cent*

	Adverse effect of the recession				
	A great deal	**Quite a lot**	**Moderate**	**A little**	**None**
Turbulent					
Both 2004 and 2011	10	9	5	0	5
2011 only	43	43	28	20	7
2004 only	7	15	10	8	14
Neither 2004 nor 2011	41	33	57	72	74
Growing					
Both 2004 and 2011	8	5	20	17	27
2011 only	3	5	10	19	38
2004 only	42	40	34	36	18
Neither 2004 nor 2011	47	50	36	28	18

Base: All private sector trading workplaces with five or more employees surveyed in 2004 and 2011. Figures are based on responses from 101 (column 1), 177 (column 2), 151 (column 3), 91 (column 4) and 52 (column 5) workplace managers.

there were any independent associations between the characteristics of workplaces in 2004 and the degree to which workplaces proved vulnerable to the recession.[6] The analysis follows Geroski and Gregg (1997) who undertook a similar investigation after the recession of the early 1990s using a survey of private sector firms. They found that it was, in fact, 'hard to predict who gets into trouble in recession' (1997: 67), adding that 'all of the pre-recession characteristics of firms that we have examined together make an extremely unimpressive contribution to explaining the incidence of vulnerability across firms'. Our analysis is somewhat more informative, as we do identify some types of workplaces that were more likely to be affected than others. However, in common with Geroski and Gregg's earlier investigation, there remains a great deal of variability that is unexplained.

In the private sector, foreign-owned workplaces were less likely than domestically owned workplaces to be adversely affected by the recession, perhaps because they were less heavily affected by credit constraints than firms owned by those based in the UK. Workplaces belonging to smaller organisations were also less adversely affected than those belonging to larger counterparts. Although larger firms can benefit from economies of scale, have greater resources to buffer them against recession and may be better able to reallocate resources within the organisation to products or services that appear more successful in the marketplace (Bernard et al., 2010), they also face greater complexity in managing more diverse entities. This complexity can lead to governance difficulties that may have made larger firms less capable of responding quickly to the challenges posed by the downturn. Workplaces recognising unions for pay bargaining were significantly less likely than non-unionised workplaces to be adversely affected by the recession – a finding that is consistent with other evidence suggesting that unionised workplaces have become more competitive in recent years relative to their non-union counterparts (Blanchflower and Bryson, 2009; Bryson et al., 2013c). One might expect the financial performance of the workplace in 2004 to be an important predictor of the extent to which workplaces were adversely affected by the recession but, although there was a simple (bivariate) association between the two, this ceased to be statistically significant after controlling for other factors. Geroski and Gregg (1997) found the same in their earlier study. There were also no statistically significant differences between workplaces in different industries, regions and market conditions, after controlling for other factors. The exception was that workplaces operating in national and international markets were less likely to be adversely affected by the recession than those operating in local and regional markets. This may be because firms in larger marketplaces rely less heavily on demand from any particular community and can shift production or sales away from poorly performing areas.

In the public sector, larger workplaces were more likely to have been adversely affected by the recession than smaller ones after controlling for other factors and, in an echo of the findings for the private sector, workplaces with high union density were less likely to be affected than those with lower union density. Unlike the private sector, however, industry and region remained important. Workplaces in the Health sector were less likely to be affected on average, after controlling for other factors, perhaps because health spending has been largely protected in the cuts to public expenditure. Looking by region, public sector workplaces in the North East and Wales were more likely to be affected than the average, while those in the East of England were least likely to be affected.

These results indicate that some types of workplaces were more likely to be affected than others but, as noted earlier, the regressions are not able to explain a large proportion of the variability in managers' assessments: they can explain around one sixth in the private sector and just over one quarter in the public sector. This suggests that, as in the 1990s, the recent recession had a sizable random component in terms of which workplaces were affected.

EMPLOYER RESPONSES TO THE RECESSION

Since the majority of workplaces were adversely affected by the recession, one would expect this to trigger action by managers intent on improving their competitive position and minimising labour costs. This seems to have been the case. Managers were guided to focus on the impact of the recession on their workforce and were asked, 'Which, if any, of these actions were taken by your workplace in response to the recent recession?' They were invited to choose from 13 specific employment-related actions, although respondents were also free to mention other unspecified actions that had been taken in their workplace. In three quarters (75 per cent) of workplaces at least one employment-related change was made in response to the recession (Table 2.3).

As one might expect, whether managers took action in response to the recession was strongly related to how adversely affected they had been by the recession. Among those workplaces that were affected 'A moderate amount', some 73 per cent took one of the actions specified in Table 2.3. This rose to 87 per cent among workplaces that were affected 'Quite a lot' and 95 per cent among those affected 'A great

Table 2.3 *Employment-related changes made in response to the recession, 2011, cell per cent*

	Private sector	Public sector	All workplaces
Freeze or cut in wages	38	<u>64</u>	41
Freeze on filling vacant posts	26	<u>44</u>	28
Change in the organisation of work	23	<u>36</u>	25
Postpone workforce expansion	22	22	22
Reduce paid overtime	19	23	19
Reduce training expenditure	14	<u>33</u>	17
Reduce agency or temporary staff	13	<u>30</u>	15
Reduce basic hours	15	<u>7</u>	14
Compulsory redundancies	14	10	13
Voluntary redundancies	5	<u>23</u>	7
Reduce non-wage benefits	7	7	7
Enforced unpaid leave	3	3	3
Increase agency or temporary staff	3	5	3
Other response	2	3	2
No action taken	27	<u>11</u>	25

Notes: An underline indicates that the difference between the figures for the private and public sectors are statistically significant from one another.
Base: All workplaces with five or more employees. Figures are based on responses from 1,842 private sector and 811 public sector workplace managers.

deal'. It is possible that the 5 per cent of workplaces that were heavily affected yet took none of the actions listed in Table 2.3 nonetheless responded in other ways that did not affect employees directly; possible examples include cutting capital expenditure, cutting in Research and Development (R&D) expenditure or reducing profit margins.

Among those workplaces that reported no adverse effect from the recession, 39 per cent still made at least one change to their employment practices. The proportion was twice as high among public sector workplaces that were not affected by the recession than it was among private sector workplaces. It is possible that managers in these workplaces either – took pre-emptive actions in expectation of a downturn that did not materialise for their particular workplace. Some may also have acted opportunistically, taking advantage of the recession to make changes that might have been more difficult or costly in benign economic conditions. A further possibility, which may be particularly relevant for public sector workplaces but may also have some salience for workplaces belonging to larger organisations in the private sector, is that individual establishments were required to share the burden of cost-cutting with others in their enterprise, even though they were not themselves directly affected by the downturn.

Turning to the types of changes that were made in response to the recession, the most common action taken by managers was to freeze or cut wages, which occurred in 41 per cent of workplaces (Table 2.3). Almost two thirds (64 per cent) of public sector workplaces were affected, compared with 38 per cent of private sector workplaces. Other common responses included introducing a freeze on filling vacant posts (28 per cent), changing the organisation of work (25 per cent) and postponing plans to expand the workforce (22 per cent). The recession prompted compulsory redundancies in 13 per cent of all workplaces and voluntary redundancies in 7 per cent (17 per cent when combined). Larger workplaces were more likely than smaller ones to have experienced some form of action so, while 25 per cent of all workplaces had seen none of the specified actions, these employed only 19 per cent of all employees.

Public sector workplaces were more likely than those in the private sector to have experienced some form of response to the recession (Table 2.3). Many of the individual actions were also more prevalent in the public sector. The only action that was more common among private sector workplaces was to reduce basic hours.[7] As this pattern suggests, public sector workplaces were then also more likely to have experienced more than one type of response – perhaps freezing wages as well as making voluntary redundancies. Overall, more than half (54 per cent) of workplaces underwent at least two employment-related changes, while one in five workplaces (21 per cent) made at least four changes. Public sector workplaces experienced the most changes in response to the recession: 40 per cent reported at least four changes, compared to 18 per cent of private sector workplaces.

THE EXPERIENCE OF INDIVIDUAL EMPLOYEES

The actions listed in Table 2.3 may not have affected all employees in the workplace, nor to the same degree. Indeed, some actions, such as reductions in training or overtime, may only affect a select group of workers. Further, actions that may not appear to impact on the remaining workforce, such as a recruitment freeze or redundancies, may have indirect repercussions. Therefore, it is useful to understand the experience of the recession from the perspective of the employees who were at the workplace at the time. Employees were asked whether they had experienced any of a list of changes as a result of the most recent recession while at their current workplace (see Table 2.4). Here the focus is necessarily on the 88 per cent of employees who indicated that they were working at the surveyed workplace during the recession.

There was a strong relationship between managers' and employees' accounts in terms of the prominence of specific actions. A freeze or decrease in wages was again the most common response, with one third of employees (32 per cent) reporting that their wages were frozen or cut in response to the recession. The second most common employee experience of the recession was an increase in workload (28 per cent) which is consistent with managers' reports of restrictions on filling vacancies. In addition to this, employees experienced changes to their working time arrangements – 18 per cent had their paid overtime restricted, 5 per cent had their basic contracted hours reduced and 2 per cent were asked to take unpaid leave. Almost one fifth (19 per cent) of employees reported directly experiencing a reorganisation of their work in response to the recession. A further 5 per cent of employees said they were moved to another job.

Some 40 per cent of employees indicated that none of the specified changes had happened to them as a result of the most recent recession. The figure was 45 per cent among private sector employees, but just 27 per cent among employees

Table 2.4 *Changes experienced by employees in response to the recession, 2011, cell per cent*

	Private sector	Public sector	All employees
Wages were frozen or cut	26	<u>49</u>	32
Workload increased	26	<u>36</u>	28
Work was reorganised	16	<u>25</u>	19
Access to paid overtime was restricted	18	<u>21</u>	18
Access to training was restricted	9	<u>19</u>	12
Non-wage benefits were reduced	5	<u>8</u>	5
Moved to another job	5	<u>7</u>	5
Contracted working hours were reduced	5	<u>3</u>	5
Required to take unpaid leave	2	2	2
None of these	45	<u>27</u>	40

Notes: An underline indicates that the difference between the figures for the private and public sectors are statistically significant from one another.
Base: Employees present in the workplace (with five or more employees) at the time of the recession. Figures are based on responses from 11,470 private sector and 7,598 public sector employees.

in the public sector. More than one third (36 per cent) of employees experienced two or more of the specified changes, including 14 per cent who reported both an increase in workload and a wage cut or freeze.

Around half (49 per cent) of employees in the public sector reported wage cuts or freezes, compared with just over one quarter (26 per cent) in the private sector. More than a third (36 per cent) of public sector employees reported an increase in workload, compared with 26 per cent in the private sector. Public administration and Construction were the industries with the highest proportions of employees reporting wage cuts or freezes (68 per cent and 48 per cent, respectively). Increases in workload were most common among employees in Public administration (49 per cent), followed by Transport and communications (35 per cent) and Financial services (34 per cent). Figure 2.2 indicated that these are among those industries that have fared the worst in the economic downturn.

Moving on to consider variations in experience between different categories of workers, Table 2.5 shows the percentage of employees reporting a pay freeze or cut, an increase in workload or any of the changes listed in Table 2.4, according to gender, age, full-time or part-time status and occupation. Men were more likely than women to have had their wages frozen or cut (34 per cent versus 31 per cent) and to have seen an increase in their workload (30 per cent versus 27 per cent). Moreover, when aggregating all of the specific changes listed in Table 2.4, men were more likely than women to have experienced some changes at work as a result of recession (63 per cent compared with 57 per cent).

Workers aged between 30 and 59 years were more likely than younger or older workers to have experienced changes as a result of recession. Full-time employees were also more likely to have experienced changes than part-time employees, although part-time employees were more likely to report that their contracted working hours had been reduced (8 per cent compared with 4 per cent among full-time employees). Some of these employees may have been previously employed on

Table 2.5 *Changes experienced by employees as a result of recession, 2011, cell per cent*

	Wages frozen or cut	Workload increased	Any change[a]
Gender			
Female	31	27	57
Male	<u>34</u>	<u>30</u>	<u>63</u>
Age			
Less than 20	2	8	24
20–29	23	24	54
30–59	36	31	63
60 or more	29	23	51
Working hours			
Full-time	35	31	63
Part-time	<u>23</u>	<u>20</u>	<u>50</u>
Occupation			
Managerial	38	37	66
Non-managerial	<u>32</u>	<u>27</u>	<u>59</u>

Notes: (a) Refers to any of the changes listed in Table 2.4.
For 'Gender', 'Working hours' and 'Occupation' an underline indicates that the difference between the two figures within each column are statistically significant from one another.
Base: Employees present at the workplace (with five or more employees) at the time of the recession. Figures are based on responses from at least 18,416 employees.

a full-time basis. Of course, some of these factors are likely to be interrelated: for example, women are more likely to be employed in part-time roles.

Employees in Associate professional and technical occupations were the most likely to have experienced wage cuts or freezes (42 per cent) while those in Elementary occupations were the least likely (17 per cent). Managerial employees were the most likely to have experienced increases in workload (37 per cent), while employees in Caring, leisure and other personal service occupations were the least likely (17 per cent).

WERE WORKPLACES WEAKER AS A RESULT OF THE RECESSION?

Thus far, the chapter has looked at changes in the external environment, the extent to which the recession adversely affected the workplace, and the types of actions that managers took in response. But how did workplaces fare overall? If the market a workplace is operating in is sent into decline or turmoil, it is likely that the workplace will suffer, at least in the short term. But even in these cases, some firms may prosper at the expense of others. For example, they may have a comparative cost advantage in delivering goods and services that, if cost becomes more important to customers during recession, gives them the edge over their competitors. In this situation they may gain market share at the expense of other producers or providers. For others, the effects of the recession may have been exacerbated – or ameliorated – by the actions that managers took in response to the recession. Short term pain (for example, in the form of wage freezes) may well have helped to secure the health of the workplace in the medium term. Some workplaces were of course

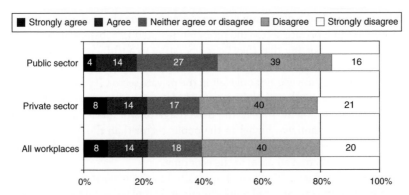

Figure 2.3 *Workplace managers' agreement with the statement: 'This workplace is now weaker as a result of its experience during the recent recession', 2011, row per cent*
Base: All workplaces with five or more employees. Figures are based on responses from 1,851 private sector and 814 public sector workplace managers.

largely unaffected by the recession, as we noted previously. Workplace managers were therefore asked how much they agreed with the statement, 'This workplace is now weaker as a result of its experience during the recent recession'.

Just over one in five managers agreed with the statement – 8 per cent 'Strongly agreed' while a further 14 per cent 'Agreed' (Figure 2.3). The majority of workplace managers (60 per cent) disagreed that their workplace was now weaker as a result of the recession, although this is an underestimate when one takes account of those workplaces that were so severely affected by the recession that they closed down altogether. Differences between public and private sector workplaces were not substantial. However, more public sector workplace managers opted to neither agree nor disagree with the statement, perhaps because it was still too early for them to make an assessment.

There was an association between the extent to which the recession had an adverse effect on the workplace and whether the workplace was weaker as a result. Of those workplaces that were adversely affected either 'A great deal' or 'Quite a lot' by the recession, 41 per cent of managers said their workplace was now weaker as a result. This compared with 13 per cent among workplaces that were only adversely affected to a 'Moderate' extent, and just 2 per cent among those that were only affected 'A little' or not at all. Nevertheless, over two fifths (44 per cent) of workplaces that were adversely affected either 'A great deal' or 'Quite a lot' *disagreed* that the workplace was now weaker as a result. The fact that groups of workplaces experienced similar effects, but reported quite divergent outcomes, indicates there were other factors that determined how well workplaces coped with the recession. It is possible that their approach to employment relations may have been informative and this is an issue that we return to in Chapter 9.

CONCLUSION

At the time of the 2011 WERS, workplaces were operating in the shadow of one of the most severe economic recessions that Britain has seen in modern times. The economic downturn had a direct and very marked effect on the majority of work-places. In the trading private sector the recession resulted in substantial increases in the proportions reporting that they were operating in a turbulent or declining market, with fewer managers saying that their market was growing. Nevertheless, the impact of the recession was not only felt in the private sector. Its direct effect on the public finances meant that public sector workplaces were by no means immune to the external environment. Indeed the percentage of workplaces reporting an adverse effect of recession was higher in the public sector than the private sector, a finding which underscores the very particular nature of this recession – the influence of which spread across all parts of the economy.

The widespread impact of the recession resulted in the majority of workplaces taking actions that directly affected employment and employees' terms and conditions, such that most employees were able to relate at least one way in which their terms or conditions of employment had been changed as a result of the recession. What is more, the recession had cast a long shadow over many workplaces and their employees such that more than one fifth of workplace managers reported in 2011 that their workplace had been weakened by the recession.

In spite of all this, it was apparent that a substantial minority of workplaces came through the recession relatively unscathed. One tenth of all workplaces reported no ill effects of the recession at all, and another one sixth said they had only been affected 'A little'. Around one quarter reported taking no actions in relation to their workforce as a result of the recession. So, for a sizeable minority of workplace managers, the recession was seemingly a relatively minor event, which could not be expected to have wrought any major influence over their thinking, their planning and their broad approach to employment relations. This is apparent even within industries and within the public and private sectors.

One of the tasks of the remainder of this book is to carefully depict those circumstances in which the recession did or did not play an important role in shaping events. Another is to identify the role played by factors other than the recession in shaping changes in employment relations since 2004. These questions form an important part of the backdrop to the analysis which is subsequently presented in Chapters 3 to 8. The discussion returns to the issue of the impact of the recession in Chapter 9.

3 Employment and Flexible Working

INTRODUCTION

Throughout the economic cycle, new workplaces spring up and grow, while others wither and die. It is often argued that job creation and destruction is necessary in order to allow economies to grow and develop. Yet these changes also have important consequences for employees – not only because of the implications for job security but also because new workplaces may provide different working environments to those that they replace.

A recession has the potential to increase the pace of change. Chapter 2 showed that between 2004 and 2011 many private sector workplaces saw the market for their main product or service move from growth or stability, to turbulence or decline. Similarly, many workplaces in the public sector had to adjust to reductions in central budgets. Such challenges may force the closure of a workplace when, in more benign circumstances, this might have been avoided. Depressed economic conditions may also cause managers to take action in ways that would not be required in less turbulent times, for example, by making compulsory redundancies rather than reducing employment through natural wastage.

Geroski and Gregg (1997: 11) have argued that the opportunity costs of introducing changes are lower in an economic downturn and so, for some, the recession may also provide the impetus to change working practices in ways that would not otherwise be considered. This may lead to the introduction of more flexible ways of working. Other influences affect these decisions, of course, including public policy. For instance, employees with parental or caring responsibilities were given the right to request flexible working in 2003, and the Government proposes to extend this right to all employees from 2014.

This chapter examines the features of workplaces that closed, declined and grew in the period from 2004 to 2011, as well as new entrants. It provides insights into the actions that employers took to adapt to the changed economic climate in order to ensure their survival. It also looks more broadly at the use of flexible working arrangements, including the use of functional flexibility (that is, multi-skilling), part-time hours, fixed-term contracts, annual hours contracts and sub-contracting.

One notable element of the context for the chapter is that this particular recession has differed from previous economic downturns because the reduction in output has far outstripped the fall in employment (see Chapter 1). A variety of possible explanations have been put forward, including greater wage flexibility (Pessoa and Van Reenen, 2013) and low interest rates which have allowed firms to continue to operate despite making low returns (Broadbent, 2012). However, there is some evidence that employers have also used flexible working arrangements to avoid job losses. Early in the recession, there were examples of efforts to reduce the scale of redundancies by introducing short-time working (for example, at Toyota) and by temporarily ceasing production (for example, at Honda) (Scott and Woodman, 2009; Webb, 2009). More generally there is some evidence of an increase in part-time and temporary working (Patterson, 2012). The chapter therefore concludes by examining the extent to which the use of flexible working arrangements may have enabled workplaces to mitigate employment losses through the recession.

WORKPLACE SURVIVAL AND CLOSURES

The chapter begins by examining patterns of workplace survival and closure between 2004 and 2011. Comparisons are made with the equivalent patterns that were seen between the two previous WERS surveys in 1998 and 2004. That earlier period was characterised by sustained economic growth and growing levels of employment. These trends continued between 2004 and 2008 before the onset of recession. This section therefore assesses the implications for workplaces of this changed set of economic circumstances.

All workplaces that take part in WERS for the first time are re-contacted at the time of the next survey to establish whether they are still in existence. The 1998 WERS only included workplaces with ten or more employees (rather than those with five or more employees as in the 2004 and 2011 surveys). It is therefore necessary to exclude workplaces with fewer than ten employees from the later surveys when comparing rates of workplace closure in the period 2004–11 with those seen in the period 1998–2004.[1]

Among workplaces with ten or more employees in 2004, 84 per cent were still in existence in 2011, while 16 per cent had closed down. Private sector workplaces were twice as likely to close as those in the public sector (18 per cent and 9 per cent, respectively). The total survival and closure rates for workplaces with ten or more employees were the same for the period 1998–2004 and the pattern of closures in the private and public sectors was also similar (at 19 per cent and 6 per cent). The difference in the length of time between surveys meant that the average annual closure rate in workplaces with ten or more employees over the period from 1998 to 2004 was 2.7 per cent, compared with 2.3 per cent over the period from 2004 to 2011, although this change was not statistically significant. This was also the case when the analysis was restricted to the private sector only (annual closure rates of 3.1 per cent for 1998 to 2004 and 2.5 per cent for 2004 to 2011).

The relative stability in the closure rate between the two periods is perhaps contrary to expectations, given the economic environment in recent years. However, the period from 2008 to 2011 followed a sustained period of growth that may have left many firms in a relatively good position from which to weather the downturn. The period from 1998 to 2004, in contrast, followed not long after the recession of 1990–93 and so many firms may still have been in a period of recovery. This is borne out by analysis from the ONS which shows that private sector companies typically operated with surpluses over the period from 2002 onwards, whereas the decade leading up to that point was characterised by both surpluses and deficits (Patterson, 2012).[2]

Which Types of Workplaces were More Likely to Close?

Although the economic downturn did not raise the overall rate of workplace closure above that seen between 1998 and 2004, it is possible that it had a more pronounced impact on some types of workplaces or employees than others. To examine the factors associated with workplace closure, the analysis turns to the full sample of workplaces surveyed in 2004 (that is, all those with five or more employees). Of workplaces with five or more employees, 17 per cent closed between 2004 and 2011 but, as in the sub-sample with ten or more employees, private sector workplaces were far more likely to close than those in the public sector (19 per cent and 7 per cent, respectively).

Whereas the private sector is exposed to fluctuations in trading conditions, the public sector is largely shielded from market pressures and closures are more likely to occur in response to changes in government policy. Given the sizeable differences in the closure rate between the public and private sectors and the small numbers of public sector workplaces which closed between 2004 and 2011, this section focuses on the characteristics associated with workplace closures in the private sector.

Regression analysis was used to identify factors that were independently associated with workplace closure and the most notable associations are presented in Table 3.1.[3] The first column of the table shows the proportion of workplaces that closed that had each specific characteristic. For instance, 18 per cent of all workplaces with five to nine employees in 2004 had closed by 2011; this compared with 11 per cent of all workplaces with 500 or more employees. The average closure rate in the former group was eight percentage points lower than that in the latter group after rounding. The second column of the table then shows how this simple difference altered after controlling for other factors. Larger workplaces tend to be older than average, for example, and the table shows that older workplaces were also less likely to close between 2004 and 2011 than younger ones. In the regression analysis, workplaces with five to nine employees were 13 percentage points more likely to close than workplaces with 500 or more employees. The negative association with workplace size therefore remained, but also became stronger after holding other features of the workplace constant. The negative association with workplace age also remained after controlling for other factors.

Recognising one or more unions for pay bargaining in 2004 increased the likelihood of closure by 11 percentage points after controlling for other characteristics. Previous evidence on the link between workplace closure and unions in Britain has been mixed, with Machin (1995) finding no association during the 1980s and Bryson (2004) finding a positive link during the 1990s which disappeared between

Table 3.1 *Characteristics of private sector workplaces that closed, 2004–11, cell per cent and percentage points*

Workplace characteristics in 2004	Closure rate 2004–11 (per cent)	Regression-adjusted difference (percentage points)
Workplace size		
5–9 employees	18	13
10–19 employees	20	17
20–49 employees	20	15
50–99 employees	10	5
100–499 employees	12	5
500 or more employees	11	Ref.
Age of workplace		
Less than 5 years	32	19
5–9 years	18	7
10–24 years	21	11
25 years or more	11	Ref.
Any recognised unions at the workplace		
Yes	19	11
No	18	Ref.
Any redundancies in 12 months prior to the 2004 survey		
Yes	25	9
No	18	Ref.

Notes: Second column shows marginal effects from probit regression. 'Ref.' indicates reference category.
Base: Private sector workplaces with five or more employees surveyed in 2004. Figures are based on responses from 1,410 workplace managers.

1998 and 2004 (Bryson and Dale-Olsen, 2008). It therefore appears that there has been a return to the pattern of the 1990s.[4]

The competitive environment that private sector workplaces faced was not found to be related to the likelihood that the workplace survived until 2011. This was also the case in the period from 1998 to 2004 (Bryson and Dale-Olsen, 2008). However, workplaces which made some redundancies in the 12 months before the 2004 survey were more likely to have closed by 2011 than workplaces which did not make cuts. This mirrored findings for the period from 1998 to 2004 (Bryson and Dale-Olsen, 2008). Clearly, the need to make redundancies indicates that the workplace was already facing some difficulties.

NEW WORKPLACES

As workplaces close they are replaced by new ones. Twenty per cent of all workplaces with five or more employees in 2011 had not existed in 2004. New workplaces were far more likely to spring up in the private sector than in the public sector, as 22 per cent of private sector workplaces came into existence in the period from 2004,

Table 3.2 *Characteristics of new private sector workplaces, 2004–11, cell per cent and percentage points*

Workplace characteristics in 2011	New workplaces established since 2004	Regression-adjusted difference
	(per cent)	(percentage points)
Workplace size		
5–9 employees	22	<u>40</u>
10–19 employees	27	<u>39</u>
20–49 employees	21	<u>33</u>
50–99 employees	15	<u>30</u>
100–499 employees	15	29
500 or more employees	1	Ref.
Industry sector (SIC 2003)		
Manufacturing	26	15
Electricity, gas and water	(6)	(–4)
Construction	21	<u>23</u>
Wholesale and retail trade	21	17
Hotels and restaurants	31	<u>29</u>
Transportation and communications	8	Ref.
Financial services	(4)	(–4)
Other business services	22	17
Public administration	N/A	N/A
Education	31	<u>38</u>
Health and social work	21	<u>29</u>
Other community services	24	<u>24</u>

Notes: Second column shows marginal effects from probit regression. 'Ref.' indicates reference category.
Base: Private sector workplaces with five or more employees surveyed in 2011. Figures are based on responses from 1,589 workplace managers.

compared with only 9 per cent of workplaces in the public sector. Among workplaces with ten or more employees new workplaces accounted for 21 per cent of the total population in 2011; this compared with 17 per cent for the period between 1998 and 2004. Again, the small number of new workplaces that sprung up in the public sector between 2004 and 2011 meant that our subsequent regression analysis of new workplaces focused only on the private sector.

Many studies in industrial economics have previously found that new workplaces tend to be very small (Caves, 1998). Overall, 22 per cent of private sector workplaces with five to nine employees in 2011 had been established after 2004. This compared with just 1 per cent of those with 500 or more employees (Table 3.2). After using regression analysis to control for other factors, this difference of 20 percentage points doubled.[5] The smallest workplaces were therefore 40 percentage points more likely to have been newly established than the largest workplaces, when holding other factors constant.

There were also variations by industry sector. Some 31 per cent of workplaces in the Hotels and restaurants industry in 2011 had been established in the previous seven years; the same figure applied among privately owned workplaces in Education. In contrast, only 8 per cent of workplaces in the Transport and communications industry had been set up in the previous seven years. These broad differences persisted after controlling for other factors.

New workplaces were more likely to serve national and international markets rather than local markets and to be UK owned rather than foreign owned. The workforce of new establishments also tended to be younger than average, even after controlling for other workplace and workforce characteristics.

As noted in the introduction to the chapter, there is particular interest in how new workplaces differ from those that have closed, as differences in their employment practices are one means by which change comes about in the broader population (the other being change over time within continuing workplaces). Previous research showed, for example, that unionisation was particularly low among new workplaces in the 1990s and this contributed to the decline in union recognition (Machin, 2003). However, new workplaces in 2011 were no less likely to recognise unions than new workplaces in 2004 (12 per cent of new workplaces did so in 2011 compared with 10 per cent in 2004), and this may go some way towards explaining why union recognition has been relatively stable over this more recent period (see Chapter 4).

EMPLOYMENT CHANGE

The previous sections have established that the rate of workplace closure between 2004 and 2011 remained similar to that for the period from 1998 to 2004, and that a similar proportion of workplaces in 2004 and 2011 were newly established. Since this occurred against the backdrop of recession, it raises the question of whether signs of distress were more evident within workplaces that remained in existence over the period. This section considers what happened to employment in such workplaces. It examines the extent to which employers reduced the size of their workforce over time and the strategies that they employed to do this, as well as whether they sought to free their hand to make future cuts by, for example, ending job security guarantees. It also assesses the characteristics of workplaces that were affected by these changes, and the impact on employees' perceptions of job security. Finally, it looks at the characteristics of workplaces that grew in size between 2004 and 2011.

Chapter 1 showed that there was no overall change in the distribution of workplaces by size between 2004 and 2011 (see Table 1.1). Indeed, in both 2004 and 2011, the median workplace had 11 employees. Yet there can be considerable change in employment levels *within* workplaces over time. Figure 3.1 uses data from the panel of workplaces surveyed in both 2004 and 2011 and shows the proportion of workplaces in which employment either fell by over one fifth, rose by over one fifth or stayed roughly the same over this period. While 20 per cent of workplaces reduced their workforce by over one fifth between 2004 and 2011, more than twice as many increased in size by over one fifth. Also, 20 per cent of workplaces grew their workforce by over a half, while only 5 per cent shrunk by this amount. These proportions were similar for workplaces in the public and private sectors.

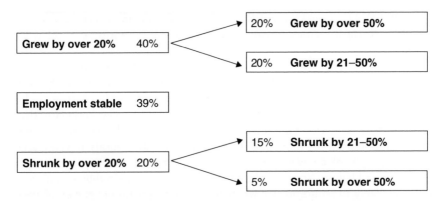

Figure 3.1 Change in the size of workforce in panel workplaces, 2004–11

Base: Workplaces with five or more employees surveyed in 2004 and 2011. Figures are based on responses from 966 managers.

Employment Contraction

The types of workplaces that experienced the largest reductions in the size of their workforce between 2004 and 2011 differed in the public and private sectors. In the private sector, workplaces were more likely to shrink by more than one fifth if their financial performance was judged by the workplace manager in 2004 to be below average for their industry (38 per cent of such workplaces shrank by 20 per cent or more, compared with 18 per cent of those where performance was judged to be about average, and 21 per cent of those where it was judged above average). The difference persisted after controlling for other factors in a regression analysis similar to those discussed earlier.[6] The impact of the recession was also evident, as workplaces which reported in 2011 that they had been affected 'A great deal' or 'Quite a lot' by the recession were more likely to have shrunk by more than one fifth than those that were less affected (28 per cent and 14 per cent, respectively).

The likelihood that a workforce shrank was lower in establishments where managers described the level of product market competition as 'Very high' compared with those where competition was 'High'. This suggests that workplaces that faced the extremes of either intense or fairly low competition were less likely to shrink than those that operate in markets somewhere towards the middle of the competitive spectrum.

Women were more likely than men to be employed in private sector workplaces that shrank, but otherwise the impact of workforce reductions was evenly spread across different groups of employees. There was little evidence that the size of the workplace in 2004 had any bearing on the likelihood that the workforce had contracted by more than one fifth by 2011. The only other workplace characteristic associated with a higher probability of employment contraction in the private sector was industry. Workplaces in Manufacturing, Construction, and Transport and communications were the most likely to experience a marked reduction in size (in each of these industries more than one quarter of workplaces had shrunk by one fifth or more). The lowest rates of shrinkage were found among privately owned workplaces in Health, Education and Other community services (each below 20 per cent).

Among public sector workplaces that continued to operate, there were few characteristics that were significantly associated with the likelihood that the workforce shrank by over one fifth between 2004 and 2011.[7] In contrast to the private sector, there was no difference in shrinkage rates between workplaces that had been more affected by the recession and those that had been less affected. There were variations by industrial sector, however, with Education workplaces least likely to shrink by over one fifth, and those engaged in Other community services most likely to do so. Continuing workplaces in the public sector were also more likely to reduce in size where a greater proportion of the employees were members of a trade union. Both associations remained in regression analysis. Together these results suggest that highly unionised workplaces and those engaged in the provision of particular local government services (for example, recreational services) may have been particularly affected by the long-running reform programme and recent budget cuts.

Redundancies

Official statistics show that the overall redundancy rate among employees in the economy was similar in 2004 and 2011, but peaked in 2009 (Office for National Statistics, 2013). However, the proportion of workplaces that made some redundancies in the year prior to the 2011 survey was higher than the proportion making redundancies in the year prior to the 2004 survey (13 per cent and 9 per cent, respectively). A further 3 per cent of workplaces had consulted over making redundancies but subsequently withdrawn the proposals before the 2011 survey – up from 1 per cent in the period before the 2004 survey.

While the proportions of workplaces that had made some redundancies in the year prior to the 2011 survey were similar in the public and private sectors (12 per cent and 13 per cent, respectively), many of the factors associated with redundancies within each sector were different. Regression analysis indicated the only common factors that contributed to the likelihood of redundancies being made were if the workplace was strongly affected by the recession and if it had a larger number of employees (Table 3.3).[8]

In the private sector there were further signs of the impact of economic conditions, as redundancies were more common among workplaces with financial performance at or below the average for their industry, and among those operating in a mature or declining market. Redundancies were less likely to occur in workplaces that offered a single product or service (9 per cent), compared with workplaces with greater diversity of product lines (16 per cent). Employers who specialise in a single product or service may find it less beneficial to reduce the size of the workforce than those with multiple products or services who may choose to cut less successful areas of business in an economic downturn. Further, those that operated in national or international markets for their goods or services were more likely to make redundancies (20 per cent) than those working in local or regional markets (9 per cent).

Table 3.3 *Workplaces that made at least one redundancy in the 12 months prior to the survey, 2011, cell per cent and percentage points*

Workplace characteristics in 2011	Private sector		Public sector	
	Any redundancies	Regression-adjusted difference	Any redundancies	Regression-adjusted difference
	(per cent)	(percentage points)	(per cent)	(percentage points)
Extent to which workplace adversely affected by recession				
A great deal/Quite a lot	17	<u>5</u>	18	<u>6</u>
A moderate amount/ Just a little/No adverse effect	10	Ref.	78	Ref.
Workplace size				
5–9 employees	7	<u>–31</u>	(4)	(–36)
10–19 employees	12	<u>–27</u>	(5)	(<u>–25</u>)
20–49 employees	18	<u>–20</u>	14	<u>–15</u>
50–99 employees	38	<u>–10</u>	10	<u>–18</u>
100–499 employees	37	<u>–10</u>	38	–8
500 or more employees	70	Ref.	65	Ref.

Notes: Columns two and four show marginal effects from probit regression. 'Ref.' indicates reference category.
Base: All workplaces with five or more employees. Figures are based on responses from 1,588 private sector and 630 public sector workplace managers.

After controlling for these and other factors, workplaces in Construction and Other business services were the most likely to have made some redundancies.

Within the public sector, the likelihood that some redundancies occurred in the 12 months prior to the 2011 survey was greater in workplaces where union density was low, suggesting that unions played a role in reducing the likelihood that redundancies occurred.[9] Only 5 per cent of public sector workplaces with density of three quarters or more had made redundancies, compared with 15 per cent of those where density was below one quarter; this difference extended to 18 percentage points after controlling for other factors. Moreover, there was little difference in the likelihood that redundancies were made across the various industries within the public sector.

Figure 3.2 shows the reasons managers gave for making redundancies in the 12 months prior to the survey, with managers being able to list multiple causes. A lack of demand for products or services was by far the most common reason given, mentioned by 47 per cent of managers in workplaces that made redundancies. However, in almost one third (30 per cent) of workplaces where redundancies had been made, the cause was a need to reorganise working methods. A similar proportion (29 per cent) made some staff redundant due to reductions in their budget, or cash limits, although further analysis showed that this was a much stronger motivator for redundancies in the public sector than in the private sector, with this reason cited in almost two thirds (63 per cent) of public sector workplaces

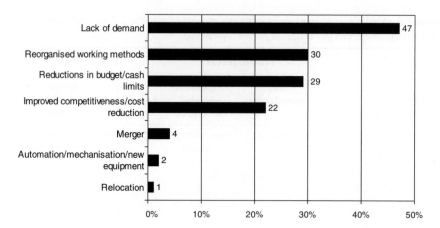

Figure 3.2 *Reasons for making employees redundant, 2011, cell per cent*

Base: Workplaces with five or more employees that made redundancies in the 12 months prior to the survey. Figures are based on responses from 852 workplace managers.

compared with 24 per cent of private sector workplaces. The need to improve competitiveness, efficiency or to reduce costs also motivated redundancies in 22 per cent of workplaces. So, while employers used redundancies to respond to pressures such as a lack of demand and budget limits that may have been heightened by the economic downturn, they also used them to adjust their methods of working and improve efficiency, which may have been part of a longer-term strategy to improve the resilience of the workplace.

Table 3.2 showed that redundancies were more common in 2010–11 in workplaces that had been strongly affected by the recession. Managers were also asked whether they had made any compulsory or voluntary redundancies in response to the recession. In this case, the time period was not specified, so the focus was on any redundancies that the manager attributed to the recession, no matter when these were made. The overall results were presented in Chapter 2 (see Table 2.4) and show that compulsory redundancies were more common in the private sector, whereas voluntary redundancies were more common in the public sector. Some 27 per cent of all public sector workplaces made some redundancies in response to the recession, but this was only the case in 16 per cent of private sector workplaces. In total 6 per cent of public sector workplaces had made both voluntary and compulsory redundancies in response to the recession, 17 per cent had made only voluntary redundancies and 4 per cent had made only compulsory lay-offs. In the private sector 2 per cent of workplaces had made both voluntary and compulsory redundancies, while 2 per cent made only voluntary redundancies and 11 per cent had made only compulsory redundancies.

Job Security Guarantees

Even if employers do not make redundancies, or reduce the size of the workforce by failing to replace staff, they may adjust staffing practices to make it easier to reduce

Table 3.4 *Private sector employment growth of more than 20 per cent, 2004–11, cell per cent and percentage points*

Workplace characteristics in 2004	Workplaces that grew by more than 20%	Regression-adjusted difference
	(per cent)	(percentage points)
Extent to which workplace adversely affected by recession		
A great deal/Quite a lot	39	−11
A moderate amount/Just a little/No adverse effect	46	Ref.
Workplace sells goods or services		
Yes	42	−30
No	(54)	Ref.
Workplace size		
5–9 employees	58	40
10–19 employees	33	24
20–49 employees	34	17
50–99 employees	28	15
100–499 employees	22	2
500 or more employees	24	Ref.

Notes: Column two shows marginal effects from probit regression. 'Ref.' indicates reference category.
Base: Private sector workplaces with five or more employees surveyed in both 2004 and 2011. Figures are based on responses from 533 workplace managers.

staff numbers in the future. They appear to have done this, since the proportion of workplaces that had a policy of guaranteed job security or no-compulsory redundancies for at least some employees fell from 14 per cent in 2004 to 7 per cent in 2011.

The rate of redundancy in the year before the 2011 survey appeared higher in workplaces without job security guarantees (13 per cent compared with 8 per cent among workplaces with guarantees), but the difference was not statistically significant. Further, a similar proportion of workplaces with and without job security guarantees made some redundancies in response to the recession (18 per cent of those with guarantees and 17 per cent of those without). There was, however, a difference in the way that workplaces made redundancies. Workplaces that guaranteed job security for some staff in 2011 were less likely to have made compulsory redundancies as a result of the recession and more likely to have had voluntary lay-offs. Some 5 per cent of workplaces with job security guarantees had some compulsory redundancies because of the recession, while 15 per cent had made voluntary redundancies. Among workplaces without job security guarantees, 14 per cent had made some compulsory redundancies and 6 per cent made voluntary redundancies. This difference is in line with evidence on the impact of job security guarantees from previous WERS surveys (Bryson and White, 2006). The main effect of a guarantee was therefore to encourage employers to make voluntary, rather than compulsory redundancies, helping employers to 'manage labour force reductions rather than avoid them' (Kelly, 2004: 281).

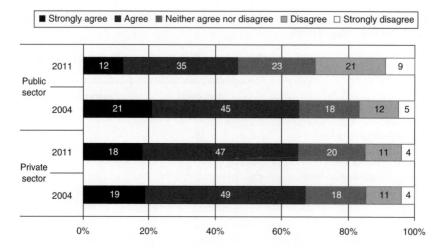

Figure 3.3 *Employee perceptions of job security, 2004 and 2011, row per cent*

Base: All employees in workplaces with five or more employees. Figures are based on responses from 21,518 (2004) and 20,994 (2011) employees.

Perceptions of job security

Given the increase in redundancies and reductions in job security guarantees between 2004 and 2011, as well as the general context of an economic downturn, it seems likely that employees' perceptions of their own job security will have fallen over time. There was a clear decline in perceptions of job security between 2004 and 2011, which is consistent with the cyclical nature of job security portrayed in other studies (Bryson and Forth, 2010b; Park et al., 2012). Two thirds (67 per cent) of employees agreed or strongly agreed in 2004 that their job was secure but, in 2011, this proportion was only three fifths (61 per cent). Figure 3.3 demonstrates that the reductions in job security were greater in the public sector, however. The proportion of employees in the public and private sectors who agreed or strongly agreed that their job was secure in 2004 was similar (at 66 per cent and 68 per cent, respectively). While the proportion of public sector employees who felt their job was secure fell dramatically between 2004 and 2011, there was only a slight drop in the proportion of private sector employees who agreed that their job was secure. As a result, by 2011, just 47 per cent of public sector employees agreed their job was secure, compared with 65 per cent of employees in the private sector.

Perceptions of job security were related to the experience of redundancies at the workplace. Where there were redundancies in the 12 months prior to the survey, 54 per cent of employees agreed or strongly agreed that their job was secure compared with 64 per cent of employees in workplaces where no redundancies occurred over this period. However, employee perceptions of job security were lower in workplaces that offered job security guarantees for some staff. While 55 per cent of employees in workplaces with job security guarantees strongly agreed or agreed that their job was secure, this compared to 61 per cent of those in workplaces that did not offer such a guarantee. This contrasts with analysis of the 1998 WERS which found that perceptions were 'virtually identical' regardless of whether workers were covered by a job security guarantee (Bryson et al., 2009b: 184). However, in a regression analysis, Bryson et al. (2009b: 187) found that job security guarantees were more likely to be adopted in workplaces where employees felt less secure, perhaps as a means of seeking to reduce the sense of employee insecurity and this may explain these latest findings.

Employment Growth

Having covered a number of indicators of employment contraction and job insecurity, the discussion now considers the other side of the coin by briefly focusing on those workplaces in Figure 3.1 that expanded their employment between 2004 and 2011. The depressed state of the economy in recent years can encourage a focus on negative outcomes for workplaces and employees – closures, redundancies, job cuts and insecurity. However, at any point in the economic cycle, some workplace managers may see opportunities for expansion. Over the period from 2004 to 2011, the median number of employees in surviving workplaces increased from 13 to 15, and 40 per cent of workplaces surveyed in both 2004 and 2011 grew by more than one fifth over this period.

Much of this growth is seen in small workplaces. Regression analysis of employment growth among private sector panel workplaces indicated that the smallest of workplaces (those with between five and nine employees) were most likely to grow by at least 20 per cent (see Table 3.4), but of course the absolute increase in employment numbers is typically small in these cases.[10] Looking across industrial sectors, growth was most common in the Manufacturing sector (where 51 per cent of workplaces grew by at least one fifth). Economic and competitive pressures had a strong association with the probability that private sector workplaces grew by more than one fifth between 2004 and 2011. After controlling for other factors, the workplace was 11 percentage points less likely to have grown where managers reported a stronger adverse impact of the recession. Although employment growth was not related to other measures of market conditions, workplaces that sold goods and services on the open market (rather than simply servicing other parts of their own organisation) were less likely to grow between 2004 and 2011 than those that did not trade externally, indicating that economic conditions did not hamper the expansion of administrative offices as much as it did front-line operations.

In summary, there was a substantial degree of change within the workplace population between 2004 and 2011, as workplaces closed, new ones opened and continuing workplaces either expanded or contracted. This contrasts with the relative stability that is apparent when comparing the two cross-sectional snapshots (see Table 1.1) and illustrates the extent to which activity occurred beneath the surface. One might expect the degree of instability to be greater in times of economic hardship. However, on average, the proportion of workplaces closing each year between 2004 and 2011 was similar to that between 1998 and 2004 in both the public and private sectors. While workplaces in the private sector were more likely to close than those in the public sector, the private sector was also more likely to be a source of new workplaces. By contrast, public and private sectors were similar in terms of the proportion of workplaces where employment grew or contracted by more than one fifth between 2004 and 2011. These findings suggest that the labour market has remained surprisingly resilient in the face of recession. Some of the possible reasons for this were outlined earlier in the chapter. The chapter now moves on to examine the extent to which the period between 2004 and 2011 saw changes to staffing practices within the workplace.

LABOUR USAGE

Having explored the changing composition of workplaces and the dynamics of job creation and loss since 2004, this section considers the ways in which employers adapt their staffing practices to economic conditions and legislative changes. The impact of the recession on employment levels has been less pronounced than might have been expected. However, there *is* evidence of employers changing employment practices. For instance, there has been a shift from full-time to part-time jobs, with an increase in the proportion of part-time employees who would prefer full-time work (Patterson, 2012; Bell and Blanchflower, 2013). Some employers have retained skilled employees while cutting labour costs by offering lower wage increases and reduced working hours (Boeri and Bruecker, 2011).

This section looks at the ways that employers use flexible working practices to achieve numerical and functional flexibility within the workplace. It considers whether the use of these practices has changed since 2004 and the extent to which employers have introduced changes in response to the recession. It also assesses changes over time in the use of subcontracting as a way of meeting staffing requirements.

Numerical Flexibility

Being able to vary the size of the workforce to reflect fluctuating levels of demand can result in substantial cost savings for employers. For example, zero hours contracts mean that employees are only paid for the hours they work. When demand for a product or service is low, the employer is under no obligation to pay staff, yet retains a pool of labour that can be called upon when needed. Other arrangements such as the use of fixed-term contracts, annual hours contracts, agency workers and shift work also allow employers to adjust staffing levels when demand for a product or service is low. The provision of part-time work provides a different form of numerical flexibility, here enabling employers (and employees) to accommodate requirements which do not require full-time hours. Flexibility over the location of work is also considered here; while it does not provide numerical flexibility in a strict sense, if employees are not permanently located within the workplace, this can nonetheless reduce the costs associated with accommodating a given number of staff.

Recent legislation governing the use of practices that create numerical flexibility has had two different emphases. On the one hand, there have been efforts to prohibit the less favourable treatment of employees in some forms of flexible work

(Part-time Workers Prevention of Less Favourable Treatment Regulations, 2000; Fixed Term Employees (Prevention of Less Favourable Treatment) Regulations, 2002; Agency Worker Regulations, 2010). On the other hand, there is an awareness that some types of numerical flexibility have benefits for employees, at least if they are applied in a way that gives the employee flexibility over their working time. The Right to Request Flexible Working Arrangements (2003) is an example of legislation that is based on an assumption that numerical flexibility can be beneficial for employees with caring responsibilities. Where the employee has a dependent child or caring responsibilities for a friend or family member, they have a right to ask the employer to seriously consider a request to use flexible working arrangements.

Workplaces used a range of ways of matching the size of the workforce to fluctuations in demand and the methods used differ markedly across the public and private sectors (Figure 3.4). There was very little change in the incidence of each type of numerical flexibility in the public sector between 2004 and 2011: only the proportion of public sector workplaces with any homeworkers increased (from 2 per cent in 2004 to 8 per cent in 2011). By contrast, the proportion of private sector workplaces using the different types of numerical flexibility rose between 2004 and 2011, with the exception of part-time working and the employment of agency workers.

Despite some convergence in the use of flexible working between the public and private sectors over time, notable differences remained in 2011. Public sector workplaces were more likely to have some employees working part-time, or on fixed-term or temporary contracts than private sector workplaces. They were also more likely to have used agency workers and annual hours contracts. In contrast, private sector workplaces were more likely to have some freelancers than workplaces in the public sector. Overall, around three quarters (76 per cent) of public sector workplaces made use of at least one of the forms of flexible working shown in Figure 3.4, compared with around two thirds (65 per cent) of workplaces in the private sector.

The prevalence of part-time working means that it is often found in combination with other types of flexibility (White et al., 2004: 33). Therefore, when seeking to identify the workplaces that made use of numerical flexibility, we focus on the use of two or more types of numerical flexibility, to ensure that workplaces had at least one type of numerical flexibility in addition to part-time staff. Public sector workplaces were more likely than private sector ones to use two or more types of numerical flexibility in both 2004 and 2011. However, the proportion of public sector workplaces with at least two practices remained stable between these two years (74 per cent in 2004 and 72 per cent in 2011), whereas there was a marked increase in the use of two or more forms of numerical flexibility in the private sector (from 43 per cent in 2004 to 57 per cent in 2011). Regression analysis indicated that in both the public and private sectors, larger workplaces were more likely to have two or more types of numerical flexibility than smaller workplaces, as one would expect, but in other respects the characteristics associated with greater numerical flexibility were different in each sector.[11]

The use of at least two types of numerical flexibility was more common among private sector workplaces that traded on the open market (56 per cent), than among workplaces which only supplied other parts of the same organisation (25 per cent), perhaps because of the need to meet external pressures from customers. The use of

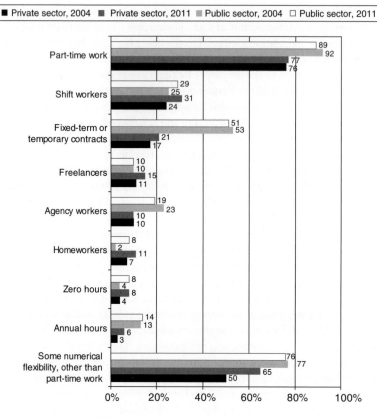

Figure 3.4 *Numerical flexibility practices, 2004 and 2011, cell per cent*
Base: All workplaces with five or more employees. Figures are based on responses from at least 2,270 (2004) and 2,646 (2011) workplace managers.

numerical flexibility also varied between different industrial sectors, with practices more common in Hotels and restaurants and Other community services than in the Construction sector. While 86 per cent of workplaces in the Hotels and restaurants sector, and 69 per cent of those in the Other community services sector used at least two types of numerical flexibility, this was the case in just 34 per cent of workplaces in the Construction sector. Workplaces that had been strongly affected by the recession were no more likely to utilise flexible working arrangements than those which had been less affected. There was an association with the demographics of the workforce, however, with private sector workplaces more likely to have at least two types of numerical flexibility where a greater proportion of the workforce was female; something which may reflect a concern to accommodate caring responsibilities.

In the public sector, there appeared to be less variability in provision. Older public sector workplaces (those that had been in existence for 25 years or more) were more likely to have at least two types of numerical flexibility than workplaces which were less than five years old (74 per cent and 45 per cent, respectively), suggesting that it took some time for new workplaces to adopt such practices. However, there was no association with the proportion of the workforce that was female, after controlling for other factors. The use of numerical flexibility was also similar across public sector workplaces in different industrial sectors.

In summary, there was some convergence between the public and private sectors in the use of many of the different types of numerical flexibility between 2004 and 2011. While private sector workplaces increased the provision of most of these arrangements, levels remained largely static in the public sector. However, the proportion of public sector workplaces which made use of at least one type of numerical flexibility in addition to part-time work remained higher than that in the private sector. There was also no evidence that workplaces that were more adversely affected by the recession, in either sector, varied in the likelihood that they used at least two types of numerical flexibility. This suggests that, having controlled for a range of other characteristics, there was no consistent pattern of those employers who were hardest hit by the recession responding by increasing the use of numerical flexibility.

Functional Flexibility

While having the ability to vary the size of the workforce to match fluctuations in demand may be a significant advantage to employers in an economic downturn, there is a potential mismatch between the interests of employers and those of employees who may want more certainty in their hours of work. An alternative approach is for employers to train staff to do a range of jobs so that they can be redeployed as needed, known as multi-skilling.

The percentage of workplaces with at least one employee from the largest occupational group who had been formally trained to do a job other than their own was stable between the 1998 and 2004 WERS surveys (Kersley et al., 2006: 92), but in the more recent period there was an increase, rising from 60 per cent in 2004 to 65 per cent in 2011. Nevertheless, the proportion of workplaces in which staff actually exhibited functional flexibility was stable over the period. Of those workplaces with multi-skilled employees, around three fifths redeployed some staff to other tasks at least once a week (61 per cent in both 2004 and 2011). The stability in the proportion of workplaces that used functional flexibility between 2004 and 2011 suggests that employers have not turned to functional flexibility in response to the economic downturn. However, there was one sector in which functional flexibility became less common: in 2011 67 per cent of workplaces in the private manufacturing sector had some employees in the largest occupational group doing a job other than their own at least once a week, compared with 84 per cent in 2004.

Flexibility and Job Cuts: Alternative Strategies to Weather the Storm?

Looking first at numerical flexibility, a regression analysis demonstrated that private sector employers used particular types of numerical flexibility as substitutes and complements for each other.[12] Private sector workplaces that had some part-time employees in 2011 were less likely to also have some employees on fixed-term or temporary contracts, or on annual hours contracts. These types of working arrangements may be less compatible with part-time work, or at least may be perceived as not likely to be open to part-time employees. Workplaces with fixed-term or temporary employees were also less likely to use homeworking.

Some types of numerical flexibility were complementary: zero hours contracts were more likely to be used in workplaces that had some staff on annual hours or part-time contracts. Annual hours contracts were also commonly combined with homeworking, and homeworking with the use of freelancers, which indicates that some workplaces have a particular need for flexibility over the hours worked by staff leading them to introduce practices which seek to meet this in a number of ways. Also, workplaces with some agency workers were more likely to have staff on fixed-term and temporary contracts, suggesting that access to a supplementary workforce for a limited period of time was important in these workplaces.

While different types of numerical flexibility appeared to be used as substitutes and complements for each other, previous evidence on whether numerical flexibility is a substitute or complement for functional flexibility is rather mixed. For example, analysis of WERS 1998 found that they were substitutes (Cully et al., 1999), while White et al. (2004) found that numerical and functional flexibility were positively correlated. There was little evidence from a regression analysis of the 2011 WERS that functional and numerical flexibility were either used to complement each other, or as substitutes. The only exceptions to this were that, where there were some freelancers the workplace was less likely to make regular use of functional flexibility, whereas functional flexibility was more common in workplaces that had some employees on annual hours contracts. This suggests that the need to employ freelancers is reduced when the existing workforce is trained to carry out a range of different tasks.

There was also only limited evidence that numerical flexibility was used to avoid redundancies. Redundancies were less likely to occur in the year prior to the 2011 survey in workplaces which had some shift workers in 2011, perhaps indicating that the flexibility to adjust shifts has a role to play in reducing costs, offsetting the need for redundancies. Conversely, redundancies were more likely to occur in workplaces which used some homeworkers and had some staff on fixed-term or temporary contracts. None of the other types of numerical flexibility were associated with the likelihood of redundancies occurring and there was also no link with the use of functional flexibility.

Subcontracting

Employers may subcontract activities as an alternative way of obtaining flexibility over staffing requirements and to meet skills needs. Workplace managers were asked whether any of a list of 11 activities were carried out by independent contractors (see Figure 3.5). The proportion of workplaces that subcontracted some activities remained similar between 2004 and 2011. There was also stability in the use of subcontracting across the 11 specific activities. Around seven in eight workplaces subcontracted at least one practice (84 per cent in 2004 and 87 per cent in 2011).

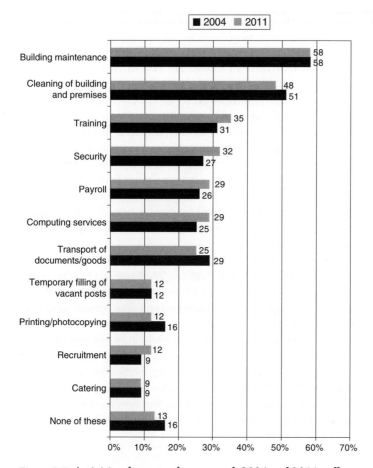

Figure 3.5 *Activities that are subcontracted, 2004 and 2011, cell per cent*

Base: All workplaces with five or more employees. Figures are based on responses from 2,290 (2004) and 2,673 (2011) workplace managers.

Only the proportion of workplaces contracting out security increased between 2004 and 2011, while the subcontracting of printing or photocopying fell.

Workplace managers were also asked whether any of these activities had been outsourced from the workplace in the previous five years (that is, the activity had previously been carried out by employees of the workplace but was now undertaken by a subcontractor). Twelve per cent of all workplaces had outsourced some activities formerly done by employees in the five years prior to the 2011 survey, compared with 14 per cent of workplaces in 2004. Outsourcing was twice as prevalent in the public sector compared with the private sector: 20 per cent of public sector workplaces outsourced some tasks formerly carried out by employees in the five years prior to the 2011 survey, compared with 11 per cent of private sector workplaces. Of the workplaces that outsourced some activities in the five years prior to the 2011 survey, the contractors were former employees in 12 per cent of workplaces, compared with 13 per cent of those that outsourced activities in the five years prior to 2004.

Managers were asked why activities were outsourced. Although making cost savings was an important motivator in more than two fifths (44 per cent) of cases where some outsourcing had occurred, this was almost twice as common in the public sector compared with the private sector (70 per cent and 38 per cent, respectively). Improving service was cited in 42 per cent of workplaces that had outsourced activities and public and private sector workplaces were fairly similar in their decision to contract activities out for this reason. Around one third (34 per cent) of workplaces that outsourced some tasks did this with the aim of being able to focus more on core business activities, but this was more usual in the private sector compared with the public sector (37 per cent and 21 per cent, respectively). One in ten (10 per cent) workplaces outsourced to improve flexibility, but this was more than three times as common in the public sector as in the private sector (23 per cent compared with 7 per cent).

There was no evidence of an increase in the extent to which employers brought previously subcontracted activities in-house between 2004 and 2011. The proportion of workplaces which had switched from external to internal provision of at least one of the activities shown in Figure 3.5 in the five years prior to survey stood at 11 per cent in 2004 and 12 per cent in 2011. Unsurprisingly, it was those activities that were most commonly subcontracted that were most likely to be brought in-house. In almost two thirds (65 per cent) of cases, when activities which were previously carried out by contractors were brought in-house, one motivation was to effect cost savings. In more than two fifths (45 per cent) of workplaces where activities were brought in-house the intention was to improve the service. Seven per cent of workplaces had stopped using external contractors because they had sufficient capability to be able to provide the service in-house.

Changes in Labour Usage during the Recession

Although private sector workplaces increased their use of many types of numerical flexibility over the period from 2004, it is not necessarily the case that the recession was the prime influence, since the change may have occurred before the start of the economic downturn. Similarly, while there was stability overall in the use of functional flexibility and subcontracting in both private and public sector workplaces between 2004 and 2011, there may have been some workplaces that altered their practices because of the changing economic conditions. In 2011 managers were explicitly asked whether they had made changes to staffing practices 'in response to the recent recession', providing a direct way of assessing the impact of the recession on staffing practices.

As noted in Chapter 2, the types of actions taken by employers in response to the recession were different depending on whether the workplace was in the public or private sector. Public sector workplaces were more likely to make changes to the organisation of work as a result of the recession than establishments in the private sector (36 per cent and 23 per cent, respectively). A reduction in the use of agency workers or temporary employees was also more than twice as likely in the public sector compared with the private sector (30 per cent and 13 per cent). However, just 3 per cent of workplaces had increased their use of agency workers or temporary staff, or required employees to take unpaid leave, in response to the recession, with public and private sectors behaving in a similar way in this respect. Private sector employers were more than twice as likely to respond to the recession by cutting basic hours compared with those in the public sector (15 per cent and 7 per cent, respectively). Although workplaces in the public and private sectors appeared to respond differently to the recession in terms of their use of labour, the findings were consistent with Geroski and Gregg's study of the 1990–91 recession which found that changes in labour organisation were sensitive to recessionary pressures (1997: 86).

The way in which the nature of the employment contract affected the employees' experiences of the recession was evident from employees' reports on the changes they experienced 'as a result of the most recent recession'. Permanent staff were most likely to have their work reorganised (17 per cent experienced this change, compared with only 9 per cent of temporary employees and 10 per cent of fixed-term staff), while fixed-term employees were less likely to experience a cut in their contracted working hours, or to be required to take unpaid leave than those on permanent or temporary contacts. Just 2 per cent of fixed-term staff had their hours cut, compared with 4 per cent of permanent staff and 6 per cent of temporary employees. While less than 1 per cent of those on fixed-term contracts were required to take unpaid leave, this was the case for 2 per cent of permanent staff, and 3 per cent of staff on temporary contracts.

CONCLUSION

This chapter has explored fundamental changes in the dynamics of workplace closure and growth in the face of the changing economic climate and legislative framework. It identified the key factors associated with the death and birth of workplaces and whether they grow or shrink. It has highlighted the fact that even during a period affected by an economic downturn, a considerable proportion of workplaces have experienced marked growth and new workplaces have continued to develop. For example, 20 per cent of workplaces in 2011 had come into existence since the 2004 survey. This demonstrates that job creation continued alongside job destruction. However, there was some evidence that employers took more drastic action in response to the recession than was necessary during more settled economic times. For example, there was an increase in the proportion of workplaces making redundancies in the year before the 2011 survey compared with the picture at the time of the 2004 survey.

In many respects, established patterns of workplace birth, death and growth in the public and private sectors have continued in the period since 2004. Private sector workplaces continued to be more likely to close than those in the public sector, while new workplaces were more likely to develop in the private sector compared with the public sector. Similar proportions of public and private sector workplaces made some redundancies in the year prior to the 2011 survey. In total, 17 per cent of workplaces made some compulsory or voluntary redundancies in response to the recession, with compulsory redundancies being more common than voluntary redundancies. While the proportion of public and private sector workplaces making some redundancies was similar, different factors were associated with redundancies in each sector, partly due to the lower exposure to market pressures in the public sector. However, within both the public and private sectors, workplaces that were more adversely affected by the recession were more likely to make redundancies.

There was also a reduction in the proportion of workplaces with job security guarantees between 2004 and 2011. However, while workplaces that offered job security guarantees were just as likely to make redundancies as a result of the recession, these were less likely to be compulsory. The reduction in the proportion of workplaces that offered job security guarantees over time could be consistent with employers either using the current economic climate to free their hand to exercise managerial prerogative at a future date, or with changes made under extreme circumstances in order to ensure the survival of the workplace. For this reason, even in a survey as detailed as WERS, it is difficult to conclude whether employers who made changes to working practices as a result of the recession were universally acting out of distress, or in a more opportunistic way.

The economic climate fed through to employee perceptions of job security. Employees were less likely to believe that their job was secure in 2011 than in 2004, and employees were less likely to feel secure in 2011 in workplaces where redundancies had been made in the 12 months before the survey. However, despite the similarities in experiences of redundancies between the public and private sectors, perceptions of job security among public sector employees fell by a far greater amount than those of private sector employees between 2004 and 2011.

Despite the uncertain economic climate, there was a considerable degree of stability of employment within workplaces. Just 20 per cent of surviving workplaces reduced their workforce by more than one fifth between 2004 and 2011, with only 5 per cent shrinking by more than 50 per cent. On the other hand, 40 per cent of workplaces grew by more than one fifth over the period. There were no notable differences between the public and private sectors as similar proportions of workplaces shrunk and grew by one fifth.

There was an increase in the use of most types of numerical flexibility in the private sector, while 15 per cent cut basic hours in response to the recession, presumably as a means of retaining staff while reducing labour costs. Employers sometimes used the different forms of numerical flexibility as substitutes for one another, and in other cases, practices were complementary. However, there was little evidence that employers took a consistent approach in using numerical and functional flexibility either together, to complement each other, or as substitutes for one another. The proportion of public sector workplaces which made use of many of the different types of numerical flexibility remained higher than that in the private sector, but the incidence of practices in the public sector changed little between 2004 and 2011.

There was evidence that the changes that employees experienced as a result of the recession depended on the nature of their contract of employment. In many respects, permanent employees were expected to provide greater flexibility than those on fixed-term or temporary contracts as they were the group most likely to have their work reorganised and were more likely to have their contracted working hours cut or be required to take unpaid leave than those on fixed-term contacts. It is likely that this reflects differences in the nature of tasks carried out by permanent, temporary and fixed-term employees, with those on fixed-term and temporary contracts carrying out discrete or time-limited tasks that offer fewer opportunities for variation.

4 The Involvement of Employees in Workplace Change

INTRODUCTION

All workplaces face the prospect of change at one time or another. Managers and employees will often be proactive in developing ideas for how to improve work processes, work organisation or working conditions. However, the stimulus may also come from outside the workplace, if developments in product or labour markets are judged to have the potential to risk the workplace's competitiveness. The recession has, of course, amplified these external pressures. Many workplaces in the private sector have seen reductions in the demand for their products and services, while many workplaces in the public sector have seen reductions in their operational budgets. These changed circumstances are likely to have led many managers to re-evaluate working processes or organisational methods in search of cost-savings, or (in some cases) to innovate proactively in search of the all-important competitive edge.

The resulting process of adaptation creates an impetus for dialogue between managers and employees within the workplace as they search for the best way forward. Ensuring that this dialogue takes place is argued by some to be an important means of arriving at decisions which are 'socially optimal' – that is, optimal for both employers and their employees (Freeman and Lazear, 1995). It is also argued that, if employees are allowed to contribute to decision-making, they will reciprocate with greater levels of engagement in their work and a more positive attitude towards the workplace as a whole (MacLeod and Clarke, 2009). Others see the question of participation primarily as one of citizenship (or power) with the employee as a stakeholder who deserves a voice over issues that affect them (Kelly, 1998; Commission of the European Communities, 2002; Budd, 2004). Yet, in spite of the potential benefits, concerns about the time required to consult with employees, or about the practicalities of sharing sensitive information, may dissuade managers from involving employees in decisions over workplace changes, particularly when the workplace's survival may be at stake.

This chapter looks at the ways in which workplaces approach the management of organisational change. On the employers' side, the chapter investigates who has day-to-day responsibility for personnel and employment relations issues at the workplace – whether it is a general manager or Human Resource (HR) specialist – and examines variations in these managers' attitudes towards consultation over workplace change. On the employees' side, the chapter investigates the extent to which workers have representatives (union or non-union) to articulate their views, and the extent to which workplaces have arrangements to facilitate direct communication between managers and their staff. This sets the scene for the second part of the chapter, which identifies the scale of organisational changes that workplaces have recently made and investigates the extent to which employees were involved in shaping those changes. In covering these issues, the chapter typically does not draw a distinction between negotiation and consultation, as both comprise involvement on the part of employees; however, the scope of bargaining is explored in Chapter 5.

Historically, there has been a great deal of variability in both the form and extent of dialogue between managers and employees over workplace change. This has led policymakers to implement rules that give employees the right to be involved in discussions over some of the main terms and conditions of employment, and in major business decisions.[1] In particular, the introduction and extension of the Information and Consultation of Employees Regulations (the ICE Regulations) between 2005 and 2008 represent a potentially important legislative change in this area since the previous WERS survey was conducted. A principal objective of the Regulations was to provide for representative structures through which dialogue would take place between employers and employees over 'substantial changes in work organisation or in contractual relations'.[2] The Regulations now seem particularly well timed, given the hardship that many workplaces have faced over the past few years, and so one objective for the chapter is to examine the effect that the regulations may have had on workplace practice.

The recession is another important contextual element for the chapter. On the one hand, it is possible that the pressure for change led managers to reduce their engagement with employees in decision-making: for instance, if they feared that consultation may slow down their reaction to the crisis. Yet it is also possible that the scale of change meant that managers increased the level of employee involvement, perhaps in identifying the best way forward. With these competing possibilities in mind, the chapter also considers how effective employees consider their managers are at informing and consulting them over organisational change and whether this has changed since 2004.

MANAGING EMPLOYMENT RELATIONS AT THE WORKPLACE

This first section of the chapter looks at the characteristics and autonomy of the manager with principal day-to-day responsibility for personnel and Employment Relations (ER) issues at the workplace. These are referred to hereafter as 'workplace ER managers'.[3] One objective is to understand who has been on the front line of employment relations as workplaces have faced up to the consequences of the recession.

Who has Responsibility for Employment Relations?

As most workplaces are relatively small (see Table 1.1), it is perhaps not surprising to find few that have a dedicated employment relations specialist, and that most workplace ER managers combine their personnel responsibilities with other duties. Only one in seven workplace ER managers in 2011 (14 per cent) had a job title that indicated they specialised in employment relations, personnel or human resources. Instead, in most workplaces (78 per cent), employment relations issues were the responsibility of the owner or the general manager; in the remainder (8 per cent) it was the responsibility of someone with another functional specialisation such as a finance manager. Nevertheless, some of these managers were spending substantial amounts of time on personnel and employment relations issues. If we adopt a broad definition of an 'ER specialist' which includes any workplace manager who *either* had an ER-related job title *or* spent more than half their time on employment relations and personnel issues, we find that over one fifth (22 per cent) of all workplaces had such a manager in 2011. This was not statistically significant from the figure of 20 per cent observed in 2004, suggesting that the increasing specialisation in personnel that was seen at workplace level in the late 1990s and early 2000s has not continued (Kersley et al., 2006: 39).

As suggested previously, small workplaces are less able to support functional specialism and, indeed, the presence of an ER specialist is strongly associated with workplace size. Only 15 per cent of all workplaces with 5 to 19 employees had a specialist ER manager in 2011, compared with 32 per cent of those with 20 to 99 employees and 71 per cent of larger workplaces. ER specialists were also more common in public sector workplaces (26 per cent) than in private sector services (21 per cent) or manufacturing (23 per cent).

Looking at the characteristics of workplace ER managers, it is apparent that they were more qualified in 2011 than had been the case in 2004. The proportion of workplaces where the ER manager had a formal qualification in personnel management or another closely related subject rose from 22 per cent to 28 per cent over the period. Around one quarter of this six percentage points increase could be accounted for by the increasing prevalence of female workplace managers, who tend to be more qualified than their male counterparts. The proportion of female workplace managers rose from 39 per cent in 2004 to 48 per cent in 2011. More than half (54 per cent) of all employees now work in an establishment with a qualified ER manager (up from 46 per cent in 2004), and the same proportion (54 per cent) work in a site with a female ER manager (up from 50 per cent in 2004).

The rise in qualifications is part of a longer-term trend that can be traced back to the mid-1980s (Guest and Bryson, 2009: 125) and is likely to be related, at least in part, to a more general trend towards certification of vocational skills. Similarly, the rise in the proportion of women managers is not a recent phenomenon (ibid.: 127) and, while it can be seen as part of the broader increase in female employment, the scale of the rise suggests that women are accessing positions of HR responsibility within the workplace more easily than many other professions.[4] This is noteworthy because analysis presented later in this chapter suggests that female ER managers are more likely than their male counterparts to see consultation as a necessary part of the management process.

In seeking to manage change, one important issue for workplace managers is the extent to which they have operational autonomy from managers at higher levels. It is possible to gauge this by looking at branch sites (which together account for around half of all workplaces) and investigating whether managers in those workplaces are able to make decisions on specific personnel issues without consulting managers elsewhere in their organisation. Table 4.1 shows that workplace ER managers in branch sites usually have autonomy to act on issues relating to staffing, recruitment and employee performance (for example, training or appraisal), but that they are much less likely to have autonomy to alter terms and conditions (that is, rates of pay, holiday entitlements and pension entitlements). The latter are, of course, often set with reference to centralised scales. The clear difference in autonomy over staffing and rates of pay suggests that many workplace managers may have had the freedom to adjust their headcount in response to recessionary pressures but that, in multi-site organisations, any wage cuts or freezes for existing staff will have typically been initiated at higher levels.

The degree of autonomy enjoyed by workplace managers has increased in recent years. Summing across all of the 13 items listed in Table 4.1, the mean number of items on which workplace managers had autonomy rose from 5.6 in 2004 to 6.4 in 2011 (see Table 4.2). Statistically significant increases were seen in respect

Table 4.1 *HR issues where decisions can be made in branch sites without consulting managers elsewhere in the organisation, 2004 and 2011, cell per cent*

	2004	2011
Training of employees	72	78
Performance appraisals	60	74
Staffing plans	66	72
Recruitment or selection of employees	63	68
Health and safety	42	63
Grievances or grievance procedures	44	55
Working hours	53	54
Disciplinary matters or procedures	46	52
Equal opportunities and diversity	34	43
Holiday entitlements	25	27
Rates of pay	30	23
Recognition of a trade union	17	18
Pension entitlements	12	7
None of these	11	9

Base: Workplaces with five or more employees, if part of a larger organisation and not the head office, and management interview conducted with on-site manager. Figures are based on responses from 1,176 (2004) and 1,163 (2011) workplace managers.

Table 4.2 *Average number of HR issues where decisions can be made in branch sites without consulting managers elsewhere in the organisation, 2004 and 2011, mean*

	2004	2011
All workplaces	5.6	<u>6.4</u>
Private sector manufacturing	8.5	7.6
Private sector services	5.5	<u>6.5</u>
Public sector	5.2	5.8
HR specialist on site	5.6	5.8
No HR specialist on site	5.7	<u>6.5</u>

Base: All workplaces with five or more employees, if part of a larger organisation and not the head office, and management interview conducted with on-site manager. Figures are based on responses from 1,176 (2004) and 1,163 (2011) workplace managers.

of appraisals, health and safety, grievances and equal opportunities, although autonomy declined in respect of rates of pay and pensions (Table 4.1).

The change was partly compositional, as those workplaces that entered the population between 2004 and 2011 (comprising new workplaces and those which grew to have five or more employees in 2011) had higher levels of autonomy, on average, than those workplaces which left the population (those which closed down or shrank to have fewer than five employees in 2011). However, the change was also behavioural: ER autonomy increased on average in workplaces that continued to be part of the survey population between 2004 and 2011. Some organisations were, then, moving from a more centralised to a more decentralised approach in respect of employment relations.

The average degree of autonomy enjoyed by local managers in the private services sector increased between 2004 and 2011 (see Table 4.2), but the changes seen in private manufacturing and the public sector were not statistically significant. The overall increase in autonomy between 2004 and 2011 was also restricted to workplaces without ER specialists (Table 4.2) and, indeed, the rise in ER autonomy among general managers wholly accounts for the overall increase in private services (where only one quarter of branch sites had an ER specialist in 2011).

A further indicator of the relationship between workplace managers and the higher echelons of their organisation is the proportion of private sector workplaces belonging to enterprises that have someone on their Board of Directors or top governing body with specific responsibility for employment relations. Guest and Bryson (2009: 128) noted that there was remarkably little movement in this percentage over the period 1980–2004 and, indeed, the figure observed in 2011 (56 per cent) is not statistically significant from that seen in 2004 (57 per cent). However, these aggregate figures mask a substantial increase among medium-sized private sector enterprises. Such enterprises account for only a small proportion of private sector workplaces (12 per cent in 2011), but within this group the proportion of workplaces covered by Boards that had someone with specific responsibility for employment relations rose from 39 per cent in 2004 to 60 per cent in 2011 (Figure 4.1).[5] This means that there is no longer a stark dichotomy

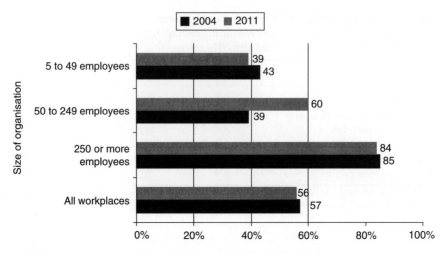

Figure 4.1 *Percentage of workplaces in UK-based, multi-site, private sector organisations for which there is an ER specialist on the board, 2004 and 2011, cell per cent*

Base: All workplaces with five or more employees, if part of a larger private sector organisation with its head office in the UK. Figures are based on responses from 1,394 (2004) and 1,539 (2011) workplace managers.

between workplaces belonging to small and medium enterprises (SMEs) and those belonging to large enterprises but, instead, the likelihood of board-level ER representation now increases monotonically between small, medium and large enterprises.

Strategic Planning over ER Issues

While there was no overall increase in the proportion of private sector workplaces belonging to enterprises with ER representation on the Board of Directors, there were other indications that ER issues were being given greater prominence at the top of organisations between 2004 and 2011. Workplace managers were asked whether their workplace was covered by a formal strategic plan that set out objectives and how they are achieved. If the workplace was covered by such a plan, managers were then asked whether specific issues are covered in the plan. Table 4.3 shows there were statistically significant increases in workplaces covered by plans that included employee diversity (28 per cent in 2004 and 33 per cent in 2011) and in workplaces covered by plans that included forecasts of staffing requirements (41 per cent in 2004 and 47 per cent in 2011). The percentages of all workplaces covered by strategic plans that set objectives for employee development or employee job satisfaction did not increase to a statistically significant extent. Nonetheless, there was a substantial increase among workplaces belonging to medium-sized private sector organisations in the coverage of strategic plans that set objectives for job satisfaction (from 26 per cent in 2004 to 45 per cent in 2011).

Table 4.3 *Workplaces with specific ER issues in formal strategic plans, by size and sector of organisation, 2004 and 2011, cell per cent*

	Employee development		Employee job satisfaction		Employee diversity		Forecasts of staffing requirements	
	2004	2011	2004	2011	2004	2011	2004	2011
Small (5 to 49 employees) private enterprise	28	35	21	23	13	17	20	<u>29</u>
Medium (50 to 249 employees) private enterprise	54	60	26	<u>45</u>	24	33	38	<u>57</u>
Large (250 or more employees) private enterprise	76	81	56	58	43	<u>52</u>	65	67
Public sector	79	78	44	46	49	49	56	64
All workplaces	53	56	36	39	28	<u>33</u>	41	<u>47</u>

Base: All workplaces with five or more employees. Figures are based on responses from 2,274 (2004) and 2,649 (2011) workplace managers.

Did the Recession Inhibit a More Strategic Approach to ER Management?

Some have argued that recessions are times when it is important for managers to maintain a long term outlook, particularly when making decisions that affect the workforce (for example, Acas-CIPD, 2009). One rationale is that there can be substantial costs incurred in replacing redundant workers if market conditions quickly improve. Yet the pressures to focus on the short term can be intense. Indeed, the recession appeared to have hindered the extension of strategic planning to some extent. We used the panel of workplaces interviewed in both 2004 and 2011 to examine how workplace experience of the recession may have affected the prevalence of strategic planning over ER issues. We divided these workplaces into three groups: workplaces that were affected 'A great deal' or 'Quite a lot' by the recession (group 1); those that were affected 'A moderate amount' (group 2); and those that were affected 'Just a little' or 'Not at all' (group 3). The coverage of plans that included forecasts of staffing requirements expanded most in group 3 (from 34 per cent of workplaces in 2004 to 52 per cent in 2011). The increase was smaller in group 2 (from 52 to 62 per cent) and smallest of all in group 1 (from 49 to 52 per cent). This suggests that the percentage of workplaces making strategic forecasts of staffing requirements would have increased by even more than it did (Table 4.3) had it not been for the recession, perhaps because it brought so much uncertainty about levels of future demand.

A similar pattern was evident in respect of strategic planning over employee development: there was a statistically significant increase among those workplaces least affected by the recession (from 47 per cent to 61 per cent) but no such increase among workplaces more severely affected. There was, however, no relationship between the impact of the recession and changes in strategic planning over job satisfaction or employee diversity. Nor was there any relationship between the impact of the recession and the other indicators of workplace management discussed so far (namely, the presence of an HR specialist and the extent of branch autonomy from higher levels).

Workplace Managers' Attitudes to Consultation

The chapter has focused thus far on the characteristics of ER management at the workplace, but the ultimate interest is in how these characteristics might affect the process of workplace change. To what extent do workplace managers vary in their attitudes towards consultation over workplace change, and are there particular types of managers who take a more positive attitude towards it?

WERS asked the management respondent for their opinion, as a manager at the workplace, on a number of issues. This included asking them the extent to which they agreed or disagreed that, 'We do not introduce changes here without first discussing the implications with employees'. Answers were invited on a five-point Likert scale from 'Strongly agree' to 'Strongly disagree'. Some 72 per cent of workplace managers either agreed or strongly agreed in 2004, but in 2011 the figure had risen to 80 per cent. Workplace managers were then, on their own accounts at least, more favourably disposed towards consultation in 2011 than had been the case in 2004.

Regression analysis revealed that views varied across many of the characteristics discussed earlier in the chapter. Female managers were seven percentage points more likely than male managers to agree that changes would only be introduced after discussing the implications with employees, while agreement also became more common as managers' length of service in the job increased. Finally, managers in workplaces with strategic plans covering employee job satisfaction were eight percentage points more likely to agree that changes were discussed than those in workplaces without such plans. These factors did not account for much of the increase in managerial attitudes towards consultation between 2004 and 2011 – after controlling for changes in the characteristics of managers and workplaces in the regression analysis, managers remained six percentage points more likely to agree that they would consult in 2011. However, the analysis does suggest that the workplace's approach to consultation is, in part, shaped by the personal characteristics of the person with day-to-day responsibility for personnel and employment relations issues at the workplace, as well as being shaped by the more formal strategic approach of the wider organisation.[6]

ARRANGEMENTS FOR EMPLOYEE VOICE

The broad arguments in favour of structures that give employees a voice at work were highlighted in the introduction to the chapter, and there are a variety of mechanisms through which employers can consult their employees. One distinction is between representative and direct mechanisms. Within representative mechanisms, one can further distinguish between union-based and non-union forms of employee representation. It is well known – not least because of data provided by the WERS series – that the proportion of all employees who are represented by trade unions has been in long-term decline, although the speed of the decline has slowed down significantly since the late 1990s (Kersley et al., 2006; Brownlie, 2012). When the last WERS was conducted in 2004, there were no substantive signs that non-union representation was expanding its coverage. Instead any growth in the late 1990s and early 2000s appeared to be restricted to arrangements for direct communication between managers and employees (Kersley et al., 2006: 135; Willman et al., 2009: 106). However, it is possible that the introduction of the ICE Regulations in 2005 may have altered the dynamic – particularly in favour of non-union forms of employee representation, as some unions were reticent to use the legislation and there were clear incentives for employers who wished to avoid union involvement to initiate their own pre-existing agreements (Hall et al., 2011).

The following discussion describes the incidence of a range of specific arrangements for employee voice before presenting a summary indicator of the availability of representative and direct voice. Differences between the public and private sectors are a key theme, not only because the coverage of employee representation has historically been much greater in the public sector, but also because the Government's attitude towards trade union representation within its own workplaces has altered in some respects since the 2010 election, as is evident through attempts to limit union representatives' facility time (see, for example, Cabinet Office, 2012; Department for Communities and Local Government, 2013).

Representation via a Trade Union

Official statistics from the Quarterly Labour Force Survey (QLFS) show that trade union membership density in Britain declined from 29 per cent in 2004 to 26 per cent in 2011, with the speed of the decline accelerating after 2009 (Brownlie, 2012). Unlike the QLFS, WERS only covers employment in workplaces with five or more employees and indicates stability in union density in this subset of the economy (the decline from 31 per cent in 2004 to 29 per cent in 2011 is not large enough to be statistically significant). However, statistically significant falls were seen in the Finance sector, where density fell from 34 per cent to 12 per cent, and in Public administration, where it fell from 65 per cent to 59 per cent. Changing attitudes among managers towards union membership may be an important factor in these sectors. Union membership density has always been particularly high in workplaces where managers are in favour of membership (see Kersley et al., 2006: 114) and WERS indicates that these workplaces have become less common since 2004. Employees were asked whether management at their workplace are 'In favour of trade union membership', 'Not in favour of trade union membership' or 'Neutral about it'. Only half (46 per cent) of all employees expressed a view but, in 2011, 13 per cent of all employees judged that managers at their workplace were in favour; this was a statistically significant decline from the 15 per cent observed in 2004. The percentage fell most substantially in Finance (from 17 per cent to 5 per cent).

It also fell substantially in Public administration (from 30 per cent to 24 per cent), Education (from 35 per cent to 31 per cent) and Health (from 22 per cent to 17 per cent).[7]

Union membership is no guarantor of voice in the workplace, however. The involvement of union representatives in consultation over workplace change is considered later in the chapter. However, one broad indicator that managers engage with the union is that it is recognised by management for negotiating pay and conditions for a section of the workforce (the content of bargaining is considered in Chapter 5). As with membership, the long-term decline in union recognition slowed in the late 1990s so there was no statistically significant fall in recognition between 1998 and 2004 among workplaces with 25 or more employees, although there was a fall among workplaces with 10 to 24 employees. Kersley et al. (2006: 122) suggest that the introduction of the Statutory Trade Union Recognition Procedure in 1999 played an indirect role in slowing the decline by prompting employers to reach voluntary agreements with unions.

Recent research suggests a sharp fall since 2004 both in applications to the Central Arbitration Committee (CAC) and in voluntary recognition agreements (Moore, 2013). Nonetheless, the 2011 WERS shows that recognition has continued to hold up overall, with the proportion of all workplaces that recognised unions in 2011 no different to the overall rate of 22 per cent recorded in 2004. Indeed, as Table 4.4 shows, there has been a statistically significant increase in recognition among workplaces with 50 or more employees (from 44 per cent in 2004 to 50 per cent in 2011). There is a suggestion that recognition may have fallen among the smaller workplaces, but the changes shown in Table 4.4 are not statistically significant (nor is the drop among *all* workplaces with fewer than 50 employees from 19 per cent in 2004 to 18 per cent in 2011). The proportion of all employees working in establishments that recognised unions was also stable between 2004 and 2011 (the slight increase from 45 per cent to 47 per cent was not statistically significant).

Overall this suggests that unions may recently have been focusing their organising efforts on larger sites, perhaps because these are more likely to have a bedrock of membership.[8] In 2011, union members accounted for at least half of the workforce in 10 per cent of all workplaces (60 per cent of those in the public sector and 3 per cent in the private sector).[9] Many of these workplaces already had recognition agreements. Only 4 per cent of all workplaces in 2011 (5 per cent in 2004) had no recognition agreement but had union membership density of at least 10 per cent (the threshold for an application to be considered by the CAC), and around one in seven of these workplaces were in the public sector. The prospects for an increase in the proportion of workplaces recognising unions therefore continue largely to be reliant on further organising.

For individual union members, their main conduit for formal representation to the employer on a day-to-day basis is typically through on-site lay representatives. Charlwood and Forth (2009: 77–81) show that workplaces with recognised unions became increasingly less likely to have on-site stewards, even as recognition rates stabilised in the late 1990s. However, this trend appears to have been arrested. There was no change between 2004 and 2011 in the proportion of workplaces with a recognised union that had a lay union representative on-site (34 per cent in 2004

Table 4.4 *Percentage of workplaces with recognised trade unions, by workplace size and sector, 2004 and 2011, cell per cent*

	2004	2011
Workplace size		
5–9 employees	15	16
10–24 employees	20	16
25–49 employees	35	30
50 or more employees	44	<u>50</u>
Sector		
Private sector manufacturing	13	9
Private sector services	13	12
Public sector	90	92
All workplaces	22	22
All employment	45	47

Base: All workplaces with five or more employees. Figures are based on responses from 2,226 (2004) and 2,621 (2011) workplace managers.

and 32 per cent in 2011). The percentage of all workplaces that recognised unions and had an on-site lay union representative was also unchanged (8 per cent in 2004 and 7 per cent in 2011). The proportion of all employees who worked in such an establishment was 36 per cent in 2011 (35 per cent in 2004); this proportion did not change in the private sector (where 24 per cent of all employees were in a workplace with an on-site union rep in 2011) or in the public sector (where the figure stood at 72 per cent in 2011).

The Worker Representative Questionnaire (WRQ) provides insights into the characteristics of the most senior union representative at the workplace. Three fifths (61 per cent) of senior workplace union representatives in 2011 were male. This compared with 51 per cent of all union members. Neither percentage had changed to a statistically significant degree since 2004. However, senior workplace representatives were older, on average, in 2011 than in 2004. Some 90 per cent were aged 40 years or older in 2011, compared with 82 per cent in 2004. This ageing of the population of senior workplace representatives was, nevertheless, consistent with the ageing of their constituents. The percentage of union members aged 40 or more rose from 65 per cent to 72 per cent over the period. These trends are not new (see Charlwood and Forth, 2009: 86) but their continuation will be of concern to those who previously argued for the need to recruit a younger generation of union representatives (Fairbrother, 2000).

The WRQ also indicates the amount of time that senior union representatives spend on their representative activities in the workplace. As noted earlier, concerns have been raised within central government about the amount of paid time that is spent on union duties by some representatives in the public sector. WERS does not make a distinction between the number of hours that are paid and the number that are unpaid for individual representatives. However, it shows that senior workplace union representatives in the public sector were spending 15 hours per week, on average, on their union duties, compared with an average of 11 hours per week in the private sector. Nevertheless, this difference is not statistically significant and can mostly be accounted for by the larger number of members that tend to be present in public sector workplaces and the greater likelihood that a recognition agreement is in place.[10]

The preceding discussion refers to lay union representatives in general. However, one area of increasing focus for unions is on the recruitment of single-issue representatives, such as Union Learning Reps (ULRs). The first ULRs emerged in 2000 following the establishment of the Union Learning Fund in 1998, and it has been estimated that over 25,000 had been trained by 2010 (Unionlearn with the TUC, 2010). Among the 8 per cent of workplaces with some on-site union representation in 2011, 16 per cent had a ULR (according to the workplace manager). This was an increase from the figure of 10 per cent in 2004. Despite this growth, only 1 per cent of all workplaces had a ULR in 2011. However, they are heavily concentrated in very large workplaces; therefore 31 per cent of all employees were located in a workplace with a ULR.

Non-Union Employee Representatives

Non-union representatives perform a representative function in their workplace – perhaps in discussions over issues such as pay and training – but do not perform their role on behalf of a trade union. As such, their statutory rights to paid time-off, training or the use of facilities are more narrowly prescribed (see Acas, 2009, 2011). In 2011 some 7 per cent of workplaces had one or more non-union representatives on site, this being no different from the figure observed in 2004. In common with all forms of employee representation, non-union representatives are more common in larger workplaces, and so a higher proportion of all employees worked in a site with a non-union representative – this stood at 17 per cent in 2011 (again unchanged from 2004). Unlike other types of representation, there is no substantial difference in the prevalence of non-union representatives between the private and public sectors. This is because they are much less common than trade union representatives in public sector workplaces, rather than being particularly prevalent in the private sector. In 2011, 13 per cent of public sector employees and 18 per cent of private sector employees worked in establishments with non-union representatives.

Joint Consultative Committees

Joint Consultative Committees (JCCs) are committees of managers and employees that are primarily concerned with consultation, rather than negotiation; in some workplaces they are known as works councils or representative forums. Union representatives often sit on JCCs but, equally, many operate with no union involvement or with a mixture of union and non-union representatives. JCCs are therefore one means by which managers may engage with the union or non-union representatives discussed earlier. The ICE Regulations were designed to provide a mechanism for creating representative structures through which employers could inform and consult their employees about significant changes, and it was expected that the Regulations would lead to an increase in the incidence of JCCs. The Regulations came into effect for organisations with at least 150 employees in April 2005, and were progressively extended to cover all those with at least 50 employees by April 2008. The requirement to inform and consult employees does not operate automatically under the Regulations; if the employer does not choose to start the process it must be triggered by a formal request from at least 10 per cent of the workforce. A comparison between the 2004 and 2011 WERS provides a valuable opportunity to contribute to the broader assessment of the Regulations' impact.

WERS seeks to identify the presence of JCCs at two levels. The survey is primarily concerned with committees that operate at the sampled workplace. However, the survey also asks about the existence of committees at a higher level in the organisation, for example, at divisional, regional or head office level. In some cases, a higher-level committee may take the form of an European Works Council: representative forums that exist at the European level in some multinational corporations.

In 2011, 8 per cent of all workplaces had a JCC on site – a figure that was not statistically significant from the figure of 9 per cent in 2004. A similar picture emerges after focusing in on workplaces belonging to organisations with 50 or more employees (that is, those now covered by the ICE Regulations) – 14 per cent had an on-site JCC in 2004 compared with 13 per cent in 2011. The figures are identical if one focuses on workplaces belonging to organisations with 150 or more employees. Subdividing workplaces into more discrete size categories indicates that there has been a statistically significant increase among workplaces in organisations with 100 to 249 employees – 18 per cent had an on-site JCC in 2011 compared with 9 per cent in 2004 (Table 4.5). It is notable that this increase has occurred in the vicinity of the original threshold for the Regulations when they were first introduced in 2005; it may then indicate some legislative influence. However, it is not clear why there has been no similar increase among workplaces belonging to larger organisations, which have also been covered since 2005. The broader picture therefore suggests that the impact of the ICE Regulations in promoting the expansion of workplace JCCs has been very limited.

There is also no evidence of any expansion of committees at a divisional, regional or head office level. Almost three fifths (58 per cent) of branch sites in 2004 reported that a consultative committee operated at a higher level in their organisation, but in 2011 the proportion had fallen to under half (46 per cent). Some caution must be attached to these figures as managers are being asked about structures outside of the workplace and their knowledge may be partial. Furthermore, the most dramatic decline was seen in the Finance sector, where there were difficulties in gaining the co-operation of some of the largest organisations. Statistically significant declines were also seen in the Wholesale and retail trade and Hotels and restaurants industries, however, and the overall decrease remains similar if the Finance sector is excluded.[11]

It is, of course, difficult to identify what would have happened in the absence of the ICE Regulations and, as the incidence of workplace JCCs was falling in the years leading up to the enactment of the Regulations (Kersley et al., 2006: 126–27), the stability in on-site JCCs seen between 2004 and 2011 may nevertheless be indicative of some impact. Even so, it is clear that the Regulations have not stimulated a growth of consultative committees as some had anticipated.

Table 4.5 *Workplaces with an on-site Joint Consultative Committee, 2004 and 2011, cell per cent*

	2004	**2011**
Organisation size		
5–49 employees	3	3
50–99 employees	10	12
100–249 employees	9	<u>18</u>
250–999 employees	14	13
1,000–9,999 employees	13	11
10,000 or more employees	17	14
All workplaces	9	8
All employment	38	37

Base: All workplaces with five or more employees. Figures are based on responses from 2,291 (2004) and 2,676 (2011) workplace managers.

At each workplace WERS also collected information about the characteristics and operation of the committee that dealt with the widest range of issues.[12] Three notable characteristics are the frequency with which the committee meets, the affiliation of the employee representatives and the approach managers take when consulting members of the committee.

One possible outcome of the ICE Regulations is that JCCs meet more frequently, but this did not appear to have happened, on average. The proportion of workplace JCCs that had met at least four times in the 12 months prior to the survey (that is, at least quarterly) was stable at around four fifths (85 per cent in 2004 and 82 per cent in 2011), while the proportion that had met at least 12 times (that is, at least monthly) was stable at around one third (30 per cent in 2004 and 33 per cent in 2011).

As the engagement of many trade unions with the Regulations has been limited (Hall et al., 2011: 6), one would not necessarily expect to see a large increase in the proportion of on-site JCCs with some union representation. Indeed one might expect more non-union committees because of the incentives for employers to take the initiative in establishing voluntary arrangements. In fact, there has been little change. In 26 per cent of workplaces with a workplace-level JCC in 2011, the employee side included at least one union representative; this was lower than the figure of 32 per cent for 2004, but the difference was not statistically significant.

One common complaint – at least from unions – has been that consultation often does not happen at a sufficiently early stage in the managerial decision-making process to allow employees to have real influence (Grell and Sisson, 2005: 10). Indeed the majority of JCCs in Hall et al.'s (2011) longitudinal case study research were described as 'communicators' of decisions that had already been taken by management, rather than as bodies engaged in active consultation. In 2011, when asked about consultation with their workplace JCC, 44 per cent of managers said their usual approach was to 'Seek solutions to problems'. A further 36 per cent said that it was to 'Seek feedback on a range of options put forward by management' and the remaining 20 per cent said that it was to 'Seek feedback on a preferred option put forward by management'. In 2004, the figures were 44 per cent for each of the first two options and 12 per cent for the latter. The rise in the percentage saying that their usual approach was only to seek feedback on a preferred option was statistically significant and suggests a narrowing of the agenda. Corroboration came from worker representatives who sat on a JCC as part of their representative role, and who were asked the same question. In 2004, 8 per cent of these representatives said that managers sought feedback on a preferred option but in 2011 this figure had risen to 28 per cent.

There was, then, no expansion of workplace JCCs between 2004 and 2011, and no substantive change, on average, in their frequency of meeting or in the composition of the employee side. In contrast, there was a clear indication that managers were more restrictive in 2011 in the way that they approached consultation with the members of the committee. Again, it is hard to conclude that the ICE Regulations have substantively enhanced the practice of joint consultation in Britain over the past seven years.

The Prevalence of Partnership Working between Employee Representatives and Managers

Having reviewed union and non-union forms of employee representation, we now compare the extent to which each works in partnership with workplace managers over organisational change initiatives. The engagement of representatives in specific instances of organisational change is considered later in the chapter, but here a more general impression is gathered from the WRQ, which asked whether representatives at the respondent's workplace 'work closely with management when changes are being introduced'. Responses were collected on a five-point Likert scale from 'Strongly agree' to 'Strongly disagree'. In 2011 two thirds (65 per cent) of union representatives agreed and one fifth (22 per cent) disagreed that they work closely with management when changes are made. The equivalent percentages among non-union JCC reps were not significantly different at 68 per cent and 11 per cent. It is then possible that, for managers, the more important distinction is between representative and direct channels of consultation.

Direct Methods of Consultation

Respondents to the WERS management questionnaire were asked whether managers at their workplace would rather consult directly with employees than with unions. Managers in 80 per cent of workplaces agreed with this statement in 2011, although this was not a statistically significant change from the figure of 77 per cent in 2004. It was noted earlier that, in the period leading up to 2004, the growth in structured arrangements for consultation and communication was primarily in arrangements for direct consultation. The latest WERS shows that this trend has only continued in some limited respects.

Alongside informal one-to-one conversations, structured arrangements for direct communication are the main method of dialogue between managers and employees in many workplaces, particularly in the private sector where employee representation is limited. The extent of informal one-to-one communication between managers and individual employees is not measured in WERS which, instead, focuses on more formal methods for direct consultation with the workforce. These take two broad forms: face-to-face meetings between managers and groups of employees, and written forms of consultation. They are not equivalent. In particular, it is argued that written methods – such as employee surveys and suggestion schemes – provide more limited means for employees to discuss plans or directly to influence changes, even though they may have the benefit of anonymity that is not available in a face-to-face meeting (Wakeling, 2010: 3).[13]

WERS distinguishes between three types of face-to-face meetings: general meetings that take place between senior managers and the *whole* workforce, either all together or in groups (hereafter called whole-workforce meetings); general meetings that take place between line managers or supervisors and all the workers for whom they are responsible (hereafter called team briefings); and finally problem-solving groups, which typically address a narrower agenda, often limited to aspects of workplace performance.

The prevalence of both types of general meeting rose between 2004 and 2011. Whole-workforce meetings were used in 75 per cent of all workplaces in 2004, rising to 80 per cent in 2011; team briefings were used in 60 per cent of workplaces in 2004, rising to 66 per cent in 2011. A summary measure that identifies the use of either type of face-to-face meeting shows that, together, they are now almost universal in their use. Some 86 per cent of workplaces used either type of meeting in 2004, rising to 90 per cent in 2011. The incidence rose above 95 per cent among workplaces with at least 20 employees.

Almost all such face-to-face meetings are found to offer at least some time for employees to ask questions or offer their views, but in some cases the proportion is relatively small. Within workplaces that offered either whole-workforce meetings or team briefings, the proportion in which at least one quarter of the meeting time was available for employee input declined between 2004 and 2011. This 25 per cent threshold is arbitrary, but serves to identify instances where there are opportunities for substantial dialogue. The decline cancelled out the overall increase in the prevalence of face-to-face meetings so that the percentage of all workplaces holding meetings in which at least one quarter of the time was available for employees was stable (57 per cent of workplaces in 2004, compared with 58 per cent in 2011) (Table 4.6). Such meetings were more widespread in the public sector than in the private sector, but the difference, although substantial, was not as great as for some of the forms of representative voice discussed earlier. In 2011, 71 per cent of public sector workplaces held face-to-face meetings, compared with 56 per cent of those in the private sector.

While the prevalence of general face-to-face meetings was stable between 2004 and 2011 (or increased if one includes those with limited time for employee feedback), the incidence of problem-solving groups declined. WERS asked about the presence of 'groups of non-managerial employees … that solve specific problems or discuss aspects of performance or quality'. Around one fifth (18 per cent) of all workplaces had such groups in 2004 but by 2011 this had fallen to 14 per cent. Again the incidence was higher in the public sector (25 per cent) than in the private sector (13 per cent).

Table 4.6 *Arrangements for direct two-way communication between managers and employees, 2004 and 2011, cell per cent*

	Private sector		Public sector		All workplaces	
	2004	2011	2004	2011	2004	2011
Meetings between senior managers and all employees with 25 per cent+ question time	45	45	54	50	46	46
Team briefings with 25 per cent+ question time	34	37	57	59	37	40
Any face-to-face group meetings with 25 per cent+ question time	*56*	*56*	*68*	*71*	*57*	*58*
Problem-solving groups	16	<u>13</u>	28	25	18	<u>14</u>
Employee survey in past two years	31	33	61	<u>75</u>	35	38
Suggestion scheme	24	23	31	40	25	25
Regular use of email to all employees	33	<u>46</u>	52	<u>73</u>	35	<u>49</u>
Any two-way written communication	*55*	<u>*65*</u>	*82*	<u>*95*</u>	*58*	*69*

Base: All workplaces with five or more employees. Figures are based on responses from at least 2,283 (2004) and 2,674 (2011) workplace managers.

The use of written forms of consultation between managers and employees was also more common in the public sector than among private sector workplaces, and the disparity between the two sectors increased between 2004 and 2011. This was because the expansion in the use of written forms was greater in public sector workplaces (see Table 4.6). The most notable growth was in the regular use of email to consult staff: some 49 per cent of workplaces used it in 2011, up from 35 per cent in 2004. Overall 38 per cent of workplaces said that they had conducted a formal survey of employees' views or opinions during the two years prior to the survey interview (35 per cent in 2004), and 25 per cent had a suggestion scheme (25 per cent also in 2004). If one combines all three written forms of consultation, over two thirds (69 per cent) of workplaces used at least one method, up from just under three fifths (58 per cent) in 2004. In the public sector the figure was 95 per cent, while in the private sector it was 65 per cent.[14]

A Summary of Representative and Direct Forms of Voice

In order to summarise developments on the prevalence of representative and direct forms of voice, a composite measure is constructed to identify: (i) whether the workplace has on-site employee representatives and (ii) whether it has face-to-face meetings at which at least one quarter of the time is available for employees' views or questions.[15] From this summary measure we see that there has been stability between 2004 and 2011 in the overall availability of representative and direct forms

Table 4.7 *Arrangements for representative and direct two-way communication: Workplace and employment coverage, 2004 and 2011, column per cent*

	Workplaces		Employment	
	2004	**2011**	**2004**	**2011**
Representative and direct	11	10	26	<u>30</u>
Representative only	6	6	24	<u>21</u>
Direct only	47	48	26	28
Neither	37	37	23	21

Note: Representative arrangements comprise either on-site trade union representatives, on-site non-union representatives, or workplace-level joint consultative committees. Direct arrangements comprise either meetings between senior managers and all employees, or team briefings, at which at least 25 per cent of the time is made available for employees' questions.
Base: All workplaces with five or more employees. Figures are based on responses from 2,262 (2004) and 2,643 (2011) workplace managers.

of voice at workplace level. In 2011, 10 per cent of all workplaces had both forms of voice, 54 per cent had one form (typically direct voice) and 37 per cent of workplaces had neither (Table 4.7). None of these figures had changed to a statistically significant extent from 2004. There were some shifts in the percentages of employees working in each type of workplace, with an increase in the percentage working in sites with representative and direct voice offsetting a decline in the percentage working in sites with only representative voice. The percentage of employees working in sites with neither form was unchanged, however (22 per cent in 2004 and 21 per cent in 2011).

One would expect the absence of formal arrangements for representative or direct voice to be most common in small workplaces and, indeed, 44 per cent of all workplaces with between five and nine employees had neither type of arrangement in 2011. Informal voice may suffice in such workplaces. However, 23 per cent of workplaces with 50 to 99 employees had neither form of voice, as did 14 per cent of those with 100 to 499 employees and 10 per cent of those with 500 or more employees. Within the private sector, the percentage of workplaces with neither representative nor direct voice was 39 per cent in 2011 and in the public sector it was 18 per cent (neither figure changed to a statistically significant extent from 2004). Public administration, Education and Health were the only industry sectors in 2011 in which at least 70 per cent of workplaces had one or other form of voice.

As Hall and Purcell (2012: 2) have pointed out there is now a varied picture in terms of the arrangements that are available for voice and participation within Britain's workplaces. In the 1990s, many (e.g. Towers, 1997) drew attention to the emergence of a 'representation gap'. Yet it is possible to take this one step further by noting that, in a large minority of workplaces and for a large minority of employees, there are not even structured arrangements to facilitate direct face-to-face participation. It may then be equally appropriate to talk of a 'participation gap' which, if it is not growing, does not appear to be diminishing either. From the point of view of employee consultation, opportunities to voice one's opinion and have it taken on board are key and, on the evidence presented previously, it seems that such opportunities have, at best, remained stable between 2004 and 2011.

Moreover, it does not appear reasonable to blame the recession for any failure in the expansion of employee voice. We repeated the type of analysis described earlier, using the panel of workplaces surveyed in both 2004 and 2011 to examine whether voice mechanisms became less prevalent in workplaces that were more adversely affected by the recession. We found no clear relationship between the adverse impact of the recession and changes in the extent to which workplaces had arrangements for representative or direct forms of voice. Specifically, when looking within each of the three categories we used earlier to identify the degree of the recessionary impact on the workplace (workplaces that were affected 'A great deal' or 'Quite a lot'; those that were affected 'A moderate amount'; and those that were affected 'Just a little' or 'Not at all'), we found no statistically significant changes between 2004 and 2011 within any of the three groups in the incidence of arrangements for representative or direct voice (as measured in Table 4.7). Of course, the presence of an arrangement does not guarantee that it will be used for active consultation: the next section will go on to consider the extent to which managers actually consulted employees or their representatives over specific instances of workplace change. However, the analysis presented here suggests that the recession did not have any substantive effect on the structures that were provided for employee consultation.

MANAGING ORGANISATIONAL CHANGE

The few attitudinal measures that have been discussed so far – whether on managers' general stance towards consultation over workplace change (p. 56), their approach to consulting with JCCs (p. 62) or their preference for direct consultation (p. 63) – have given some indication that many managers remain committed to consultation but that they increasingly favour a direct approach. This section considers the extent to which employees are actually consulted over specific events, and the mechanisms that are used for such consultation. It looks at three scenarios, assessing the extent to which managers consulted employees when (i) a workplace was faced with redundancies; (ii) there was major organisational change; and (iii) there were changes prompted specifically by the recession. The objective is to assess the extent and form of any consultation, rather than to investigate the quality of the outcome.[16]

Consultation over Redundancies

Legislation is in place that seeks to ensure managers consult employees in a meaningful way when large-scale redundancies are planned. When the intention is to make 20 or more employees redundant, they must be consulted at least 30 days in advance. However, such consultation does not always take place and claims to the Employment Tribunal system about inadequate redundancy consultation rose during the recession (see Ranieri, 2011). Moreover, survey evidence suggests that many employees are unhappy at how redundancies have been handled (CIPD, 2010).

In this section we examine the extent to which managers consulted employees over planned redundancies, and who was involved in any consultation that took place.

The WERS management questionnaire focuses on redundancies that were made in the 12 months prior to the survey or proposals that were withdrawn in the same period (for the median interview, this means the period from October 2010 to September 2011). This misses the substantial spike in redundancies which came in late 2008 and early 2009, but the Office for National Statistics (ONS) annual redundancy rates indicate that the rate during the WERS fieldwork period was still higher than the level seen before the onset of the recession.[17]

Some 13 per cent of all workplaces made redundancies in the year preceding the 2011 survey. A further 3 per cent had not made any redundancies but had withdrawn proposals at some point during the year. The percentage of all workplaces that had therefore either made redundancies or withdrawn proposals (16 per cent) was an increase from the 10 per cent observed in 2004. Managers consulted with employees or employee representatives in 83 per cent of workplaces that had considered making redundancies in the year before the 2011 interview. This was not statistically significant from the 76 per cent observed in 2004. In 2011, consultation took place in 68 per cent of workplaces where proposals were withdrawn, in 76 per cent of workplaces that made one employee redundant, and in 94 per cent of workplaces that made two or more employees redundant.

In workplaces where consultation took place, managers were asked whom they consulted. The percentage of workplaces consulting with any type of representative was 34 per cent in 2004 and 27 per cent in 2011, but this decline was not statistically significant. In 2011, 16 per cent consulted with trade unions, 7 per cent consulted with a JCC, 11 per cent consulted with other employee representatives, and 95 per cent consulted directly with employees. None of these individual figures were significantly different from 2004, except that the percentage of workplaces consulting with a JCC was higher at 12 per cent.[18]

Managers did not always consult with representatives when structures for employee representation were in place at the establishment. In 2011, 33 per cent of workplaces that consulted over redundancies had on-site representative structures as measured in Table 4.7. In just over half (54 per cent) of these, managers said that they consulted with at least one type of employee representative (68 per cent in 2004). Consultation with representatives was more likely to have occurred when more than one person was being made redundant, but it was still not universal. Available employee representatives were consulted in 44 per cent of workplaces that made one redundancy, 63 per cent of those that made 2 to 19 redundancies, and 84 per cent of those that made 20 or more people redundant in the year.[19]

HR specialists may have a pivotal role to play in workplaces that consider making redundancies in view of their role as 'stewards of the social contract at work' (Kochan, 2003: 2). Striking the right balance between employer and employee interests may conceivably be more difficult if daily responsibility for employment relations lies with the owner or general manager. This seems to be the case. In 2011, when redundancies were considered, some consultation took place with either employees or their representatives in 94 per cent of workplaces with an HR specialist, but in only 75 per cent of those without.[20] In a regression analysis that controlled for the total number of redundancies and the size of the workplace, the presence of an HR specialist at the workplace was associated with an 11 percentage point higher probability that consultation occurred. In previous research, which did not consider redundancy consultation, Guest and Bryson (2009) failed to find any association between the presence of an HR specialist and a range of HR practices or indicators of workplace performance. Consultation over redundancies is, then, at least one area where the presence of an HR specialist appears to make a tangible difference.

Consultation over Workplace Change

In addition to asking managers about redundancies over the year prior to the survey, WERS explored a range of organisational changes that may have occurred over the previous *two* years (that is, for the median interview, the period October 2009 to September 2011). These changes included alterations in terms of employment (such as the introduction of performance-related pay) and changes in the production process (such as the introduction of new technology). Table 4.8 provides a full list of possible changes. In workplaces that had made more than one of the specified changes, managers were asked to focus on the one that had the greatest impact on employees at the workplace; this is the change we focus on here when assessing the degree of consultation.

Overall 79 per cent of workplaces had made one of the specified changes in the two years prior to the 2011 survey. The change that had the greatest impact on employees was most commonly the 'Introduction or upgrading of new technology (including computers)' (19 per cent). This was followed by 'Changes in the organisation of work' (17 per cent) and 'Changes in work techniques or procedures' (16 per cent). The 'Introduction of new, or significantly improved, products or services' was the most important change in 10 per cent of workplaces, followed by 'Changes in working time arrangements' (8 per cent), the 'Introduction of initiatives to involve employees' (7 per cent) and the 'Introduction of performance-related pay' (3 per cent). The pattern of changes was similar to that found in 2004, with the exception that technological innovation was more commonly cited in 2004, when 35 per cent of workplaces named it as the most important change. However, it is possible that this decline may be an artefact of alterations in the questionnaire, which included separate items for 'new technology' and 'computers' in 2004 but grouped them together in 2011.

Managers were asked about the level of involvement afforded to employees when the most important change was being made; they were also asked the same question regarding the involvement of trade unions and the workplace JCC covering the widest range of issues. Five response options were given: they decided; they negotiated; they were consulted; they were informed; or they had no involvement at all.

In 2011, managers in 50 per cent of workplaces that had made at least one of the specified changes consulted over the most important change with employees or their representatives and a further 13 per cent negotiated with employees. Overall, managers either consulted or negotiated with employees or their representatives in 61 per cent of workplaces (a figure that was identical to that observed in 2004).[21]

Managers were more likely to consult or negotiate with employees when the most important change involved alterations to terms and conditions (the introduction of

Table 4.8 *Workplaces where managers consulted or negotiated with employees over specified organisational changes, 2004 and 2011*

	Most important change in previous two years		Managers consulted or negotiated with employees		Managers consulted with employees		Managers negotiated with employees	
	2004	2011	2004	2011	2004	2011	2004	2011
	Column per cent				Cell per cent			
Introduction of performance-related pay	4	3	62	79	37	45	28	35
Introduction or upgrading of new technology (including computers)[a]	35	19	53	51	42	45	11	7
Changes in working time arrangements	6	8	88	69	55	50	39	22
Changes in the organisation of work	11	17	71	71	67	62	6	11
Changes in work techniques or procedures	11	16	59	62	51	52	10	11
Introduction of initiatives to involve employees	7	7	69	70	59	52	13	22
Introduction of technologically new or significantly improved product or service	8	10	56	50	47	42	11	8
None of the specified changes made	18	21						

Note: (a) Combines two separate items in 2004 – one covering computers and the other covering new technology other than computers. These two items were combined onto a single item – 'new technology (including computers)' – in 2011.
Base: All workplaces with five or more employees. Figures for the first two columns are based on responses from 2,279 (2004) and 2,654 (2011) workplace managers. The bases for the cells in columns three to eight vary between each row.

performance-related pay or changes in working time) or changes to the organisation of work, than they were to consult or negotiate when it involved issues to do
with the production process (work techniques, technology or changes in product
or services) (Table 4.8). Comparing the prevalence of employee involvement on
each item between 2004 and 2011, the only statistically significant change was the
decline in the incidence of negotiation over working time arrangements, although
this may partly reflect a heightened level of engagement over working time just prior
to the 2004 survey, since the Working Time Directive had recently been extended to
some previously excluded groups.

It was shown earlier in the chapter that many managers profess a preference
for consulting employees directly rather than via trade unions. Such attitudes are
most prevalent in workplaces without unions. They are also common in workplaces
where unions are present, but the evidence that managers bypass unions when
consulting over workplace change is limited. For simplicity, the various changes
listed in Table 4.8 can be categorised into two groups: employment-related changes
(those concerning performance-related pay, working time, work organisation or
employee involvement) and production-related changes (those concerning new
technology, work techniques and product innovation). In 2011, an employment-
related change was the most important change to have been made in 44 per cent
of workplaces, and managers involved individual employees to some extent in 68
per cent of such changes (Table 4.9). A production-related change was the most
important in 56 per cent of workplaces, and here managers involved individual
employees to some extent in 53 per cent of such changes. Within the subset of
workplaces that had an on-site union representative, there was little to suggest that
managers were any more likely to consult individual employees over employment-
related changes than they were to consult the union. However, the union was less
likely than individual employees to be involved in production-related changes.
When the comparison was repeated for JCCs, there was a similar level of involvement for the JCC and for individual employees, in both employment-related and
production-related changes.

In summary, managers usually involve employees in important workplace
changes, but this is more common if the change directly affects employees' terms
and conditions or patterns of work organisation, than if it affects issues that are
concerned with production or service delivery. When employees are involved, this
typically takes the form of consultation rather than negotiation, although negotiation over employment-related changes is more common. Employee representatives
are only involved in a minority of cases, but this is typically because they are not
present in the workplace. When they are present, there appear to be relatively few
instances in which representatives are bypassed in favour of direct consultation with
the affected employees.

The comparison between the private and public sectors has been a continual
theme throughout the earlier parts of the chapter, and here it is apparent that
consultation over organisational change was more prevalent in the public sector.
When the most important change was employment related, managers consulted or
negotiated with employees (or their representatives) in 92 per cent of public sector
workplaces, but in only 67 per cent of private sector establishments. When the most

Table 4.9 Engagement with employees, trade unions or Joint Consultative Committees over organisational changes in the previous two years, 2011, column per cent

Managers' engagement with:	All workplaces making some organisational change in the previous two years		All workplaces with on-site union representatives (where change was made)		All workplaces with JCC (where change was made)	
	Employment-related change	Product/service-related change	Employment-related change	Product/service-related change	Employment-related change	Product/service-related change
The employees likely to be affected						
Negotiated/Let them decide	15	8	17	16	20	10
Consulted	52	45	61	50	50	49
Informed/Did nothing	32	47	22	34	30	41
Employee representatives			*Engagement with union reps*		*Engagement with JCC*	
Negotiated/Let them decide			18	9	25	17
Consulted			59	37	46	41
Informed/Did nothing			23	54	30	41

Base: All workplaces with five or more employees. Figures for column one are based on responses from 803 workplace managers, and those for column two are based on 882 workplace managers.

important change was production related, the figures were 78 per cent for the public sector and 52 per cent for the private sector.

The role of HR specialists has been another theme. In a regression that controlled for workplace size, organisation size, industry and private or public sector, the presence of an HR specialist at the workplace made no statistically significant difference to the likelihood that managers consulted employees (or their representatives) over employment-related changes, or to the likelihood that they consulted employees over production-related changes. But workplaces with on-site employee representatives were 16 percentage points more likely to consult over production-related changes than workplaces without any on-site employee representatives and ten percentage points more likely to consult over employment-related changes. The involvement of employees in production-related changes is, then, particularly unusual in the absence of arrangements for employee representation.

The Management of Change in the Recession

The information presented in the preceding section does not tell us specifically about the extent of consultation when changes came about as a result of the recession; some of the changes reported by managers – maybe even the majority – may have taken place in the absence of any economic downturn. However, WERS does provide some information on the extent of consultation over recession-induced changes via the WRQ. The negotiation of agreements between managers and employees over changes in working time or staffing was a feature of the recession which captured the headlines in the early stages of the downturn and, indeed, Acas-CIPD issued guidance for managers emphasising the importance of communicating and taking an inclusive approach (Acas-CIPD, 2009). How prevalent was such an approach?

The previous section used a question asked of managers to identify organisational changes that had taken place in the two years prior to the survey. Worker representatives were asked a similar question, but were also asked which of these changes had taken place *as a result of the recession*. In addition, they were asked whether employees or their representatives were involved in management decisions on the proposed changes.

Consultation or negotiation with on-site employee representatives was relatively widespread in respect of recession-induced redundancies (83 per cent), and in respect of recession-induced changes in the organisation of work (79 per cent) (Table 4.10). However, it was less common when the workplace was faced with a wage cut or freeze, even though this was the most common type of change reported by worker representatives. Only 53 per cent of worker representatives reporting a recession-induced wage cut or freeze said that it had been the subject of consultation. Similarly, only 63 per cent reported consultation over recession-induced changes in working time and 57 per cent reported consultation over changes in the use of agency workers. There were no statistically significant differences in the extent of consultation between the private and public sectors.

Table 4.10 Nature of engagement with employees or their representatives over recession-induced organisational changes in the previous two years, 2011, cell per cent

	Any change	Recession-induced change	Employees or reps consulted over recession-induced change
Wage cut/freeze	51	40	53
Change in organisation of work, work techniques or procedures	46	21	79
Redundancies	34	23	83
Changes in working time	32	15	63
Change in use of agency workers	29	14	57
Introduction of performance-related pay	10	3	(92)
Other changes	4	1	(33)
None of these	15		

Base: Workplaces with five or more employees and an eligible worker representative. Figures are based on responses from 995 worker representatives.

DO EMPLOYEES WANT MORE INVOLVEMENT?

Having considered the steps that managers took to consult employees, it is appropriate to ask whether they were perceived by workers as being effective. To address this question we first looked at the percentage of all employees who said that managers were generally either 'Very good' or 'Good' at allowing them to influence decisions. Some 35 per cent of all employees gave this opinion in 2011 (an increase from 32 per cent in 2004). Regression analysis was conducted on this indicator controlling for the extent of employee involvement in the most important workplace change (discussed earlier), as well as the type of this change, workplace size, industry sector and year.[22] Managers who had consulted employees or negotiated with them over the most important change were three percentage points more likely to be rated as 'Very good' or 'Good' than those who only informed employees, and five percentage points more likely to be rated as 'Very good' or 'Good' than those who did not involve employees at all. This indicates that employees take note when they are not involved in key decisions at the workplace. But do they actually want greater levels of involvement?

Employees were also asked whether they were satisfied with the amount of involvement they have in decision-making at their workplace. The percentage of all employees who either strongly agreed or agreed rose slightly from 40 per cent in 2004 to 43 per cent in 2011. In a similar regression to that outlined before, employees located in workplaces where managers had consulted or negotiated over the most important workplace change were three percentage points more likely to agree that they were satisfied with the level of involvement than employees in workplaces where managers had only given information, and four percentage points more likely to agree than employees in workplaces where managers had not involved employees at all. These differences are not substantial, but they are statistically significant, and so there is some indication that employees without representation have a desire for more influence in the workplace.

CONCLUSION

The period between the two previous WERS surveys, in 1998 and 2004, saw stability in the prevalence of arrangements for representative voice in the workplace, following years of decline. It also saw a continuation of growth in the prevalence of direct methods of consultation. This occurred in relatively benign conditions characterised by continual economic growth. In the period between 2004 and 2011, however, workplaces experienced a different context, as midway through this period the economy entered a deep recession. When faced with a need to react to the economic downturn, it is possible that workplace managers may have been less inclined to consult their workforce over intended changes than would be the case in more comfortable times, despite the urgings of bodies such as Acas and the CIPD to the contrary. One possible countervailing influence on any such tendency was the presence of the ICE Regulations, which were first introduced in 2005. These provided a substantial opportunity to establish new mechanisms for consultation, if employees or their employers were inclined to take it. The earlier period between 1998 and 2004 had seen the introduction of the Statutory Recognition Procedure (SRP) in 1999 but, in contrast, the ICE Regulations did not rely on union presence at the workplace, and so ICE might have been expected to have had more widespread influence on workplace practice.

In fact, while there was considerable change in the way that some workplaces operated (see Chapter 2 for example), there was no substantial change in the prevalence of arrangements that were available for employee involvement in managerial decision-making, or in the way that managers approached the issue of consultation. The prevalence of arrangements for employee representation remained broadly stable, despite the phased introduction of the ICE Regulations in 2005–08. Furthermore, arrangements for direct consultation continued to grow in prevalence. However, there remained a minority of workplaces with neither type of formal arrangement for employee voice – signifying the persistence of what we termed a 'participation gap' in some British workplaces.

Despite these patterns, managers were slightly more likely in 2011 than they had been in 2004 to say that they would always consult employees before introducing changes – an increase which was partly explained by changes in the characteristics of workplace managers (for example, the increased proportion who are women). And indeed this positive stance was largely borne out in practice. Managers continued to involve employees in most workplace changes, although this was more common if the change directly affected the wage/effort bargain (payment systems, working time or patterns of work organisation), than if it was production related. The involvement of employees was usually through direct methods of consultation, rather than via representatives, but this largely reflected the absence of representative arrangements from many workplaces; representatives were not typically bypassed by managers where they were present.

The recession did not therefore appear to have prompted employers to seek to avoid engaging with employees or their representatives. However, this is not to imply that consultation was (or is) always effective. Only one third of all employees in 2011 said that managers were either 'Very good' or 'Good' at allowing them to influence decisions; only two fifths were satisfied with the amount of involvement they had in decision-making. These proportions were not much changed from 2004. As with Hall et al.'s (2011) research into consultation forums set up under the ICE Regulations the impression is that, while consultation may typically happen to some degree or another, the opportunities for extensive formal involvement and influence on the part of employees may often be limited.

5 Pay and Rewards

INTRODUCTION

In some of Britain's main competitor countries, employees have faced stagnant or declining real wages for over a decade. In Germany, for example, real wages were stable for median earners in the years that preceded the recession and fell for those at the lower end of the earnings distribution, with the demise of sectoral collective bargaining being a key contributing factor (Dustmann et al., 2009). In the United States real hourly wage growth has been sluggish for three decades for many workers, and has actually been negative for the bottom fifth of earners (Mishel, 2013). Union weakness and the declining real value of the minimum wage are contributory factors (Mishel et al., 2012). In contrast, full-time British employees saw real wages grow by almost two thirds since the mid-1980s, with the lowest paid experiencing higher than average real wage increases (Office for National Statistics, 2012a). This was despite declining union bargaining coverage (Brown et al., 2009), with the advent of the statutory minimum wage acting as a countervailing force. But in Britain this real wage growth came to an end with the recession: real earnings have fallen since then (Levy, 2013; Bryson et al., 2013a).

Keen to remain competitive by containing labour costs, private sector employers have been looking at how they reward their employees. Prior to the recession they had already begun taking action to limit long-term pension liabilities by reducing the generosity of pension plans or changing the terms for new entrants. But new cost pressures from the economic downturn led some employers to take more radical action on pay and rewards. Reports of employees being forced to take substantial pay cuts or face redundancy were not uncommon. Although many low-paid production and service workers were deeply affected, so too were professionals and consultants (Brignall, 2009). Some of these cases were highlighted in the media, but just how typical were they of what was happening in the private sector as a whole?

In the few years leading up to the recession, earnings growth in the public sector was roughly similar to that in the private sector. However, with the onset of recession, real earnings fell markedly in the private sector, but not immediately in the public sector. This resulted in the emergence of a public sector pay premium in 2009–10 for men and a growth in that premium for women. These premia remain even when controlling for age, education and qualification differences between the two sectors (Bozio and Disney, 2011). In June 2010 the government announced a two-year pay freeze for many public sector employees starting in 2011–12, but their real earnings had already begun to fall before the pay freeze took effect (Levy, 2013). Since then the government has announced a further 1 per cent cap on pay increases for the period through 2015–16. On top of this public sector pensions were under scrutiny following Lord Hutton's review, which had profound consequences for public sector employees (Pensions Commission, 2011).

This chapter examines pay setting and employees' pay and rewards across Britain. First it describes what has happened to pay determination in Britain since the last WERS in 2004. We consider the incidence, coverage and scope of collective bargaining and the extent to which its demise since the 1980s has continued in the 2000s. We identify factors that account for shifts in pay determination over time, and the implications for trade unions' involvement in negotiating terms and conditions. The private and public sectors are discussed separately because the nature of pay determination differs fundamentally in the two sectors.

The chapter then looks specifically at the latest pay settlement or review for the largest occupational group at the workplace: how was it reviewed, who was involved in the review, what was the size of the settlement and the main influences on it? The chapter goes on to explore entitlements to non-pay, or fringe, benefits among managerial and non-managerial employees: how widespread are they and how have entitlements changed since 2004? A subsequent section is devoted to the role played by the recession in pay determination and the types of employees that suffered most from the recession in terms of pay freezes or cuts to their fringe benefits. Finally the chapter turns to pay systems more generally and, in particular, the extent to which employers rely solely on the payment of fixed wages as opposed to using incentive or performance-related pay. In concluding the chapter reflects on employees' desire for representation in having their pay determined.

PAY DETERMINATION IN THE PRIVATE SECTOR

Collective Bargaining Coverage

Throughout much of the post-war period, the majority of employees had their pay set via collective bargaining between employers and trade unions. Coverage peaked at around 70 per cent of employees in the 1970s and early 1980s, at around the same time that union membership also peaked (Milner, 1995). But from the mid-1980s onwards collective bargaining coverage started to decline in the private sector. It began with the demise of sectoral collective bargaining and continued in the 1990s as many workplaces chose to dispense with collective bargaining resulting in what Millward et al. (2000: 234) termed a 'transformation' in the system of collective employment relations that had been dominant in the post-war period. They argued that the system which had been 'based on the shared values of the legitimacy of representation by independent trade unions and of joint regulation [had] crumbled ... to such an extent that it no longer represents a dominant model'.

With the turn of the century, collective bargaining coverage continued to decline, albeit at a slower rate than in the 1980s and 1990s (Kersley et al., 2006: 187–88). Between 2004 and 2011 the percentage of private sector employees covered by pay bargaining was stable according to WERS (Table 5.1). This stability in coverage in the

Table 5.1 *Employee collective bargaining coverage and union presence in WERS and the LFS, 2004 and 2011, cell per cent*

	Public sector		Private sector		All workplaces	
	2004	**2011**	**2004**	**2011**	**2004**	**2011**
WERS						
Employees covered by collective bargaining	68	<u>44</u>	16	16	28	<u>23</u>
Employees in workplaces with recognised unions	94	96	29	31	45	47
LFS						
Employees covered by collective bargaining	71	68	21	17	35	31
Employees in workplaces with unions	87	87	33	29	48	45

WERS Base: All workplaces with five or more employees. WERS figures are based on responses from at least 2,226 (2004) and 2,621 (2011) workplace managers.
Notes: The WERS estimate of collective bargaining coverage is based solely on occupation-level 'collective bargaining'. See note 1 for details.

Table 5.2 *Workplace collective bargaining coverage and union recognition in WERS, 2004 and 2011, cell per cent*

	Public sector		Private sector		All workplaces	
	2004	**2011**	**2004**	**2011**	**2004**	**2011**
Any employees covered by collective bargaining	70	<u>57</u>	7	7	15	13
All employees covered by collective bargaining	49	<u>37</u>	4	4	10	8
At least one union recognised	90	92	13	12	22	22
Last pay settlement for core employees negotiated with a trade union	40	<u>24</u>	5	4	9	7

Base: All workplaces with five or more employees. Figures are based on responses from at least 2,226 (2004) and 2,621 (2011) workplace managers.

private sector marks something of a break with the WERS series which has shown a decline in union involvement in private sector pay setting for over a quarter of a century (Brown et al., 2009; Bryson and Forth, 2011). In 2011 just under one third (31 per cent) of private sector employees were located in a workplace with a recognised union. However, the percentage whose pay was set by collective bargaining was around half of this (16 per cent).[1] The Quarterly Labour Force Survey (QLFS) provides an alternative measure of collective bargaining coverage. Although the samples and survey questions differ, one would expect the estimates to be similar, and the 2011 QLFS coverage estimate is almost identical to that for WERS at 17 per cent of employees. Although the 2011 WERS did not reveal a statistically significant decline, the QLFS figure has fallen significantly by four percentage points since 2004.[2]

Just over 1 in 20 (7 per cent) private sector workplaces engaged in collective bargaining with at least some of their employees in 2011 (Table 5.2). They tended to be larger workplaces, which is why they accounted for coverage among 16 per cent of employees (as shown in Table 5.1). Around half these workplaces – just 4 per cent of all private sector workplaces – used collective bargaining to set the pay of all their employees. These figures for collective bargaining coverage in private sector workplaces do not differ significantly from their equivalents in 2004, suggesting no change in union involvement in pay determination in the private sector over the last seven years.

Scope of Collective Bargaining

Only in circumstances where union recognition is obtained via statutory procedures does the employer have a clear legal obligation to negotiate over core aspects of the employment contract, namely pay, holiday and hours worked. But the statutory recognition procedure is rarely invoked (Moore et al., 2013). In other particular circumstances, such as transfers of undertakings and large-scale redundancies, the employer has a legal duty to consult or inform employees regarding change at the workplace. But, for the most part, whether negotiation, consultation or information provision takes place between an employer and employee representatives is a matter for the parties concerned. Earlier research has shown that it is common for unions to be formally recognised for bargaining purposes yet to have little or no influence over setting employees' terms and conditions (Millward et al., 2000: 167–73; Kersley et al., 2006: 193–96).

Whereas the incidence of collective bargaining in the private sector remained stable since 2004, there was a significant diminution in the scope of items over which employers negotiated. In workplaces with union members, workplace managers were asked whether they normally negotiated, consulted or informed the union – or did not involve them at all – on the issues of pay, hours, holidays, pensions, training, grievance procedures, and health and safety. If any of the issues were dealt with at a higher level in the organisation or through an employers' association, the manager was asked to record the nature of union involvement at that level.[3] Where union members were present, the percentage of private sector workplaces that normally negotiated with unions over at least some terms and conditions fell from 43 per cent to 38 per cent (upper panel of Table 5.3). Although this was not a statistically significant change, the fall in the mean number of items over which they negotiated did fall significantly from 1.6 to 1.1.

In the private sector, unions were much more likely to be involved in negotiating terms and conditions where they were formally recognised by the employer for bargaining purposes (lower panel of Table 5.3). Nevertheless, there was a marked decline in the scope of collective bargaining in these private sector workplaces. The proportion of workplaces in which managers did not normally negotiate with their recognised unions over any of the seven items rose from just over one quarter (28 per cent) to over one third (37 per cent). Although this difference was not statistically significant the mean number of items over which negotiations took place fell significantly from 2.7 to 2.0. Some of this decline in negotiation over terms and

Table 5.3 *Scope of collective bargaining, 2004 and 2011, column per cent and mean*

	Public sector		Private sector		All workplaces	
	2004	**2011**	**2004**	**2011**	**2004**	**2011**
All workplaces with union members						
All seven items	4	7	5	1	5	4
One to six items	59	57	39	36	47	45
None	37	36	57	62	49	51
Mean number of items	2.3	2.4	1.6	<u>1.1</u>	1.9	1.6
Workplaces with recognised unions and members at the workplace						
All seven items	5	8	8	3	7	6
One to six items	62	58	63	61	63	59
None	33	35	28	37	31	35
Mean number of items	2.5	2.4	2.7	<u>2.0</u>	2.6	2.5

Notes: The seven items are pay, hours, holidays, pensions, training, grievance procedures, and health and safety.
Base: Workplaces with five or more employees and at least one union member present. Figures are based on responses from at least 999 (2004) and 1,178 (2011) workplace managers.

Table 5.4 *Negotiation and consultation over specific terms and conditions in workplaces recognising unions, 2004 and 2011, cell per cent*

	Public sector		Private sector		All workplaces	
	2004	**2011**	**2004**	**2011**	**2004**	**2011**
Pay	56 (71)	52 (72)	61 (81)	56 (70)	58 (76)	54 (71)
Hours	55 (74)	45 (72)	50 (75)	37 (61)	52 (74)	<u>42</u> (68)
Holidays	51 (65)	44 (66)	52 (72)	41 (61)	51 (68)	43 (64)
Pensions	34 (54)	38 (62)	38 (59)	24 (55)	36 (56)	33 (59)
Training	10 (48)	<u>17</u> (54)	13 (32)	6 (42)	11 (40)	13 (49)
Grievance procedures	29 (72)	30 (71)	31 (73)	<u>19</u> (68)	30 (72)	25 (70)
Health and safety	16 (69)	22 (69)	18 (65)	10 (59)	17 (67)	17 (65)

Notes: No parentheses indicate the incidence of negotiation and parentheses indicate the incidence of negotiation or consultation. For each item employers are asked, 'Does management normally negotiate, consult, inform or not inform unions?' In 2011 'grievances' covers 'grievance and disciplinary procedures' whereas 2004 refers to grievances only (see note 4).
Base: Workplaces with five or more employees with at least one union member present and recognise a union for bargaining purposes. Figures are based on responses from at least 1,008 (2004) and 1,218 (2011) workplace managers.

conditions might have been due to an increased propensity to consult with unions or inform them of changes. There is some indication that this may have happened but the increase in the mean number of items over which recognised unions were consulted or informed by the employer (from 3.0 in 2004 to 3.5 in 2011) was not statistically significant.

Pay is the item that is most commonly subject to negotiation with a trade union. Yet in 2011 the employer had negotiated over pay in only 56 per cent of private sector workplaces where unions were formally recognised for negotiation (Table 5.4).

The low incidence of pay bargaining in much of the unionised sector, even when unions are recognised for this purpose, is an important feature of employment relations in Britain.

The incidence of negotiation with recognised unions in the private sector appears to have fallen across a range of items between 2004 and 2011. These include hours and holidays which, together with pay, are treated as core terms under the statutory union recognition procedure. However, none of the changes are statistically significant, with the exception of negotiation over grievance procedures which fell from 31 per cent to 19 per cent.[4] Nevertheless, taken together, these findings on the scope of collective bargaining in the private sector are reminiscent of those in earlier WERS studies (for example, Millward et al., 2000) in suggesting that formal recognition of unions for pay bargaining may often resemble a 'hollow shell' in which unions and their members have little influence over the setting of terms and conditions.

Methods of Pay Determination

Employers may choose a variety of methods to determine pay for their employees. WERS provides information on the methods used to determine the pay of each occupational group at the workplace, which allows us to obtain a more detailed picture of how workplaces set pay. The survey identifies whether any of seven different methods of pay determination were used and, if so, whether they were one of multiple methods used at the workplace. Four in five private sector workplaces use a single method (83 per cent in 2004 and 2011) (Table 5.5). In 7 per cent of workplaces collective bargaining is used for pay determination (penultimate two rows of the table). Instead, pay is usually determined by management. The only statistically significant change since 2004 is the shift away from pay being decided by management at workplace level to decisions being taken at a higher level beyond the workplace.

Although only 7 per cent of private sector workplaces used collective bargaining to set pay for any of their employees, these workplaces accounted for almost one fifth (19 per cent in both years) of employees. This is because collective bargaining tends to occur in larger workplaces.

PAY DETERMINATION IN THE PUBLIC SECTOR

The previous section indicated that the coverage of collective bargaining in the private sector was at a low level and fairly stable between 2004 and 2011, though there were signs of a reduction in the number of items over which employers and unions bargained. The contrast between pay setting arrangements in the private and public sectors is stark. In the private sector nine in ten employees were in workplaces where management unilaterally set the pay of at least some employees in 2011 and 2004 (88 per cent in both years), with the single most common form of pay determination being workplace-level management pay setting. In contrast, the most common form of pay determination in the public sector is collective bargaining (Table 5.5).

Table 5.5 *Pay determination methods in workplaces, 2004 and 2011, cell per cent*

	Public sector		Private sector		All workplaces	
	2004	**2011**	**2004**	**2011**	**2004**	**2011**
Collective bargaining						
Any multi-employer	58	<u>43</u>	2	2	9	7
Any single employer	14	17	4	3	5	5
Any workplace level	1	1	2	2	1	2
Other pay determination methods						
Any set by management, higher level	23	24	36	<u>42</u>	35	<u>40</u>
Any set by management, workplace	11	9	60	<u>53</u>	54	<u>48</u>
Any set by individual negotiations	2	2	14	15	12	13
Any Pay Review Body	28	35	0	0	4	5
Single method used	68	71	83	83	81	82
Pay set by collective bargaining for every occupational group present at the workplace	51	<u>38</u>	5	4	10	<u>8</u>
Mix of collective bargaining and other forms of pay determination	19	18	2	3	4	5
Pay not set by collective bargaining for any occupational group	30	<u>43</u>	93	93	85	87

Notes: Note 1 provides details of the derivation of time-consistent estimates of collective bargaining coverage. *Base:* All workplaces with five or more employees. Figures are based on responses from at least 2,207 (2004) and 2,561 (2011) workplace managers.

Pay determination in the public sector is dominated by the presence of trade unions. In 2011, 96 per cent of public sector employees worked in a workplace with at least one union recognised for pay bargaining (second row, Table 5.1) and 92 per cent of public sector workplaces recognised unions for pay bargaining (third row, Table 5.2). Collective bargaining remains the primary method for pay determination and, where it does occur, it is usually sectoral bargaining (first row, Table 5.5). However, pay determination is more complex in public sector workplaces than it is in private sector workplaces: they are more likely to use a mixture of methods (eighth row, Table 5.5), in part, because public sector workplaces are on average larger than those in the private sector. In addition, many public sector workplaces have employees whose pay is set by an Independent Pay Review Body (seventh row, Table 5.5). These are bodies, set up under statute, to consider evidence from employers and unions before making a recommendation to the government as to the appropriate pay settlement. It is arguable as to whether their activities constitute collective bargaining but, since they operate within guidelines set by government and their recommendations are subject to ministerial approval before implementation, it is typically the case that their deliberations are not akin to collective bargaining.

Collective Bargaining Coverage

There has been a gradual decline in bargaining coverage over time in the public sector since the mid-1990s but, whereas the WERS and QLFS coverage estimates for 2004 are comparable with roughly seven in ten public sector employees covered by collective bargaining, the QLFS suggests coverage declined only three percentage points in the period to 2011, whereas in WERS it fell dramatically by over one third to 44 per cent (Table 5.1).[5] The incidence of collective bargaining among public sector workplaces declined from 70 per cent in 2004 to 57 per cent in 2011 (first row, Table 5.2). This is not as steep as the decline in employee coverage shown in Table 5.1 because the decline in the incidence of bargaining is most pronounced among larger public sector workplaces like hospitals. This decline appears all the more surprising given the stability of union recognition for pay bargaining in the public sector in WERS (second row, Table 5.1). The decline is due to a fall in the percentage of public sector workplaces using multi-employer bargaining, which fell significantly from 58 per cent in 2004 to 43 per cent in 2011 (first row, Table 5.5). Instead, a growing percentage of public sector workplaces had some of their employees' pay set by a Pay Review Body. The percentage of public sector workplaces with some employees whose pay was set by a Pay Review Body was 28 per cent in 2004 and 35 per cent in 2011. Although this difference is sizeable, it is not statistically significant. However, the percentage of employees working in workplaces where Pay Review Bodies set pay for at least some employees rose from 21 per cent in 2004 to 47 per cent in 2011, a difference that is statistically significant. Despite the decline in collective bargaining in the public sector, it was in place for *all* employees in over one third (38 per cent) of public sector workplaces (ninth row, Table 5.5).

There are two reasons why WERS records a substantial decline in collective bargaining coverage in the public sector whereas the QLFS does not. First, it reflects a rise in the incidence of pay setting via Pay Review Bodies. The QLFS does not collect detailed pay arrangements and it can be expected that many employees do not make a distinction between collective bargaining and the Pay Review Body process whereas, as noted earlier, such a distinction is made in our analysis of WERS. The percentage of public sector employees covered by collective bargaining in Health fell from 75 per cent in 2004 to 14 per cent in 2011 in WERS, largely because the Pay Review Body resumed responsibility for pay after Agenda for Change negotiations were completed.[6] However, even if the Health sector is excluded, the percentage of public sector employees covered by collective bargaining fell from 65 per cent in 2004 to 55 per cent in 2011.

A second reason why fewer public sector managers report collective bargaining coverage is that the survey was conducted at a time when many public sector employees were subject to a pay freeze. This led many public sector managers to state that union representatives had not been involved in the last pay settlement (see further). In these instances managers may have chosen to say that employees were not covered by collective bargaining, even though the underlying apparatus of union recognition remained in place.

Closer inspection of industries within the public sector reveals there had been little change in union involvement in pay bargaining in Education since 2004. Rather the decline in union influence over pay bargaining was driven by trends in Public administration, Health and Other community services. The percentage of public sector workplaces with any collective bargaining fell from 58 per cent to 30 per cent in Health, 84 per cent to 68 per cent in Public administration and 72 per cent to 66 per cent in Other community services. In Education the figures were 68 per cent in 2004 and 66 per cent in 2011.

Scope of Collective Bargaining

As noted earlier, workplace managers were also asked whether they normally negotiated with unions over a range of specific terms and conditions. Almost two thirds of public sector workplaces with union members (63 per cent in 2004 and 64 per cent in 2011) normally negotiated over at least some of the seven specified items (Table 5.3). These figures do not vary a great deal if one focuses on workplaces recognising at least one union for bargaining purposes (lower panel in Table 5.3) because a higher proportion of unions in the sector are recognised by employers.

There appear to have been increases in negotiation over pensions, training, grievance procedures, and health and safety in the public sector since 2004, but the only increase that is statistically significant is negotiation over training. The mean number of items over which bargaining occurred was constant, whereas it had fallen in the private sector (fourth and eighth rows, Table 5.3). This stability in the scope of bargaining contrasts with the decline of bargaining coverage in the public sector. There was also little change in whether unions normally bargained over pay (first row, Table 5.4). This serves to illustrate the point that the temporary pay freezes that were in place in large parts of the public sector at the time of the survey affected managers' responses to questions regarding the incidence of collective bargaining. The pay freeze had less of an effect on managers' perceptions of whether bargaining *normally* occurred over pay.

PAY SETTLEMENTS

Traditionally pay settlements are the agreements managers and employees reach periodically regarding pay rises. These settlements were usually associated with annual pay bargaining with trade unions, but the demise of collective bargaining in the private sector means this is no longer the typical case. Instead, the term 'pay settlement' may cover a range of disparate arrangements whereby the employer comes to a decision about whether to raise or even lower pay and, if so, by how much.

The frequency with which employers review pay and the pay settlements that are finally agreed are two of the clearest indicators of the way in which the economy responds to changed economic circumstances. As the only source of information on pay settlements that is nationally representative of workplaces in Britain, WERS provides information on the nature of pay settlements that complements the ongoing monitoring undertaken by organisations such as Income Data Services (IDS), the Labour Research Department and the Confederation of British Industry.

The slow down and reversal in real earnings growth referred to at the beginning of the chapter is in large part due to employers responding to the recession by freezing pay. At the height of the recession in 2009, IDS estimated that around one third of private sector employers had frozen pay in their reviews, with the remaining two thirds increasing pay. However, the proportion freezing pay fell throughout 2010 and 2011 such that most medium- to large-sized firms were awarding pay increases in 2011 (IDS, 2011). In the public sector, on the other hand, pay freezes began in 2010 and continued for two years followed by a 1 per cent cap on pay increases to run through to 2015–16. Based on their sample of over 1,000 employers, IDS estimated median pay settlements of 3 per cent in the private sector in 2011, with a median settlement of zero in the public sector (IDS, 2011).

WERS fieldwork took place between March 2011 and June 2012, with management respondents being asked about the most recent review or negotiation of basic pay for the largest occupation at the workplace. Although the survey does not identify precisely when settlements occurred, most are likely to have occurred in 2010. Managers were asked who had been involved in the last pay settlement for the group of non-managerial employees in the largest occupation at the workplace, and whether that settlement had been negotiated with trade unions. In the private sector, the percentage of managers saying that they negotiated with unions in the last pay settlement for the largest occupational group of employees was 4 per cent in 2011 and had not changed significantly since 2004 (Table 5.2). In the public sector, on the other hand, one quarter (24 per cent) of managers had negotiated the most recent pay settlement with trade unions, compared with 40 per cent in 2004.

Two further notable changes had occurred between 2004 and 2011. First, the frequency of pay reviews fell. Managers were asked, 'How frequently is basic pay for [the largest occupational group] at this workplace reviewed or negotiated?' If pay was set at head office or national level rather than at the workplace, the respondent was asked how frequently pay was reviewed at that level. Across the economy, the percentage of workplaces in which the pay of the largest occupational group was reviewed less than once a year rose from 6 per cent to 10 per cent. In the private sector the percentage rose from 6 per cent to 9 per cent, but in the public sector it doubled from 8 per cent to 16 per cent, reflecting the introduction of a pay freeze in the public sector and, in some cases, agreement to long-term pay deals.

Second, the incidence of pay freezes rose markedly. Managers were asked, 'At the last review or settlement, was basic pay for [the largest occupational group] increased, decreased, or did it see no change?' Less than 1 per cent of workplaces had resorted to nominal wage decreases in 2004 and 2011, but the percentage instituting a pay freeze rose from one in ten (11 per cent) in 2004 to three in ten (29 per cent) in 2011. The percentage doubled in the private sector (from 12 per cent to 26 per cent) but rose 14-fold (5 per cent to 58 per cent) in the public sector. With inflation running at over 2 per cent per annum these settlements entailed real wage reductions for all employees affected.

The likelihood of a pay freeze or cut varied with the industry to which the workplace belonged (Table 5.6). Nearly four fifths (78 per cent) of Public administration workplaces had instituted a pay freeze or cut in 2011, as had around two fifths of workplaces in Education, Health and Other community services, all of which are dominated by public sector employers.[7] Forty-four per cent of Construction sector workplaces were subject to a pay freeze, but other sectors dominated by the private sector, such as Hotels and restaurants, were less likely to have had a pay freeze in

Table 5.6 *Incidence of pay freezes or cuts at the workplace, 2004 and 2011, cell per cent*

	2004	2011
All workplaces	11	<u>30</u>
Organisation size		
Small (5–49 employees) private enterprise	12	<u>31</u>
Medium (50–249 employees) private enterprise	7	<u>34</u>
Large (250 or more employees) private enterprise	14	15
Public sector	5	<u>58</u>
Industry		
Manufacturing	17	25
Electricity, gas and water	(0)	12
Construction	6	<u>44</u>
Wholesale and retail trade	11	<u>21</u>
Hotels and restaurants	10	12
Transportation and communication	11	26
Financial services	18	(17)
Other business services	13	<u>25</u>
Public administration	9	<u>78</u>
Education	13	<u>45</u>
Health	7	<u>40</u>
Other community services	10	<u>43</u>
Union recognition		
No recognised union at the workplace	12	<u>26</u>
Recognised union at the workplace	8	<u>41</u>
Adversely affected by recession		
'A great deal'	–	41
'No adverse effect'	–	21

Base: Workplaces with five or more employees. Figures are based on responses from at least 2,277 (2004) and 2,647 (2011) workplace managers.

2011. As IDS evidence indicates, pay freezes had been much more common in the private sector in 2009 (IDS, 2011).

Pay freezes became much more common between 2004 and 2011 in both unionised and non-unionised workplaces, but the unionised sector experienced a five-fold increase in pay freezes compared to only a two-fold increase in the non-unionised sector. A regression analysis that controlled for industry sector, workplace size, enterprise size and the largest occupation at the workplace found that workplaces recognising trade unions had no greater probability of a pay freeze in 2011 than non-unionised workplaces, whether in the public or private sector.

Managers in unionised workplaces were asked whether the decision to have no pay rise was 'agreed by recognised unions here'. In 2011, unions had agreed to the cut or freeze in roughly half of all cases (55 per cent in the public sector and 48 per cent in the private sector). The number of incidents in which pay freezes or cuts were made in unionised workplaces was too small in 2004 to make comparisons over time. However, the implication is that unions often sought to accommodate pay freezes or cuts, even in the public sector where calls for strike action have been increasingly common (see Chapter 8).

Where pay settlements for employees in the largest occupation at the workplace resulted in a pay increase, the settlements were around 1.5 percentage points higher in the private sector: the mean settlement in the private sector was 3.8 per cent, compared to 2.4 per cent in the public sector. Managers were asked whether the settlement for the largest occupational group was higher, lower or the same as the settlements for other non-managerial employees and for managers. The settlements for employees in the largest occupation at the workplace were typical of settlements for other non-managerial employees: in 84 per cent of cases the settlement for the largest occupational group was the same as that for other groups, something that had not changed since 2004. However, in the private sector the settlement for employees in the largest occupation in the workplace was only identical to that for managerial employees in two thirds of cases (65 per cent in 2004 and 63 per cent in 2011); it was higher than the managerial settlement in just over one quarter of cases (26 per cent in 2004 and 30 per cent in 2011), and lower in 8 per cent of cases in 2004 and 7 per cent in 2011. In the public sector, where pay equity considerations are more apparent and pay compression is pursued by unions, managers had received the same pay award as the employees in the largest occupation at the workplace in 83 per cent of cases in 2004. But by 2011 this had fallen to 59 per cent due to the increasing proportion of cases in which the managerial settlement lay below that for the largest occupational group (rising from 8 per cent in 2004 to 31 per cent in 2011).

Influences on pay settlements

Managers were asked about the factors that had influenced the size of the pay settlement for the employees in the largest occupation at the workplace and were given six specific response options (see Figure 5.1) but managers were also free to specify other factors where relevant. The financial performance of the firm dominated in the private sector, where it was mentioned by 62 per cent of managers, but it was also a salient factor in the public sector, where it was cited in 26 per cent of cases. One third of private sector workplaces had regard to the National Minimum Wage in 2011, compared with only 13 per cent of public sector workplaces. The cost of living was also mentioned by around one third of workplaces in both sectors, but the proportions were significantly lower than in 2004 when the cost of living was mentioned by 75 per cent of public sector workplaces and 54 per cent of private sector workplaces.[8]

Managers who said their workplace had been adversely affected 'A great deal' by the recession generally listed similar influences on pay settlements to those who said the recession had had 'No adverse effect'. The primary difference was in the public sector, where those adversely affected a great deal were more likely to cite financial performance than those who said recession had had no adverse effect (32 per cent compared with 14 per cent).

In summary, the frequency with which managers reviewed pay had fallen since 2004 and, where pay was reviewed, it was more likely to lead to a pay freeze in 2011, especially in the public sector. Throughout the period, union involvement in pay settlements was rare in the private sector and, although more common in the public sector, had fallen significantly. The influences on pay settlements differed

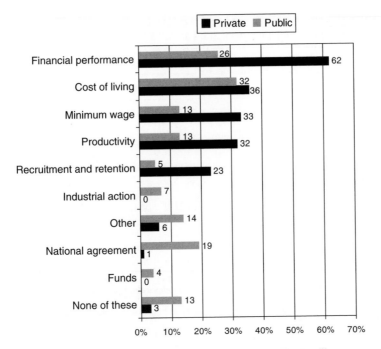

Figure 5.1 *Influences on the size of pay settlements, 2011, cell per cent*
Base: All workplaces with five or more employees. Figures are based on responses from 2,606 workplace managers.

markedly between the public and private sectors in 2011, but the degree to which workplaces had been directly affected by the recession was not strongly linked to the nature of those influences.

FRINGE BENEFITS

Research indicates that non-pay fringe benefits are often valued more highly by employees than their pay equivalent (Dale-Olsen, 2006). Although employers can defray some of the costs of providing such benefits via the tax system, the costs of provision mean employers often limit entitlement to more valued employees such as managers. In both 2004 and 2011 managers were asked which of five non-pay terms and conditions were available to employees in the largest non-managerial occupational group, and which were available to managers at the workplace (Table 5.7). Four of the five items were directly comparable in 2004 and 2011, the exception being the annual leave item which had its wording adjusted to reflect amendments to the Working Time Regulations in 2007 and 2009 which brought the leave entitlement up to 28 days per year for full-time workers.

In both 2004 and 2011, public sector workplaces were more likely to offer their employees fringe benefits than those in the private sector (Table 5.7). This was the case for both non-managerial employees in the largest occupational group and for

Table 5.7 *Entitlements to non-pay fringe benefits among employees in the largest occupation at the workplace and managers, 2004 and 2011, cell per cent*

	Public sector		Private sector		All workplaces	
	2004	2011	2004	2011	2004	2011
Employer contribution to pension scheme	94 (94)	92 (90)	52 (60)	41 (49)	57 (64)	47 (54)
Company vehicle or vehicle allowance	18 (30)	16 (22)	13 (42)	15 (31)	13 (40)	15 (30)
Private health insurance	5 (7)	4 (4)	16 (36)	17 (33)	15 (32)	16 (30)
Sick pay in excess of statutory	72 (74)	81 (80)	48 (57)	44 (51)	51 (59)	49 (55)
None of the above	4 (4)	5 (7)	31 (19)	38 (27)	28 (17)	34 (25)
More than 28 days paid annual leave (including public holidays)[a]	87 (90)	79 (81)	53 (59)	44 (49)	57 (63)	48 (53)
None of these	2 (4)	4 (4)	24 (17)	31 (24)	21 (15)	28 (22)

Notes: [a] In 2004 this category was 'more than *four weeks* of paid annual leave *excluding* public holidays'. No parentheses indicate employees in the largest occupation at the workplace and parentheses indicate managers.
Base: Workplaces with five or more employees. Figures are based on responses from at least 2,290 (2004) and 2,673 (2011) workplace managers.

managers at the workplace. Public sector workplaces were more likely than private sector ones to make contributions to an employee's pension scheme, provide sick pay above statutorily required levels and offer paid annual leave beyond the statutory entitlement. However, private sector employers were more likely to offer private health insurance. In the public sector there was little difference in the fringe benefits to which managers and non-managerial employees were entitled, the exception being a vehicle or vehicle allowance, a benefit to which managerial employees were more likely to be entitled. In the private sector, on the other hand, managers were more likely than non-managerial employees to be entitled to each of the five benefits.

Trends in the provision of fringe benefits differed by sector. There was little sign of a decline between 2004 and 2011 in the provision of fringe benefits in the public sector.[9] In the private sector, on the other hand, there was a significant decline in the mean number of fringe benefits to which managers and employees in the largest occupation at the workplace were entitled. The decline in the percentage of private sector workplaces that paid pension contributions was statistically significant for both managerial and non-managerial employees. Managers also experienced a decline between 2004 and 2011 in their entitlement to a company vehicle or allowance.

THE IMPACT OF RECESSION ON PAY AND BENEFITS

In previous recessions firms were fairly reluctant to freeze or cut pay for employees, preferring instead to adjust the quantity of labour they used, rather than its price (Geroski and Gregg, 1997). There can be many good reasons for this, including unions' ability to have a greater influence over wages than employment, and employers' need to make quite drastic reductions in labour costs which can only come with adjustments to the number of employees. Nevertheless, evidence from the recession in the 1990s indicates that employers were much more likely to resort to wage freezes when they said they were 'extremely severely' affected by recession (Geroski and Gregg, 1997: 80–81).

Earlier it was noted that pay freezes were quite common in the last pay settlement or review prior to the 2011 survey. The recession appeared to play an important part in employers' decisions to institute a pay freeze or cut in that pay settlement. Only one fifth (21 per cent) of employers who said the recession had had no adverse effect on their workplace had frozen or cut pay, compared to 41 per cent of those who said they had been adversely affected 'A great deal'. In workplaces where pay had been frozen or cut, the gap between those affected a great deal and not at all was larger in the private sector (35 per cent versus 15 per cent, respectively) than it was in the public sector (78 per cent versus 62 per cent, respectively). The fact that close to two thirds of public sector workplaces had instituted a pay freeze even when the workplace manager said the recession had no impact on their workplace is an indication of the degree to which pay decisions in the public sector are centralised and reflect central government priorities such as tackling the public sector deficit.

Turning to the actions that workplace managers had taken specifically in response to the recession, Chapter 2 showed that two fifths (41 per cent) of managers identified a freeze or cut in wages as one response to the recession (Table 2.3). The percentage was much higher in the public sector than the private sector (64 per cent compared to 38 per cent) but in both sectors it was the most commonly cited response to recession. Reducing non-wage benefits was far less common (7 per cent of workplaces did so in either sector).

It is clear, then, that employers were keen to adjust the price of the labour they were employing. But those undertaking pay freezes or cuts were doing so as part of a package of measures in response to the recession. In just 18 per cent of workplaces instituting a pay freeze or cut was the only action (of the 13 specified) that had been taken. In all other cases, wage freezes or cuts were combined with other responses to the recession (typically with two or three other actions). Wage freezes or cuts were most strongly correlated with reductions in non-wage benefits, followed by a temporary freeze on recruitment to fill vacant posts, then reduction in training expenditure and voluntary redundancies.[10] These associations point to wage freezes or cuts being instituted as part of a wider cost-containment strategy for coping with the recession.

Unsurprisingly, freezing and cutting wages in response to the recession was more likely in workplaces that had been more severely affected. Six in ten workplaces (62 per cent) affected by the recession 'A great deal' had frozen or cut wages, compared with 25 per cent of those which had not been adversely affected. This begs the question as to why some managers reported that they had frozen or cut wages in response to the recent recession when their workplace had experienced no adverse effect from it. One reason is that decisions over wages are often taken above the workplace level in multi-site organisations and in the public sector, so that managers follow policies that are not directly connected with the fortunes of the workplace. Yet even among single-site firms in the private sector, 17 per cent had frozen or cut wages in response to the recession in spite of reporting no adverse effect of recession. This could be because some firms had behaved opportunistically in taking advantage of the opportunity presented by the recession to contain wage costs. Alternatively, they may have been taking pre-emptive actions which successfully averted the worst effects of recession.

Industry affiliation played an important role in explaining the incidence of pay freezes/cuts in response to the recession. In the private sector wage freezes or cuts were least likely to occur in Hotels and restaurants (20 per cent) and were most likely to occur in Construction (63 per cent). In the public sector, workplaces in Public administration were by far the most likely to institute a wage freeze or cut in response to the recession, with 87 per cent doing so. In multivariate analyses controlling for workplace size, single-establishment organisation, region, industry and union recognition, these differences between industries remained statistically significant. The other variables explained little of the variability in the likelihood of instituting a wage freeze or cut, with the exception of union recognition. The presence of a recognised union significantly reduced the likelihood of wage cuts/ freezes in the private sector, but not in the public sector. Thirty-nine per cent of non-unionised private sector workplaces had frozen or cut wages in response to the recession compared with 27 per cent of those recognising trade unions with union members on site. This 12 percentage point gap persisted controlling for other factors in a multivariate regression.[11]

As in the case of pay freezes or cuts, reductions in non-wage benefits tended to be deployed as part of a package of cost-cutting measures, rather than in isolation, and they were most likely to be used in workplaces that had been the most adversely affected by the recession. In the private sector, one sixth (18 per cent) of workplaces affected 'A great deal' by the recession had reduced non-wage benefits, compared with fewer than 1 per cent of workplaces that were not affected at all. They were also more likely to occur in larger workplaces, an association that was apparent in both the public and private sectors. In the private sector, as in the case of pay freezes/ cuts, reductions in non-wage benefits were less likely in the presence of unions with members recognised for pay bargaining. Three per cent of workplaces recognising unions with members on site implemented cuts in non-wage benefits, compared to 7 per cent of workplaces without members of a recognised union. This difference remained statistically significant in a multivariate analysis.

As reported in Chapter 2, employees were also asked whether their wages had been frozen or cut as a result of the recession. Among employees who had been at their workplace throughout the recession, one third (32 per cent) said their wages had been frozen or cut as a result of the recession (Table 2.4), but they were almost twice as likely to say so if they worked in the public sector (49 per cent compared with 26 per cent in the private sector). Reductions in fringe benefits were far less common than a freeze or cut in wages.

Employees subject to wage freezes or cuts tended to experience other adverse effects on their jobs and conditions of employment. These employees were subject to an average (mean) of 2.4 actions out of the possible nine (2.5 in the public sector and 2.3 in the private sector), with one fifth (22 per cent) experiencing four or more changes. Wage cuts or freezes were positively correlated with the other recession responses listed. The strongest correlations were with reductions to non-wage benefits and restrictions to access to training (the correlation coefficients being 0.44 and 0.39, respectively).

There was a positive association between workplace managers' and employees' report of wage freezes or cuts as a result of the recession, but the association was not perfect. Only two thirds (67 per cent) of employees reporting that their wage had been cut or frozen were employed in workplaces where the manager said they had frozen or cut wages in response to the recession. This may indicate the difficulties for employees in determining the ultimate determinant of managerial actions. Conversely, among those in workplaces where the manager said that a wage freeze or cut had been instituted, about half (49 per cent) of employees reported that this had happened to their own wages, indicating that wage freezes were not always applied to the whole workforce.

Which workplace an employee worked in played a key role in determining whether the employee had been subject to a wage freeze or reduction as a result of the recession. This explained 37 per cent of the variability in the likelihood of experiencing a wage freeze or cut among private sector employees. In the public sector it accounted for 28 per cent, a differential that partly reflects the more centralised decision-making in employment relations in public sector organisations.

There were a number of workplace features which contributed to the likelihood that an employee reported being subject to a wage freeze or cut. Where the employer said the workplace had been adversely affected 'A great deal' by the recession, 43 per cent of employees said their wages had been cut or frozen, compared to only 20 per cent where the employer said the recession had had no adverse impact. Variation across industries was also substantial. In the private sector wage freezes or cuts were most likely to be experienced by employees in the Construction industry (43 per cent) while those in Electricity, gas and water and Financial services were the least likely to be affected (both 14 per cent). In the public sector, employees in Public administration were most likely to report wage freezes or cuts with over two thirds (69 per cent) doing so. These industry differences continued to be statistically significant when entered into a regression analysis alongside the size of the workplace, whether it was part of a larger organisation, the region in which it was located and whether it had a recognised union. Employees in workplaces with a recognised union were significantly less likely to say their wages had been frozen or cut. The impact of the presence of a recognised union was twice as large in the private sector as it was in the public sector (an eight percentage point reduction in the likelihood of reporting a wage freeze or cut, compared to a four percentage point reduction in the public sector).

To find out which types of employee were more or less likely to have received recession-induced wage cuts in a given workplace, we conducted a regression analysis that incorporated an individual's demographic and job characteristics alongside the workplace in which they worked.[12] In both the private and public sectors, men were more likely than women in the same workplace to say their wages had been frozen or cut as a result of the most recent recession. The probability of a wage freeze or cut rose with age in the private sector until employees reached their 50s, whereas this age effect peaked in one's 30s in the public sector, declining thereafter. In the private sector there was no significant difference between white and non-white employees in the likelihood of having their wages frozen or cut, but in the public sector white employees were more likely than non-white employees to have experienced a freeze or cut. In both sectors those with higher academic qualifications were more likely to have been affected. In the public sector, union members were more likely to face wage freezes or cuts than their non-member counterparts in the same workplace. Membership was not independently associated with wage freezes for employees in the private sector.

Whether employees in the same workplace faced a wage freeze or cut also depended in part on the job they performed. Managers were the occupational group most likely to face wage cuts or freezes. Those on higher earnings were more likely to face a wage freeze or cut than those on lower earnings, while those on permanent contracts were more likely than those on temporary or fixed-term contracts, and higher tenured employees were more likely than lower tenured colleagues. The general picture emerging from this analysis of employees' demographic and job traits is that it was those employees who were perhaps relatively advantaged, rather than those with the least bargaining power, who were most likely to experience a freeze or cut in their wages as a result of the recession.

We ran parallel analyses for the probability that an employee reported a reduction in their non-wage benefits as a result of the recession. The workplace was also a dominant factor in determining who was subject to cuts in their fringe benefits: in both the public and private sectors the workplace accounted for nearly one quarter of the variability in the likelihood that an employee had their fringe benefits reduced. Adding job and workplace characteristics barely improved the explanatory power of these models, whereas they had done so in the case of wage freezes or cuts. This suggests that non-wage benefits are likely to be more standardised across the workplace than pay, because they form part of the standard terms and conditions of employment and are not typically subject to annual reviews or discretionary awards. Nevertheless, many of the demographic and job-related characteristics of individuals were significantly and independently correlated with individuals' reporting of cuts in their fringe benefits, even within the same workplace. As in the case of wage cuts or freezes, it was those employees traditionally seen as more advantaged in the labour market, such as managers, males, white people and those with higher academic qualifications, who were more likely to have had their fringe benefits reduced. On the other hand, in contrast to the analysis of wage cuts, neither wages nor tenure were independently associated with the likelihood of having had a reduction in fringe benefits.

PAYING FOR PERFORMANCE

How much employees are paid can influence how they feel about their jobs, as shown in Chapters 6 and 7; it can also affect an employee's productivity. However, the way in which employees are paid also matters. In particular, employers may choose whether to pay employees a simple fixed rate of pay for the time they spend on the job, or else they may choose to tie some or all of the payment to the employee's performance.

In the two decades to 2004, an increasing proportion of workplaces tied pay to performance. More workplaces used payments by results (PBR) based on individual or team-level performance, and there was increasing financial participation through profit-related pay (PRP) and employee share ownership (Pendleton et al., 2009). The increased use of incentive pay may reflect a growing realisation on the part of employers that it can encourage greater employee effort, enable them to recruit the most able employees, and facilitate wage flexibility (Kruse et al., 2010; Bryson et al., 2013b). In addition, during recession financial participation might be an attractive way for firms to share risk with their employees. In this section we explore the incidence and correlates of employer use of incentive pay using workplace-level data, before turning to new data only available for 2011 that allow us to identify which employees received different forms of incentive pay.

Employer Use of Incentive Schemes

The management survey in WERS allows us to distinguish between financial participation (PRP schemes and share plans) and PBR, and between objective and subjective assessments of performance (Box 5.1). Over half (55 per cent) of all workplaces used at least one incentive pay scheme in 2011, but private sector workplaces were nearly three times as likely as public sector workplaces to do so (Table 5.8).

BOX 5.1   TYPES OF EMPLOYEE INCENTIVE SCHEMES

Payments by Results (PBR)

Any method of payment determined by objective criteria – *the amount done or its value* – rather than just the number of hours worked. It includes commission, and bonuses that are determined by individual, workplace or organisation productivity or performance. It does not include profit-related pay schemes.

Merit pay

Pay related to a *subjective assessment* of individual performance by a supervisor or manager.

Profit-related Pay (PRP)

Payments or bonuses related to profit levels of all or part of the organisation.

Share schemes
Any Share Incentive Plan (SIP); Save As You Earn (SAYE or Sharesave); Enterprise Management Incentives (EMI); Company Share Option Plan (CSOP); or other employee share scheme.

Table 5.8 *Workplaces using incentive schemes, 2004 and 2011, cell per cent*

	Public sector		Private sector		All workplaces	
	2004	2011	2004	2011	2004	2011
Any Payments by Results or merit pay	17	17	43	45	40	41
Any PBR	10	8	34	32	31	29
Any merit pay	10	10	15	23	15	21
Any profit-related pay	1	5	34	33	30	29
Any share schemes	1	4	19	10	16	9
At least one of the above	17	21	59	59	54	55

Base: All workplaces with five or more employees. Figures are based on responses from at least 2,294 (2004) and 2,676 (2011) workplace managers.

The percentage of workplaces that use any one of these incentive schemes has remained broadly stable since 2004 as the changes in the private and public sectors are not statistically significant. But there have been changes in the types of schemes used by employers. In the private sector a growth in the use of merit pay has been offset by a reduction in the use of PBR so that the proportion of all workplaces using either PBR or merit pay has remained constant at just over two fifths (45 per cent in both years). The most notable change in the private sector has been the halving of the proportion of workplaces with employee share plans from 19 per cent in 2004 to 10 per cent in 2010. The decline was most apparent in large private sector enterprises with at least 250 employees – 45 per cent of workplaces in these organisations had share plans in 2004 and in 2011 it was 21 per cent. The sectors experiencing the biggest decline in the use of share plans were Financial services; Electricity, gas and water; Wholesale and retail trade; and Other business services. Only the smallest workplaces with fewer than ten employees saw the incidence of share plans decline significantly where it fell from 16 to 4 per cent. Consequently, the fall in the proportion of employees in workplaces with share plans fell less steeply than the workplace incidence of share schemes: one fifth (20 per cent) of all employees belonged to workplaces with share plans in 2011 compared to one quarter (24 per cent) in 2004. In the public sector there have been small but statistically significant increases in the percentage of public sector workplaces with share plans and PRP schemes. These increases are due to the growth of financial participation schemes in the postal service.

The proportion of non-managerial employees covered by incentive schemes has changed little since 2004, although there was a small rise in those covered by PRP schemes. For instance, the percentage of workplaces with PRP covering all non-managerial employees rose from 7 per cent to 10 per cent (Figure 5.2).

Studies up to the early 2000s indicated that incentive pay schemes had become increasingly common – particularly collective schemes linking pay to the performance of teams or organisations (Pendleton et al., 2009; Bryson et al., 2013b). However, the analyses presented here indicate broad stability between 2004 and 2011 in the incidence of incentive schemes, with some increase in merit pay, a decline in share plans and some growth in financial participation in the public

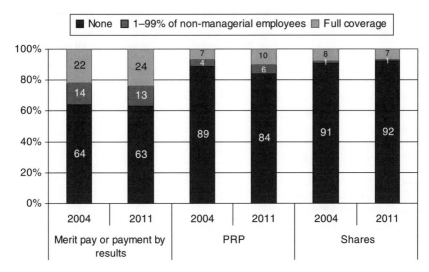

Figure 5.2 *Coverage of incentive payments for non-managerial employees within workplaces, 2004 and 2011, column per cent*

Base: All workplaces with five or more employees. Figures are based on responses from at least 2,158 (2004) and 2,456 (2011) workplace managers.

sector. Pendleton et al.'s (2009) analyses of WERS between 1984 and 2004 were based on workplaces with 25 or more employees, whereas the analyses presented here are for workplaces with five or more employees. Nevertheless, if we confine our analyses to workplaces with at least 25 employees, the incidence of incentive schemes is higher overall, as one might expect, but the trends are similar to those presented previously.

How Many Employees are Paid for Performance?

For the first time in WERS, the 2011 survey asked employees whether they received payments based 'on your individual performance or output', 'on the overall performance of a group or team' or 'on the overall performance of your workplace or organisation (e.g. profit sharing scheme)'. The question did not identify how performance was assessed and so, in this section, we use the catch-all term 'performance-related pay' without making the distinctions between PBR, merit pay and PRP that were made in the previous section. Nor did the question ask employees whether they were in a share plan.

One fifth (20 per cent) of employees received performance-related pay in addition to their fixed wages and 3 per cent were solely reliant on it; the remaining three quarters (77 per cent) were on a fixed wage only. There is substantial variation across industries – two thirds (65 per cent) of employees were in receipt of performance-related pay in Financial services compared with only 4 per cent in Education.

Only 7 per cent of public sector employees received performance-related pay, compared with 28 per cent of private sector employees (Table 5.9). Individual

Table 5.9 *Employee receipt of performance-related pay, 2011, cell per cent*

	Public sector	Private sector	All workplaces
Employees in receipt of any performance-related pay	7	28	23
Employees in receipt of two or more forms of performance-related pay	1	9	7
Basis for payments			
Individual performance or output	5	15	13
Overall performance of a group or team	2	9	8
Overall performance of the workplace or organisation (e.g. profit-sharing scheme)	1	15	11

Base: All employees in workplaces with five or more employees. Figures are based on responses from 20,556 employees.

performance-related pay was the dominant form in the public sector. However, much of this was accounted for by employees in Public administration, some of whom may have been reporting receipt of non-consolidated bonuses in the wake of a pay freeze. In the private sector, individual and organisation-level performance-related pay were equally common. In private manufacturing, employees were most likely to have their pay tied to workplace or organisation performance (18 per cent), followed by individual performance (11 per cent). In private services individual performance was the more common basis (16 per cent of employees) followed by workplace or organisation performance (14 per cent).

Performance Appraisal

How employees perform is important not only because it can affect their pay directly, but also because managers are increasingly likely to be monitoring their performance and making decisions on careers and promotions accordingly. This, in turn, can have important longer-term effects on employees' pay.

A growing proportion of non-managerial employees have their performance formally appraised (Figure 5.3). The percentage of workplaces formally appraising at least some non-managerial employees rose from 43 per cent in 2004 to 70 per cent in 2011. Furthermore, the percentage of workplaces formally appraising *all* of their non-managerial employees increased from 38 per cent to 63 per cent over that period.

The percentage of workplaces directly linking pay to the outcome of performance appraisal also rose so that, by 2011, non-managerial pay was partly determined by performance appraisal in one quarter (25 per cent) of workplaces (Figure 5.3). An increase was apparent in both the public and private sectors. There was also an increase in appraisals that were not linked to pay, indicating that employers were increasingly concerned to assess their employees' performance, irrespective of whether a direct link was made with employees' pay.

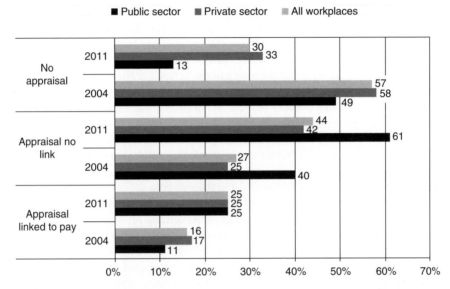

Figure 5.3 *Incidence of appraisal for non-managerial employees, 2011, cell per cent*
Base: All workplaces with five or more employees. Figures are based on responses from 2,291 (2004) and 2,660 (2011) workplace managers.

CONCLUSION

This chapter has considered trends in pay and rewards across Britain's workplaces in the last seven years. The central themes have been the importance of distinguishing between the public and private sectors, and the impact that recessionary pressures have had on the pay setting process and the terms and conditions of employees. In the private sector, pay setting arrangements were found to be fairly stable, thus marking a break with the decline in collective bargaining coverage that has characterised the last few decades. But underneath that stability in formal arrangements for pay determination, the scope of collective bargaining was found to have diminished in the private sector, suggesting a further hollowing out of union influence over the setting of terms and conditions.

The picture was different in the public sector in two ways. First, depending upon the definition one uses to capture collective bargaining, the incidence of bargaining fell quite substantially in the public sector, a trend that is in part due to the increased use of Independent Pay Review Bodies to set pay in the sector. Although the Pay Review Body procedures are akin to collective bargaining in some respects, they are bodies that are ultimately subject to government control and, as such, they are considered to be distinct from collective bargaining in our analysis. Second, in contrast to the private sector, and despite the diminution in collective bargaining coverage, the scope of union negotiation over non-pay terms and conditions was stable in the public sector.

The recession played a significant role in determining pay outcomes for employees. Pay settlements leading to actual cuts in pay were very rare in the public and private sectors, but pay freezes were fairly common. Pay freezes were much more likely in workplaces that had been adversely affected by the recession, although a sizeable percentage of workplace managers reported pay freezes even when they said the recession had had no adverse effect on them. Managers confirmed that wage freezes or cuts frequently occurred as a direct result of the impact of recession. Indeed they were the most common response to the recession, but this action was often taken as part of a broader cost-cutting exercise involving other actions such as restricting entitlements to training.

Employees also testified to widespread pay freezes or cuts. They were particularly common among public sector employees. It was employees who were perhaps relatively advantaged, rather than those with the least bargaining power, who were most likely to suffer from a freeze or cut in their wages.

In the public sector there was little change between 2004 and 2011 in the provision of fringe benefits, although the forthcoming reforms to public sector pensions mean that the nature of pension provision may change in the near future. In the private sector some erosion of fringe benefit provision was apparent, with much of the impact falling disproportionately on managerial employees. Here the Government's workplace pension reforms are intended to arrest the decline in the coming years.

The last seven years have been particularly challenging for trade unions. In the public sector, they have had to negotiate wages and play a role in Pay Review Bodies while the Government is committed to pay freezes and widespread reductions in public expenditure. Furthermore, the diminution of the scope of collective bargaining in the private sector suggests a continuing hollowing out of union influence over terms and conditions, even where they maintain a formal presence at the workplace. And yet, employee-level analyses for the private sector suggest that the presence of a recognised trade union reduced the chances of a recession-induced pay freeze or cut and cuts in fringe benefits.

A final question is whether employees themselves still value trade union representation in joint regulation of workplaces, or whether they prefer alternative arrangements. When employees were asked, 'Ideally, who do you think would best represent you in dealing with managers about getting increases in your pay?', one third (32 per cent in 2004 and 30 per cent in 2011) said a trade union.[13] This rose to one half in workplaces with a union recognised for pay bargaining (55 per cent in 2004 and 52 per cent in 2011) and two thirds among union members (69 per cent in both years). These numbers may not provide a ringing endorsement for trade unions. Nevertheless, they do suggest that employees' perceptions of union effectiveness in bargaining on their behalf have remained fairly stable since 2004, something that is arguably a reasonable achievement in the face of the challenges unions have faced.

6 The Quality of Jobs and Employment

INTRODUCTION

The quality of jobs, particularly in terms of the inequalities between different groups of workers and those in different types of employment, forms a critical strand of employment relations debates. The issue of job quality has also risen in prominence in national labour market policy over the past 15 years. In Britain this increasing focus was fuelled in part, in the late 1990s and early 2000s, by a diminished concern with the level of unemployment in a context where the economy was performing well. However, there has also been an increasing acknowledgement that job characteristics, such as the intensity of work and the degree of autonomy that workers have in their jobs, affect employees' physical and mental health (Commission on Social Determinants of Health, 2008). This link in turn implies that job quality has an influence on workers' productivity, and so aggregate levels of job quality have also become important in understanding international differences in economic performance (Green, 2013).

Existing studies show that job quality in Britain declined in the 1990s, with a rise in work intensification and a decline in task discretion being charted in reputable national surveys (Green, 2006). The decline was reversed in the late 1990s and early 2000s, however, which saw improvements in task discretion and no further increase in work intensity, alongside improvements in job security (Green and Whitfield, 2009). Improvements in job quality were attributed primarily to the favourable economic climate rather than specific policy interventions (Brown et al., 2007). The economic climate has clearly been less favourable of late, and the attention of policymakers has again turned more to the *quantity* as much as the *quality* of employment.

This chapter considers overall changes in job quality between 2004 and 2011. It explores the effects of the economic downturn, considers changes for different groups of workers, and explores the association with particular employee and workplace characteristics. The focus is principally on features of the job and working environment that Karasek (1979) and others have identified as important for employee well-being. The chapter is then complemented by Chapter 7, where the role of job quality in explaining variations in employee well-being forms a prominent theme.

This chapter begins by exploring the job demands faced by employees. These may have risen where employers responded to recession by cutting the size of their workforce. However, job demands may have fallen where employers hoarded labour, despite falling demand for goods and services, as some have suggested. Next the chapter examines trends in the control that employees have over their jobs and how secure they feel in their jobs. Chapter 3 showed a sizeable decline in perceived job security since 2004. This chapter extends that analysis to identify which employees this affected most, and in which workplaces.

The chapter then explores changes in a range of job supports. These include the provision of off-the-job training, managerial encouragement for employees to develop their skills, flexible working arrangements to help employees balance their work and non-work lives, and practices to promote equal opportunities in the workplace. The degree of health and safety risks in the workplace and the degree of control employees have over these risks is also considered. Additionally, we explore changes in the extent of employees' trust in their managers.

The last element of job quality to be considered in this chapter is pay. Real earnings have been shown elsewhere to have fallen since the onset of recession (Levy, 2013). We focus on the relationship between pay and job quality. We examine whether employees appear to receive higher pay to compensate for other less desirable aspects of the job, or whether employees in higher quality jobs also receive higher rates of pay. The chapter concludes by considering the relative importance of an employee's choice of workplace in determining their level of job quality.

JOB DEMANDS

Work intensity increased during the 1990s (Green, 2006) then remained fairly stable between 1998 and 2004 (Kersley et al., 2006; Brown et al., 2007). Hours worked provide one measure of work intensity and the QLFS shows a decline in average hours worked from the early 1990s onwards (Office for National Statistics, 2011a), but this has been gradual and the overall distribution of hours worked by employees in WERS was very similar in 2004 and 2011. The pattern of working hours – and particularly the incidence of long hours working – was discussed in van Wanrooy et al. (2013). Here the focus is on work intensity, which may differ for any given hour of work.

Analysis of the 2011 WERS data revealed a mixed picture of changes in work intensity. The percentage of employees agreeing or strongly agreeing with the statement, 'My job requires that I work very hard' increased from 76 per cent in 2004 to 83 per cent in 2011. In contrast, the proportion agreeing or strongly agreeing with the statement, 'I never seem to have enough time to get my work done' remained at around two fifths in both years (41 per cent in 2011). These trends mirror those found for Britain in the European Social Survey between 2004 and 2010 (McManus and Perry, 2012).

There was an increase in the proportion of employees that reported their job required them to work very hard in both the public and private sectors, but public sector employees were more likely to do so (Table 6.1). However, the magnitude of the

Table 6.1 *Employees' perceptions of work intensity and working hours, 2004 and 2011, cell per cent*

Employees agreeing that	'My job requires that I work very hard'		'I never seem to have enough time to get my work done'		'People in this workplace who want to progress usually have to put in long hours'
	2004	2011	2004	2011	2011
Sector of ownership					
Private sector	74	<u>83</u>	36	<u>38</u>	42
Public sector	80	<u>85</u>	51	48	37
Usual weekly hours					
Less than 10 hours	67	<u>76</u>	26	29	39
10–29 hours	70	<u>80</u>	31	34	37
30–48 hours	77	<u>83</u>	41	41	40
More than 48 hours	85	<u>90</u>	51	<u>55</u>	55
Occupation					
Managers and senior officials	85	<u>89</u>	55	52	49
Professional	84	<u>88</u>	58	55	59
Associate professional and technical	77	<u>85</u>	44	45	43
Administrative and secretarial	73	<u>80</u>	39	38	32
Skilled trades	71	76	35	31	32
Caring, leisure and other personal services	77	<u>85</u>	33	36	31
Sales and customer service	71	<u>79</u>	30	29	45
Process, plant and machine operatives	71	<u>76</u>	27	31	33
Elementary occupations	70	<u>79</u>	24	<u>28</u>	35
Gender					
Male	74	<u>81</u>	39	38	43
Female	78	<u>85</u>	40	<u>43</u>	39
All employees	76	<u>83</u>	40	41	41

Base: All employees in workplaces with five or more employees. Figures are based on responses from at least 21,502 (2004) and 20,682 (2011) employees.

increase was greater among private sector employees, such that by 2011 the difference between the sectors was smaller than it was in 2004, but still statistically significant.

As in 2004, employees who worked longer hours were more likely to report that their job required them to work very hard; this applied for 90 per cent of those working more than 48 hours per week in 2011. However, increases in the proportion of employees stating that they were required to work very hard occurred across all bands of work hours (Table 6.1). Occupational differences also remained apparent, with Managers and senior officials and Professionals the most likely to report working very hard. These relationships remain significant when controlling for a range of employee and workplace characteristics.[1]

While there was no change in the overall proportion of employees stating that they never had enough time to get their work done, there were changes for some groups of employees. Among private sector employees there was a small increase in the percentage agreeing that they never had enough time to get their work done; there was no statistically significant change for public sector employees. The percentage of employees who felt they never had enough time to get their work done had fallen in the smallest workplaces (those with five to nine employees), from 36 per cent in 2004 to 29 per cent in 2011. Among employees aged 60 or over the percentage agreeing or strongly agreeing that they never had enough time to get their work done rose from 32 per cent in 2004 to 37 per cent in 2011, while there were no statistically significant changes for younger employees. A small increase was also apparent for women (rising from 40 per cent to 43 per cent) but not for men.

One potential reason for differences in work intensity between workplaces may relate to the presence of a long-hours culture, particularly if long hours are seen as necessary to gain promotion or progress within the workplace. With this in mind, employees were asked in the 2011 WERS whether they agreed that, 'People in this workplace who want to progress usually have to put in long hours' – two fifths (41 per cent) of all employees agreed or strongly agreed with this statement (Table 6.1). This was more common among employees who worked longer hours, with 55 per cent of employees working more than 48 hours a week agreeing with this statement compared with 39 per cent of all other employees. While women were more likely than men to report working very hard or never having enough time to get their work done, men were more likely to believe that long working hours were required for progression. This remained the case after controlling for hours worked. The perception that long hours were required for progression was also more common among employees in larger workplaces than those working in smaller workplaces, in private sector workplaces compared with the public sector, and in particular industries, including Financial services (where 51 per cent agreed with this statement), Education (49 per cent) and Hotels and restaurants (48 per cent).

Employees who felt long hours were necessary for progression were more likely to report that their job required them to work very hard (90 per cent of this group, compared with 79 per cent of all other employees) and that they never had enough time to get their work done (52 per cent compared with 32 per cent among all other employees).

When asked directly about their experiences of recession in their workplace (as discussed in Chapter 2), an increase in workload was reported by 28 per cent of employees, the second most common response after a pay freeze or cut. Employees who reported their workload increased as a result of the recession were more likely, than those who did not, to strongly agree that their job required them to work very hard (45 per cent compared with 30 per cent of those who did not report an increase in workload). They were also more likely to agree or strongly agree that they never had enough time to get their work done (61 per cent compared with 34 per cent of those not reporting an increase in workload as a result of the recession).

To explore the impact of recession further we can consider changes in work intensity within the panel workplaces that were surveyed in both 2004 and 2011 according to managers' reports of the adverse effect of recession on the workplace.

In fact, the proportion of employees who strongly agreed that their job required them to work very hard increased between 2004 and 2011 regardless of the extent of the adverse effect of recession on the workplace. Further, the proportion of employees who never had enough time to get their work done did not change in workplaces affected to a lesser or greater extent by recession. Both these findings also apply when considering workplaces where the recession led to actions that may be expected to affect work intensity, namely redundancies, or recruitment freezes. So while some employees attributed increasing work intensity to the recession, the broader responses suggest that the increase in work intensity between 2004 and 2011 may have been part of a wider phenomenon, rather than purely driven by the economic downturn. It could also be the case that workloads increased only for particular jobs within a workplace, rather than across the workplace as a whole. Managers in particular were more likely than employees in other occupations to report an increase in workload as a result of recession, even when controlling for other characteristics.

JOB CONTROL

As predicted by Karasek (1979), affording employees greater influence over their work has been associated with better workplace performance and employee well-being (Wood, 2008; Wood et al., 2012). WERS gauges the level of autonomy afforded to employees in two ways. First, workplace managers are asked to what extent employees in the largest occupation at the workplace have control over some specific aspects of their work, with responses on a four-point scale: 'A lot', 'Some', 'A little' and 'None'.[2] Second, all employees, regardless of their occupation, are asked how much influence they have over specific aspects of their work, using the same aforementioned four-point scale.

Information gathered from workplace managers in the 2011 WERS suggested no change in autonomy since 2004. The proportion of workplaces in which employees in the largest occupation at the workplace were considered by managers to have a lot of 'discretion over how they do their work' stood at 29 per cent in both 2004 and 2011. In around one quarter of workplaces in both years such employees were considered to have a lot of 'control over the pace at which they work' (25 per cent in 2004 and 24 per cent in 2011), while the proportion of workplaces where employees had a lot of 'variety in their work' remained at around one half (49 per cent in 2011 and 48 per cent in 2004). These measures were stable in both the public and private sectors. These job autonomy measures were also stable between 1998 and 2004 (Wood and Bryson, 2009), suggesting there has been little change since the late 1990s.[3]

Autonomy over the organisation of work is a key element of many conceptions of teamwork. Here information from workplace managers indicated that there had been an increase in the percentage of workplaces where any employees in the largest occupation at the workplace worked in formally designated teams, rising from 62 per cent in 2004 to 71 per cent in 2011. In two thirds (67 per cent) of teams, the members jointly decided how the work was to be done, a proportion that had not changed significantly since 2004. But combined with the rise in the incidence of

Table 6.2 *Employees who reported 'A lot' of influence over their work, 2004 and 2011, cell per cent*

	Private sector		Public sector		All employees	
	2004	2011	2004	2011	2004	2011
How the work is done	52	55	45	47	50	53
The order in which tasks are carried out	50	52	46	47	49	51
The pace of work	40	43	32	35	38	41
The tasks done in the job	38	44	31	36	36	41
Start and finish times	26	31	28	30	27	31
All of the above items	13	16	10	12	12	15

Base: All employees in workplaces with five or more employees. Figures are based on responses from at least 21,630 (2004) and 21,287 (2011) employees.

workplaces with any formally designated teams, this resulted in an overall increase in the percentage of all workplaces with teams where members jointly decided how the work was to be done (referred to from here on as semi-autonomous teams), from 39 per cent in 2004 to 47 per cent in 2011.

The increase in the prevalence of semi-autonomous teamwork was confined to the private sector, however, with an increase in the percentage of workplaces with any employees in such teams from 37 per cent in 2004 to 45 per cent in 2011. Although there was no statistically significant increase in semi-autonomous teams in public sector workplaces, they remained more common throughout (in 57 per cent of public sector workplaces in 2004 and 61 per cent in 2011). While larger workplaces remained more likely than small workplaces to have some employees in semi-autonomous teams (56 per cent of workplaces with 100 or more employees and 43 per cent of workplaces with 5–19 employees), both had seen an increase in teamworking since 2004.

Turning to information on autonomy collected from employees, a small but statistically significant increase was observed on each individual measure between 2004 and 2011, and also in the proportion of employees reporting a lot of influence over all five items (Table 6.2).

Private sector employees reported greater autonomy than public sector employees over all dimensions except for start and finish times. Job control rose in both sectors between 2004 and 2011, but while the increase was statistically significant for all individual items in the private sector, in the public sector, this only applied for the tasks done in the job and the pace of work. These increases were still evident after controlling for change in the composition of workplaces and the workforce over time.

The responses from employees point then to some increase in autonomy between 2004 and 2011, which contrasts with the information from managers which suggested relative stability. The questions asked of managers relate only to employees in the largest occupation and also relate to two of the five aspects covered in Table 6.2 ('How the work is done' and 'The pace of work'). If we restrict the analysis of employees to those in the largest occupation at the workplace, we still see a rise in the percentage of employees reporting 'A lot' of influence over the

Table 6.3 *Employees who reported 'A lot' of influence over their work by impact of the recession, 2004 and 2011, cell per cent*

	Workplace adversely affected by recession			
	'A great deal' or 'Quite a lot'		'A moderate amount', 'Just a little' or 'No adverse effect'	
	2004	2011	2004	2011
How the work is done	49	52	48	51
The order in which tasks are carried out	49	51	45	48
The pace of work	37	38	35	<u>40</u>
The tasks done in the job	35	<u>41</u>	33	<u>40</u>
Start and finish times	29	<u>37</u>	25	28
All of the above items	14	<u>17</u>	10	<u>13</u>

Base: All employees in panel workplaces. Figures are based on responses from at least 7,656 (2004) and 7,046 (2011) employees.

pace at which they work, from 33 per cent in 2004 to 36 per cent in 2011, but no statistically significant increase for how the work is done (45 per cent in 2004 and 47 per cent in 2011).[4] This may go some way to explaining the discrepancy between managers' and employees' responses, but also there may be differences within the group of employees in the largest occupation and perhaps some genuine differences in perceptions between managers and employees.

As in 2004, autonomy was highest among employees in managerial occupations. Not all occupation groups saw a statistically significant increase in autonomy between 2004 and 2011; this being the case only for Managers and senior officials (26 per cent reported 'A lot' of influence over all items in 2004 rising to 30 per cent in 2011), Professionals (10 per cent to 14 per cent), employees in Sales and customer service occupations (5 per cent to 9 per cent) and those in Elementary occupations (10 per cent to 14 per cent).

Other studies have shown little change in autonomy over a similar time period. The Skills and Employment Survey 2012 (Inanc et al., 2013) revealed that task discretion has remained relatively stable since 2001; but divergent trends for men and women since 2006, with a small increase for women but a fall for men. The European Social Survey points to an increase in job control in Britain between 2004 and 2010, but again only for women (McManus and Perry, 2012). The 2011 WERS also shows some differences by gender, with increases in influence over how employees did their work and the order in which they carried out tasks only statistically significant for women (rising from 49 per cent in 2004 to 52 per cent in 2011, and 50 per cent to 54 per cent, respectively). However, both men and women saw an increase in the other dimensions of autonomy considered in WERS.

The increase in employee-reported autonomy has occurred against the backdrop of recession. Focusing on employee accounts of job autonomy in the panel of workplaces surveyed in both 2004 and 2011, a similar increase in the proportion of employees reporting 'A lot' of influence over all five items is apparent in workplaces affected by the recession to both a greater and lesser degree (Table 6.3). There were some differences on individual items. Autonomy over the tasks done in the job increased regardless of the impact of recession, autonomy over the pace of work only increased to a statistically significant extent in workplaces less affected by the recession, while the reverse applied for autonomy over start and finish times. Overall, the percentage of employees reporting 'A lot' of influence over all items increased to a similar extent (3 percentage points) in both groups shown in Table 6.3. As we only observe two discrete time points, that is, 2004 and 2011, it is not possible to tell whether this increase in autonomy occurred after 2004, but prior to the onset of recession. However, the absence of a consistent relationship with recession in Table 6.3 suggests that job autonomy was not impaired, on average, where recession hit hardest.

JOB SECURITY

The findings presented so far have shown a mixed picture of trends in job quality between 2004 and 2011, with some evidence of an increase in work intensity, but also some improvements in autonomy. In this section we consider changes in perceived job security. The cyclical nature of perceived job security – falling in times of economic uncertainty and improving when the economy is more buoyant – has been documented in several studies (Green, 2006; Bryson and Forth, 2010a; Park et al., 2012). Reflecting this, perceptions of job security increased over the period 1998–2004 (Brown et al., 2007), with more recent studies indicating a fall during the current economic downturn (McManus and Perry, 2012).

Chapter 3 discussed the decline in employee perceptions of job security between 2004 and 2011 and showed that employees were less likely to feel their job was secure in work-places that had made redundancies in the year prior to the survey compared with those workplaces where no redundancies had been made. Here we explore further the work-places and groups of employees for which perceptions of job security changed the most.

While perceived job security fell among employees in both the private and public sectors, the fall was much greater among public sector employees, with the percentage agreeing or strongly agreeing that their job was secure falling from 66 per cent to 47 per cent (Figure 6.1). In contrast, it fell from 68 per cent to 65 per cent among private sector employees. The decline in job security in the public sector was particularly substantial for employees working in Other community services, where it fell by 34 percentage points. The percentage of employees agreeing their job was secure fell by around 20 percentage points each in Public administration and Health and social work, but by only eight percentage points in Education.

Looking across all employees, falls in perceived job security were apparent for both men and women, although there was a greater decline among women – falling from 71 per cent in 2004 to 62 per cent in 2011. The proportion of men that agreed that their job was secure stood at 63 per cent in 2004 compared with 59 per cent in 2011. The disparity was partly because women were more likely than men to be working in the public sector (where perceptions of job security fell by a similar extent for both women and men), but also because in the private sector it was only women (and not men) who reported a fall in job security.

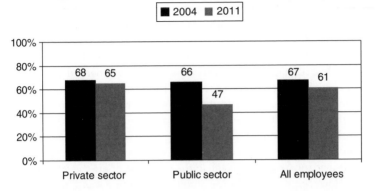

Figure 6.1 *Employee perceptions of job security, by sector, 2004 and 2011, cell per cent*
Base: All employees in workplaces with five or more employees. Figures are based on responses from 21,518 (2004) and 20,994 (2011) employees.

Perceptions of job security were lower in workplaces adversely affected by the recession and fell with the number of changes employees had experienced as a result. The proportion of employees agreeing or strongly agreeing that their job was secure fell considerably in workplaces adversely affected 'A great deal' by the recession, from 69 per cent in 2004 to 45 per cent in 2011. In contrast, there were no statistically significant changes in the proportion of employees who considered their job was secure in workplaces less adversely affected by the recession. Both the extent to which the workplace was adversely affected by the recession and whether the employee experienced any change as a result remained significant predictors of perceived job security when controlling for a range of employee, job and workplace characteristics. These findings provide further evidence that perceptions of job security are related to the real chances of job loss, as also found, for example, in Dickerson and Green (2012).

JOB SUPPORTS

The relationship between working in a supportive environment and employee well-being was first discussed in research by Payne (1979) and added to the original demands-control model developed by Karasek (1979), on the basis that support at work could counter the effect of excessive job demands (Wood, 2008). In this section we explore changes in a range of job supports, in particular, the provision of off-the-job training, flexible working arrangements to aid employees in achieving a balance between work and life outside, equal opportunities policies and practices, and health and safety in the workplace. Additionally, we explore changes in employees' perceptions of the extent to which their managers are fair and trustworthy.

Training and Skill Development

Earlier surveys in the WERS series indicated an increase between 1998 and 2004 in the proportion of workplaces providing some off-the-job training (Kersley et al.,

2006: 82). We might expect some cuts in provision of training between 2004 and 2011, as in Chapter 2 we saw that a sizeable minority of employers reported that they had reduced expenditure on training in response to the recession (see Table 2.3).

However, responses from managers in the 2011 WERS indicated that four fifths (81 per cent) of workplaces had given at least some of their experienced employees in the largest occupation at the workplace time off from their normal work duties to undertake training in the year prior to the survey. This represented an increase since 2004 when this stood at 76 per cent. Furthermore, there was an increase in the percentage of workplaces that provided this training for at least 80 per cent of this group of employees, rising from 34 per cent in 2004 to 42 per cent in 2011. On this basis, there is little evidence to suggest a fall in the provision of off-the-job training over this period. However, some fall in the amount of training was apparent; the percentage of workplaces providing an average of ten or more days of training for experienced employees in the largest occupation in the year prior to the survey had fallen from 14 per cent in 2004 to 10 per cent in 2011. It is therefore uncertain as to whether the overall volume of training for employees in the largest occupation at the workplace actually rose between 2004 and 2011.

As in 2004, public sector workplaces remained more likely than those in the private sector to provide training to a large proportion (at least 80 per cent) of experienced employees in the largest occupation at the workplace, but the increase between 2004 and 2011 was observed only for the private sector (Table 6.4). Differences between the public and private sectors, in part, reflect variations by industry. When controlling for workplace and organisation size, industry, sector of ownership, union recognition and the largest occupation at the workplace, the key determinants in 2011 were organisation size (with workplaces in larger organisations more likely to have provided training to the majority of their employees than those in smaller organisations), industry (with provision highest in Financial services and Health and social work), and occupation (lowest in workplaces where the largest occupation at the workplace was Administrative and secretarial or Elementary occupations).[5]

In Chapter 5 it was shown that there was a notable increase in workplaces where performance appraisals were carried out for at least some non-managerial employees. In the vast majority (95 per cent) of these workplaces, the appraisal resulted in an evaluation of employees' training needs. This proportion had remained stable since 2004 (94 per cent), but combined with the rise in workplaces that conducted formal appraisals resulted in an overall increase in the percentage of workplaces where at least some non-managerial employees received an appraisal that led to an evaluation of training needs from 41 per cent in 2004 to 66 per cent in 2011.

Which employees benefited from the increased coverage of training within workplaces? All employees were asked about training they received regardless of their level of experience or whether they were employed in the largest occupation at the workplace; employees were specifically asked to exclude health and safety training, but otherwise the definition of training mirrored that used in the management survey. Responses from employees showed similar trends to those of the managerial respondents. The proportion of employees who had received any training in the 12 months prior to the survey increased from 63 per cent in 2004 to 68 per cent in

Table 6.4 *Workplaces providing off-the-job training to at least 80 per cent of experienced employees in the largest occupation at the workplace, 2004 and 2011, cell per cent*

	2004	2011
Sector of ownership		
Private sector	31	<u>40</u>
Public sector	56	57
Organisation size		
Less than 50 employees	19	<u>36</u>
50–249 employees	43	44
500 or more employees	48	50
Industry		
Manufacturing	20	34
Electricity, gas and water	(81)	66
Construction	24	43
Wholesale and retail trade	23	<u>36</u>
Hotels and restaurants	16	25
Transport and communications	48	40
Financial services	80	(72)
Other business services	38	37
Public administration	58	46
Education	64	61
Health and social work	46	<u>70</u>
Other community services	35	43
All workplaces	34	<u>42</u>

Base: All workplaces with five or more employees. Figures are based on responses from at least 2,251 (2004) and 2,583 (2011) workplace managers.

2011. However, this increase was concentrated on shorter periods of training: the percentage of employees receiving up to two days of training increased from 24 per cent to 30 per cent, while the percentage of employees receiving ten days or more fell from 8 per cent to 6 per cent. The percentage of employees receiving any training rose from 58 per cent to 66 per cent in the private sector, but remained stable in the public sector (around 75 per cent in both years). However, both sectors saw a fall in the proportion of employees receiving ten or more days of training.

In both 2004 and 2011, similar patterns were found in the employee and job characteristics that were associated with receipt of training. Training remained more common among younger employees compared with older employees, among those who had most recently joined the workplace compared with those with longer job tenure, and among those working at least 30 hours per week compared with those working fewer hours. While employees with higher academic qualifications remained more likely to receive training than those with no or low levels of qualifications, the increase in training between 2004 and 2011 appeared to be concentrated among those with no or lower levels of qualifications, increasing from 55 per cent to 64 per cent among employees whose highest qualification was equivalent to below A-level. This is also reflected in changes in training by occupation; increases in training between 2004 and 2011 were experienced by employees working in

Skilled trades; Caring, leisure and other personal services; and as Process, plant and machine operatives.

Employees were asked their level of agreement as to whether managers at their workplace, 'Encourage people to develop their skills'. There was no overall change between 2004 and 2011 in the proportion of employees who agreed or strongly agreed – about three fifths of employees in both years. However, while this remained stable in the private sector (58 per cent in 2004 and 60 per cent in 2011), the proportion of employees in the public sector who agreed fell (from 61 per cent in 2004 to 55 per cent in 2011). As in 2004, employees were more likely to agree that managers encouraged skill development when they had received more days of training within the past year, standing at 78 per cent among those receiving at least five training days. Nevertheless, even among those who had received no days of training in the past year, 44 per cent thought managers encouraged development of skills; this may reflect training the employee had received in prior years, or the presence of other forms of skill development, such as on-the-job training.

Overall then, more employees received at least some training in 2011 compared with 2004, although there was a reduction in the amount of training individual employees received. But how did employers change training specifically in response to recession? Felstead et al. (2012) found that employers cut expenditure on training in response to the recession but with a minimal impact on rates of training participation. In the 2011 WERS, 17 per cent of managers stated that training expenditure had been reduced in their workplace as a result of the recession, while 12 per cent of employees stated that their own access to training had been restricted. These reductions in expenditure and access, in conjunction with the increase in the proportion of employees receiving some training, albeit of shorter duration, lend support to the idea that employers may have reacted to the recession by training 'smarter', or in other words that training budgets may be being used more cost-effectively (Felstead et al., 2012).

Finally in this section we consider the extent to which employees feel their skills match those required for their jobs. A number of sources, including previous WERS surveys, have suggested that many employees' qualifications and skills are under-used (Alpin et al., 1998; Green et al., 2002; Chevalier, 2003; Kersley et al., 2006). The skills mismatch remained evident in the 2011 WERS. Just under one fifth (19 per cent) of employees gauged that their skills were 'Much higher' than those required to do their job while 32 per cent thought that their skills were 'A bit higher' than the skills required for their job. Forty-four per cent of employees considered that their skills matched the level required for their job and 4 per cent said their skills were below the level required to do their job. However, there has been a small but significant reduction in the mismatch since 2004. The percentage of employees that said their skills were about the same as those required by the job rose from 42 per cent to 44 per cent in 2011, offsetting a reduction in the percentage who felt their skills were much higher than those required by their job (from 22 per cent in 2004 to 19 per cent in 2011). This pattern is consistent with trends shown by the 2012 Skills and Employment Survey (Felstead et al., 2013).

Work–Life Balance Practices and Work–Life Conflict

Flexible working arrangements can play a critical role in allowing employees to balance their work with commitments in their non-work life. Currently, employees with parental or caring responsibilities have the right to request flexible working; however, the government has announced plans to extend this right to all employees from 2014. Managers were asked whether any of a specified list of working time arrangements, such as flexi-time or working from home, were available to any employees at the workplace. We focus our comparison on the six arrangements that were included in both 2004 and 2011, which results in a mixed picture (Table 6.5).[6] While there had been an increase in the proportion of workplaces allowing at least some employees to work from home and to compress their working hours, there had been a reduction in the proportion allowing employees to reduce their working hours and where job-sharing was available. There were no significant differences in the availability of term-time working or flexi-time. Broadly similar patterns are observed when we focus the analysis on the panel of workplaces that were surveyed in both 2004 and 2011.[7]

The fall in the proportion of workplaces allowing employees to reduce their working hours was driven mainly by a decline in the private sector – where the percentage of workplaces offering this arrangement fell from 60 per cent to 54 per cent. There was no significant change in the public sector. The private and public sectors fared similarly on the other practices shown in Table 6.5.

In 2011, term-time working and job-sharing were less common in private sector workplaces than in the public sector, even after controlling for industry and other workplace characteristics. However, for the other working time arrangements, no statistically significant differences by sector remained when controlling for these other factors. As in 2004, larger workplaces were more likely to offer the aforesaid arrangements than smaller workplaces.

In 2011, employees were also asked for a specified list of arrangements, 'In the last 12 months, have you made use of any of the following arrangements, and if not, are they available to you if you needed them?' (Figure 6.2). As the question wording was changed from 2004, we focus only on 2011 responses here. For many of the

Table 6.5 Availability of flexible working arrangements, 2004 and 2011, cell per cent

	Private sector		Public sector		All workplaces	
	2004	2011	2004	2011	2004	2011
Reduce working hours	60	<u>54</u>	76	75	62	<u>56</u>
Flexi-time	34	32	43	49	35	34
Working from home	24	<u>29</u>	35	42	26	<u>30</u>
Compressed hours	10	<u>17</u>	21	<u>36</u>	11	<u>19</u>
Job-sharing	19	<u>11</u>	67	<u>53</u>	25	<u>17</u>
Term-time working	9	12	49	51	14	16

Base: All workplaces with five or more employees. Figures are based on responses from 2,292 (2004) and 2,662 (2011) workplace managers.

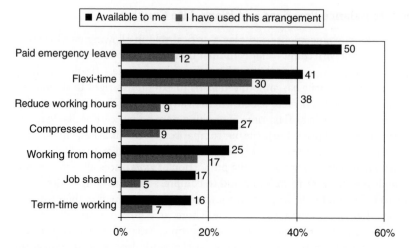

Figure 6.2 *Employees' reports of availability and use of flexible working arrangements, 2011, cell per cent*

Base: All employees in workplaces with five or more employees, excluding those who did not know whether an arrangement was available to them. Figures are based on responses from at least 15,141 employees.

arrangements, a sizeable proportion of employees did not know if the arrangement would be available to them. This was most common for paid leave to care for dependants in an emergency, where three in ten respondents (31 per cent) did not know whether this would be available to them. In contrast, just 6 per cent did not know whether they would be able to work from home.[8] Excluding those employees who did not know, the most commonly available arrangements were paid leave to care for dependents in an emergency (available to 50 per cent of employees), flexi-time (41 per cent) and the chance to reduce working hours (38 per cent). The most commonly *used* arrangements were flexi-time (used by 30 per cent of all employees) and working from home (17 per cent of all employees). Both arrangements were used by around 70 per cent of those to whom they were known to be available.

Employees' take-up of flexible working practices may depend not only on their availability but also on whether they feel managers look favourably on such arrangements. There was a small but statistically significant increase in the proportion of employees who felt managers understood 'about employees having to meet responsibilities outside work' from 60 per cent in 2004 to 62 per cent in 2011. However, this rise was confined to employees in the private sector (59 per cent to 63 per cent) and fell in the public sector (61 per cent to 58 per cent).

At the same time, there was an increase in the proportion of managers who agreed or strongly agreed with the statement, 'It is up to individual employees to balance their work and family responsibilities', from 66 per cent in 2004 to 77 per cent in 2011. This has partly reversed the downward trend seen between 1998 and 2004 – the percentage stood at 84 per cent in 1998.[9] An increase is also seen if we confine our attention to the panel of workplaces surveyed in both 2004 and 2011, where it increased from 66 per cent to 74 per cent. This increase was notably larger

Table 6.6 *Employees' perceptions of work–life conflict, 2011, row per cent*

	'I often find it difficult to fulfil my commitments outside of work because of the amount of time I spend on my job'		
	Agree or Strongly agree	**Neither agree nor disagree**	**Disagree or Strongly disagree**
Hours worked			
Less than 10 hours	19	21	60
10–29 hours	13	21	66
30–48 hours	26	26	47
More than 48 hours	57	22	21
Organisation size			
Less than 50 employees	21	24	54
50–249 employees	27	25	49
500 or more employees	29	25	47
Any dependent children			
No	26	24	50
Yes	30	26	44
All employees	27	25	48

Base: All employees in workplaces with five or more employees. Figures are based on responses from at least 21,034 employees.

among managers in the public sector, increasing from 48 per cent to 67 per cent, although a rise was also seen in the private sector (from 69 per cent to 78 per cent). One possible explanation is that managers may feel that, as they have improved their provision of flexible working arrangements, the individual increasingly has the responsibility for achieving a balance between work and home. Analysis of change in the panel workplaces provides some support for this, with an increase in the proportion of managers agreeing with this statement – from 62 per cent in 2004 to 75 per cent in 2011 – in workplaces where there had been an increase in the provision of flexible working arrangements between these years. In contrast, there was no statistically significant rise in agreement in workplaces where provision had not increased between 2004 and 2011.[10]

Flexible working arrangements may aid employees to manage the conflict they feel between their work and their outside commitments. The 2011 WERS asked employees their level of agreement with the statement, 'I often find it difficult to fulfil my commitments outside of work because of the amount of time I spend on my job'. Around one quarter (27 per cent) of employees agreed or strongly agreed with the statement (Table 6.6). Employees who worked longer hours were more likely to agree that work interfered with their outside commitments. Controlling for hours worked, conflict was also more commonly reported by employees with dependent children, those working in managerial occupations and those with higher academic qualifications. Employees working in smaller organisations were less likely to report conflict than those working in larger organisations; variations were also apparent by industry, with the greatest levels of conflict in Transport and communications, Hotels and restaurants, and Education. The presence of flexible working arrangements (as measured by whether the employee reported that any of the specified arrangements were available to them) was not significantly associated with reported levels of work–life conflict. However, the level of autonomy reported by employees was significantly associated with work–life conflict – greater autonomy was related to lower levels of work–life conflict.

In summary there was a mixed picture of changes in work–life balance between 2004 and 2011. Responses from managers indicated that some forms of flexible working had become more common, but others less so. An increasing proportion of managers felt that it was up to the individual to balance their work and family responsibilities, but there were some signs that this reflected a transfer of responsibilities to employees as provision of flexible working arrangements increased. Nevertheless, employees felt managers were more understanding of their responsibilities outside work, at least among those in the private sector. However, a sizeable minority of employees still reported conflict between work and their commitments outside.

Equal Opportunities Policies and Practices

Ensuring all employees have equal rights at work, regardless of their demographic characteristics, forms one important aspect of fair treatment in the workplace. Equal opportunity at work continues to remain an important issue on the policy agenda, especially in the face of growing diversity in the composition of the workforce (see van Wanrooy et al., 2013: 34). Equality legislation has been extended to cover more grounds throughout the past decade, introducing protection against discrimination on the grounds of religion and sexual orientation since 2003, and age since 2006. The Equality Act 2010 harmonised and replaced previous legislation, extending some rights and ensuring consistency in what employers need to do to make their workplaces a fair environment for all employees.

The proportion of workplaces with a formal written policy on equal opportunities or managing diversity rose from 66 per cent in 2004 to 77 per cent in 2011. This continued the increase in the prevalence of such policies seen between 1998 and 2004 (Kersley et al., 2006; Dex and Forth, 2009). In the public sector, the presence of an equal opportunities policy was almost universal, found in 99 per cent of these workplaces in 2011, an increase from 94 per cent in 2004. While such policies remained more common in the public sector, the private sector saw a greater increase in the presence of equal opportunities policies, rising from 62 per cent of workplaces in 2004 to 74 per cent in 2011. Policies were more common in larger workplaces, such that 92 per cent of all employees worked in a workplace where an equal opportunities policy was in place in 2011 (an increase from 84 per cent in 2004).

The majority (75 per cent or more) of written equal opportunities policies explicitly mentioned gender, ethnic group, disability, religion or belief, age, or sexual orientation. Both age and sexual orientation were more likely to be explicitly mentioned within written policies than in 2004. Two thirds (66 per cent) of formal written policies explicitly mentioned age in 2004, increasing to 77 per cent by 2011, while the percentage mentioning sexual orientation had risen from 69 per cent to 75 per cent.

Table 6.7 *Equal opportunities workplace practices, 2004 and 2011, cell per cent*

	Private sector		Public sector		All workplaces	
	2004	**2011**	**2004**	**2011**	**2004**	**2011**
Monitor recruitment and selection	20	18	60	57	25	23
Review recruitment and selection procedures	14	14	46	46	18	18
Monitor promotions	6	6	30	28	9	9
Review promotion procedures	7	8	29	28	10	10
Review relative pay rates	6	5	15	19	7	7

Notes: Figures indicate percentage of workplaces where practices are in place for any of the following employee characteristics: gender, ethnic background, disability or age.
Base: All workplaces with five or more employees. Figures are based on responses from at least 2,258 (2004) and 2,623 (2011) workplace managers.

Managers were also asked about the presence of various practices in relation to discrimination, namely monitoring recruitment, selection and promotions according to various employee characteristics; reviewing recruitment, selection and promotion procedures to identify indirect discrimination, and reviewing relative pay rates. Overall there had been little change in the prevalence of such practices since 2004, despite the increase in the presence of formal equal opportunities policies.

In 2011, recruitment and selection was monitored by at least one of the characteristics of gender, ethnicity, disability or age in 23 per cent of workplaces; in 14 per cent monitoring was carried out on the basis of all four characteristics. Just under one fifth (18 per cent) of workplaces reviewed recruitment and selection procedures to identify indirect discrimination by at least one of these four characteristics. The prevalence of either practice had not changed since 2004 (Table 6.7). Both practices were more common in the public sector compared with the private sector. There was no change in the proportion of private sector workplaces with either practice between 2004 and 2011; however, there was an increase in the percentage of public sector workplaces monitoring recruitment and selection on the basis of *all* four characteristics from 36 per cent in 2004 to 46 per cent in 2011.

Monitoring promotions and reviewing promotion procedures were less common than monitoring and reviewing recruitment and selection. Around one in ten workplaces (9 per cent) monitored promotions by any of the four characteristics; a similar proportion (10 per cent) reviewed promotion procedures. Just 7 per cent of workplaces reviewed relative pay rates by any of the four characteristics. Again, all three practices were more common in the public than private sector, but the prevalence of practices had not changed since 2004 in either sector.

Overall, the public sector continued to fare better in terms of provision for equal opportunities at work, with both formal policies and practices more common than in the private sector. While some improvement in the private sector was apparent, with an increase in the proportion of workplaces with a formal policy, little appeared to have changed in actual practice. Further, the proportion of employees who felt managers treated employees fairly had not changed since 2004, remaining at around three fifths (57 per cent in 2004 and 58 per cent in 2011). This stability was apparent in both the private and public sectors; however, employees in the private sector remained more likely than those in the public sector to agree that managers treated employees fairly.

Health and Safety

Workplace managers were asked to rate the potential health and safety risks faced by employees at their workplace, for the first time in the 2011 WERS. Managers were asked, 'How would you rate the potential health and safety risks faced by employees in this workplace?' and invited to respond using a ten-point scale, where one indicated no risk at all and ten indicated a high degree of risk.[11] Health and safety risks were rated as relatively low in the majority of workplaces. Around one in ten managers (12 per cent) considered there to be no health and safety risks at the workplace, with a further half (53 per cent) rating the risks at two or three on the ten-point scale. Health and safety risks varied by industry, with workplace managers in Construction and Electricity, gas and water reporting the highest average level of risk (Table 6.8). Risks were rated lowest on average in workplaces in Other business services and Financial services.[12]

The average level of risk also varied according to the largest occupation at the workplace, this being highest where it was Skilled trades or Process, plant or machine operatives. Risks were also rated as higher in workplaces with a recognised union, even when controlling for ownership, industry, largest occupation at the workplace and workplace size. One potential explanation could be that union presence is associated with greater awareness of risks at the workplace.

Workplace managers were also asked, 'How would you rate the control that employees have over the health and safety risks that could affect them?', again on a scale from one to ten, where one indicated no control at all and ten indicated a high degree of control. In the majority of workplaces, managers considered employees to have a high degree of control over health and safety risks – 80 per cent of managers rated this at eight or higher.

Employees may be considered to be most vulnerable in those workplaces where they face not only a high degree of risk but also have a low level of control over those risks. If workplaces are classified as 'high risk' where health and safety risks were rated above the median (at four or above), and as 'low control' where control is rated below the median (a rating of seven or lower), 8 per cent of workplaces were deemed to have both a high level of risk and a low level of control over those risks. On average, such workplaces were more commonly found in the public sector than private sector, with 12 per cent of public sector workplaces reporting both high risks and low control compared with 7 per cent of private sector workplaces. However, this conceals further variation by industry, with 13 per cent of workplaces in each of Health and social work, and Hotels and restaurants, deemed to have both high risks and low control (Table 6.8). Controlling for ownership, industry and other workplace characteristics, the co-existence of high risks and low control was most common where the largest occupation at the workplace comprised employees in Caring, leisure and other personal service occupations.

Table 6.8 *Health and safety risks and control over risks by industry, 2011, mean and cell per cent*

	Health and safety risk	Control over risk	High risk and low control
	Mean	Mean	Cell per cent
Construction	5.26	8.44	5
Electricity, gas and water	4.68	9.02	1
Manufacturing	4.08	8.58	6
Transport and communications	4.01	8.79	8
Public administration	3.79	8.49	9
Health and social work	3.53	8.11	13
Hotels and restaurants	3.51	7.84	13
Other community services	3.34	8.31	8
Wholesale and retail trade	3.28	8.28	9
Education	2.97	8.45	4
Other business services	2.63	8.54	5
Financial services	(1.88)	(8.98)	(2)
All workplaces	3.41	8.36	8

Notes: Response scales for columns one and two range from 1 (low) to 10 (high). High risk and low control (final column) refers to workplaces where risks were rated above the median (four or above) and control was rated below the median (seven or below).

Base: All workplaces with five or more employees. Figures are based on responses from at least 2,659 workplace managers.

Managers' ratings of health and safety risks can be compared with the actual incidence of injury and illness at the workplace. There had been no increase since 2004 in the percentage of workplaces reporting that any employee had sustained any of a specified list of injuries during working hours in the year prior to the survey, at 7 per cent of workplaces in both years.[13] Injuries were more common where managers considered there to be higher health and safety risks at the workplace; in 10 per cent of workplaces where the manager rated risks at four or above at least one employee had sustained an injury in the year prior to the survey, compared with 5 per cent in workplaces rated as lower risk. However, this proportion did not differ to a statistically significant extent according to the degree of control employees had over risks, even when considering higher risk workplaces alone. Managers were also asked whether any employees had suffered from any of a specified list of illnesses caused or made worse by their work in the year prior to the survey.[14] This was the case for 20 per cent of workplaces in 2011, a fall from 25 per cent in 2004. Work-related illness was more common in workplaces deemed to have at least some health and safety risks; in 22 per cent of such workplaces at least one employee had suffered from a work-related illness, compared with 12 per cent among those judged by the workplace manager to have no level of risk. Again this did not differ to a statistically significant degree according to the level of control employees had over risks. This suggests that managers' perceptions of risk were associated with actual risk at the workplace both in terms of injury and illness.

Trust in Management

One means by which managers can provide support to employees in the workplace is by seeking to understand their needs and by acting in a trustworthy manner. WERS measures this dimension of job quality using a set of questions aimed at measuring management's behavioural integrity, their behavioural consistency and their demonstration of concern for employee needs; it is built around some of the measures of Whitener et al.'s (1998) trustworthy behaviours (Guest et al., 2007). The related issue of the quality of collective relations between managers and the workforce, and the incidence of manifest conflict, are discussed in Chapter 8.

Between 2004 and 2011 there were increases in the proportion of employees who agreed or strongly agreed that managers were sincere in attempting to understand employees' views, and in the percentage who agreed that managers dealt with employees honestly (Table 6.9). However, in both cases the increase was only seen in the private sector, and not in the public sector. There was no statistically significant increase in the proportion of employees agreeing or strongly agreeing that managers could be relied on to keep their promises in either sector.

As in 2004, employees in smaller workplaces were more likely than those in larger workplaces to agree or strongly agree that managers were trustworthy. Three fifths (61 per cent) of employees in workplaces with five to nine employees agreed or strongly agreed with all three statements in 2011, compared with just over one third (36 per cent) of employees in workplaces with 100 or more employees. However, improvements in trust between 2004 and 2011 were seen only in larger workplaces (those with 100 or more employees), where the percentage of employees agreeing or strongly agreeing with all three statements had increased from 31 per cent in 2004.

It is conceivable that employees in workplaces worst affected by the recession may feel managers are less trustworthy, particularly if cutbacks have been made. However, we find no clear association between the managers' report of the impact of recession on the workplace and the extent of change in employees' ratings of trust in management.

Table 6.9 Employees' trust in management, 2004 and 2011, cell per cent

	Private sector		Public sector		All employees	
	2004	**2011**	**2004**	**2011**	**2004**	**2011**
Employees agree that managers ...						
Are sincere in attempting to understand employees' views	56	<u>59</u>	52	51	55	<u>57</u>
Deal with employees honestly	58	<u>60</u>	52	51	56	58
Can be relied upon to keep their promises	51	53	44	42	49	50

Base: All employees in workplaces with five or more employees. Figures are based on responses from at least 21,575 (2004) and 21,423 (2011) employees.

PAY

At the time of the previous WERS in 2004, real wages had been growing for the previous decade (Fitzner, 2006). More recently, average earnings have been falling in real terms; the Annual Survey of Hours and Earnings (ASHE) shows median earnings of employees in the UK have been declining since 2009 (Levy, 2013). While employees in both the public and private sectors have experienced a decrease in average real earnings since the onset of the recession, the decline began later in the public sector. This fall in earnings has been highlighted as one potential reason why employment has held up relatively well despite the recession; Gregg and Machin (2012) find evidence that real earnings in the UK have become more sensitive to unemployment since the early 2000s. In overall terms, this decline in average real earnings suggests that job quality in terms of pay has been falling in recent years, although of course this aggregate picture hides variations for different groups of employees.

WERS collects no continuous wage data that can add substantially to the picture of general wage trends shown by other sources such as ASHE. Instead, the comparative advantage of WERS is in its ability to show how pay levels vary between different types of employees, jobs and workplaces. Hence the focus here is on the relationship between pay and other dimensions of job quality, examining whether employees receiving higher levels of pay also enjoy greater quality in other aspects of their jobs, and how job quality has changed between 2004 and 2011 for employees at different points in the wage distribution.

Analysis of the 2011 WERS data shows higher rates of pay were associated with lower job quality in some respects. Employees reporting greater work intensity were more highly paid – those who agreed that their job required them to work very hard received higher rates of pay on average. While employees who agreed they never had enough time to get their work done also received higher pay on average compared to those who disagreed, or neither agreed nor disagreed; this relationship was no longer significant once other factors were controlled for. In 2004, higher pay was associated with greater work intensity on both measures. Greater job security was associated with lower rates of pay in 2004; however, this relationship was not statistically significant in 2011 controlling for other factors. Other aspects of job quality were positively correlated with pay. Employees reporting greater autonomy over their work received higher pay on average, compared with employees with lower levels of autonomy. Similarly, pay was higher among employees who had received any training in the 12 months prior to the survey compared to those who had received no training.

Looking at changes in job quality for employees within different points of the wage distribution, the proportion of employees agreeing that they never had enough time to get their work done increased between 2004 and 2011 among those in the lowest quartile of the pay distribution, but did not increase to a statistically significant extent among more highly paid employees. Perceived job security had fallen among employees in all quartiles of the pay distribution between 2004 and 2011, but by a greater extent for employees in the bottom half of the pay distribution.

Autonomy had increased among employees in all quartiles of the pay distribution. Employees in the highest pay quartile remained the most likely to have received any training in the 12 months prior to the survey compared to lower paid employees, but were the only group not to have seen an increase in the likelihood of receiving training compared with 2004.

Overall the relationship between pay and other aspects of job quality is varied. Some aspects of job quality appear to be compensated for by higher pay, such as greater work intensity, and to some extent lower job security. But in terms of other dimensions of job quality, employees who received higher rates of pay on average also had greater influence over their work and were more likely to receive off-the-job training.

CHANGES IN JOB QUALITY, 2004–11

The aforesaid has shown a number of changes in job quality between 2004 and 2011, and in particular noticeable differences between trends in the public and private sectors. In terms of job demands, both the public and private sector saw an increase in the proportion of employees who agreed their job required them to work very hard, but the extent of this increase was greater in the private sector. The proportion of employees reporting that they never had enough time to get their work done also increased in the private sector, but showed no change in the public sector. Job demands on the basis of both measures remained higher in the public sector than the private sector in 2011.

Employees in the private sector considered that they had higher job control and more trustworthy managers than employees in the public sector in 2004. While job control increased in both the public and private sectors between 2004 and 2011, the extent of this rise was greater in the private sector. Employees' trust in management improved only in the private sector over this period. Employees' perceptions of job security were similar in the public and private sectors in 2004; but it was employees in the public sector who experienced a considerable decline in job security in the period to 2011.

It is useful to compare the magnitude of these changes, so that we can assess which elements of job quality have changed the most over this period. We do this by constructing indices for four key aspects of job quality: job demands, job control, perceived job security and job supports. These indices are based on a selection of those measures from the employee survey that have been discussed earlier in the chapter; the exact measures used are listed in Box 6.1. The most notable omission is a measure of wages but, as noted previously, WERS cannot indicate changes in earnings with the precision of other surveys such as ASHE, and the broad trends are described elsewhere (Levy, 2013). To cover job supports, we combine the responses from employees on trust in management with indicators of the extent to which employees are treated fairly, and are supported in skill development and in managing work–life conflict, in order to form an overall measure of supportive management.

For each aspect of job quality we first form an additive scale, summing together the responses from each question listed in Box 6.1.[15] So that these aspects of job

---

BOX 6.1   COMPONENTS OF JOB QUALITY INDICES

Index	Component items
Job demands	• My job requires that I work very hard • I never seem to have enough time to get my work done
Job control	In general, how much influence do you have over the following: • The tasks you do in your job • The pace at which you work • How you do your work • The order in which you carry out tasks • The time you start or finish your working day
Job security	• I feel my job is secure in this workplace
Job supports (supportive management)	Managers at the workplace: • Understand about employees having to meet responsibilities outside work • Encourage people to develop their skills • Can be relied upon to keep their promises • Are sincere in attempting to understand employees' views • Deal with employees honestly • Treat employees fairly

Notes: Responses to each of the items for job demands, job security and job supports are on a five-point scale from 'Strongly agree' to 'Strongly disagree'. Responses for the items relating to job control are on a four-point scale from 'A lot' to 'None'.

---

quality can be more readily compared with one another, we then convert the resulting scales into standardised indices (also known as z-scores). Each standardised index is constructed so that its mean value is equal to zero in 2004. A positive score on the 2011 index then indicates an increase in that measure of job quality (for example, an increase in job control), while a negative sign indicates that this has fallen. The range of the index is then calibrated so that a one-unit change between 2004 and 2011 is equivalent to a movement of one standard deviation in the 2004 distribution of the index. So if the resulting index were to have a mean value of +0.25 in 2011, this would indicate that this particular element of job quality has improved by an amount that is equivalent to one quarter of a standard deviation from the mean value in 2004. This calibration is undertaken on the basis that a small change in a tightly distributed variable is as notable as a larger change in a scale which already shows greater variation within the population. It is these

Table 6.10 *Changes in job quality, 2004–11, mean index value*

	Private sector		Public sector		All employees	
	2004	**2011**	**2004**	**2011**	**2004**	**2011**
Job demands	0.00	<u>0.15</u>	0.00	0.05	0.00	<u>0.12</u>
Job control	0.00	<u>0.15</u>	0.00	<u>0.07</u>	0.00	<u>0.13</u>
Job security	0.00	−0.03	0.00	<u>−0.41</u>	0.00	<u>−0.13</u>
Supportive management	0.00	<u>0.08</u>	0.00	−0.04	0.00	<u>0.05</u>

Base: All employees in workplaces with five or more employees. Figures are based on responses from at least 20,619 (2004) and 20,705 (2011) employees.

standardised measures that form the basis of the analysis relating to job quality when examining change in well-being over time in Chapter 7.

The resulting indices are presented in Table 6.10. Focusing first on the results for all employees, as explained previously, each index is constructed so that its average value in 2004 is zero. In 2011, the mean value of the job demands index is 0.12, reflecting an increase in job demands since 2004. More precisely, this indicates that the mean for this measure has increased by 0.12 of a standard deviation in the 2004 distribution. Increases are also seen in job control and in supportive management, but job security has fallen. These findings reflect the changes in absolute terms that we have seen earlier: an increase in job demands, job control and supportive management, but a decline in job security. But these standardised measures allow us to compare change in the different measures in relation to their 2004 distributions. On this basis, we see that the magnitude of the changes in job demands and job control are similar in size, relative to their 2004 distributions. However, the increase in supportive management is smaller, with an increase of 0.05 of a standard deviation, around half that observed for job demands and job control. The fall in job security (0.13) is of a similar magnitude to the rise in job demands and job control.

Given the differences observed for the private and public sectors throughout this chapter, the indices are also presented separately for each sector (Table 6.10). Here we standardise the indices within sectors so that, again, in each case the mean value of each index in 2004 is equal to zero.

The most notable change is the sizeable decline in job security in the public sector, with a fall in mean job security equivalent to 0.41 of a standard deviation in the 2004 distribution. This serves to indicate the magnitude of the fall in job security, relative to changes in other elements of job quality in the public sector. There were no statistically significant changes in the indices of job demands or supportive management. Job control, as reported by employees, increased between 2004 and 2011, rising by 0.07 of a standard deviation of its 2004 distribution.

Within the private sector, the largest changes between 2004 and 2011 were observed for job demands and job control, both of which increased by a similar magnitude in relation to their 2004 distributions. Supportive management also increased, but the extent of this rise was around half that for job demands and job control. The decline in job security is not statistically significant.

HOW IMPORTANT IS THE WORKPLACE?

Differences in job quality can arise through differences in jobs themselves, but WERS also allows us to explore how important the workplace is as a determinant of job quality. Individuals with similar characteristics, and in similar jobs, may experience differing levels of job quality as a result of the workplace they are in. The continuous nature of the job quality indices allows us to more easily explore the role played by the workplace than when considering the distributional measures reported earlier in the chapter. In the case of job demands, in 2011 the workplace accounted for around 12 per cent of the variance in this aspect of job quality, while employee demographic and job characteristics explained around a further 14 per cent. In terms of employee-reported autonomy, the workplace explained a similar proportion of the variance, at around 13 per cent, with employee and job characteristics explaining around 9 per cent. For job security, however, the workplace played a much more significant role in explaining variation, accounting for around 21 per cent, while employee and job characteristics accounted for 5 per cent of the variation. A similar picture was apparent for supportive management, around 21 per cent of the variation being explained by workplaces, and a further 6 per cent by employee and job characteristics.[16] While the workplace in which an employee works therefore plays an important role in variation in all four aspects of job quality, it is of particular significance in terms of job security and supportive management.

CONCLUSION

This chapter has examined changes in job quality between 2004 and 2011. There is some evidence to suggest a decline in job quality between 2004 and 2011, with increasing work intensity and falling job security. However, other dimensions of job quality have seen some improvement, with increases in the level of autonomy – at least from the perspective of employees, and some aspects of support.

One clear pattern emerging from the analysis is the different experiences of employees in the private and public sectors. Work intensity increased most for employees in the private sector, although overall job demands remained higher for public sector employees. But in terms of job control, job security and supportive management, there has been a widening of the gap between the public and private sectors, with the private sector faring better on all three of these aspects of job quality.

The economic downturn appears to have played a part in some of this change, but does not explain the full extent of developments between 2004 and 2011. Job demands rose in workplaces affected to both a greater and lesser extent by recession, as did employee-reported autonomy. Of all the elements of job quality considered in this chapter, it is job security that demonstrates the clearest relationship with the economic downturn, declining most in those workplaces most adversely affected.

The decline in average real earnings seen in recent years, documented by other sources, suggests job quality in terms of pay has been falling. Looking at the relationship between pay and other aspects of job quality, higher rates of pay appear to compensate for lower job quality with respect to some aspects, such as greater work intensity. But on other dimensions of job quality, such as autonomy, employees who enjoyed greater job quality also received higher rates of pay.

Finally, this chapter has shown the importance of the workplace as a determinant of job quality. Thus individuals with similar characteristics, and in similar jobs, may experience differing levels of job quality as a result of the workplace in which they are employed. The workplace plays an important role in explaining variation in job demands and job control, but is of particular significance in determining levels of perceived job security and supportive management.

7 Employee Well-being

INTRODUCTION

In recent years employees' well-being has come to the fore in public policy with Dame Carol Black's review of the health of the working age population (Black, 2008; Black and Frost, 2011) and the review of the Commission on the Measurement of Economic Performance and Social Progress (Stiglitz et al., 2009) raising its visibility as an issue. Consequently, governments and their statistical agencies are developing well-being metrics by which to judge national progress, taking seriously the Commission's contention that gross domestic product alone is insufficient. Some have gone further, arguing that maximizing well-being should be the primary goal of public policy (for example, Layard, 2009, 2011).

Paid work is a central part of most people's lives, so it is not surprising to find that it is critical to our sense of well-being. It contributes to overall life satisfaction and general happiness (Warr, 2007; Blanchflower and Oswald, 2011). Its loss through unemployment also results in a precipitous decline in well-being which – unlike most other changes in personal circumstances – individuals do not recover from until they leave that state (Warr, 2007; Clark et al., 2008). However, the content of an employee's job and the type of workplace in which it is carried out are also important determinants of well-being for those who are in work. Psychological theories, in particular, highlight the importance of job demands, control and support as influences of employee well-being (Karasek, 1979).

This chapter considers three dimensions of employee well-being: job-related contentment, job-related enthusiasm and job satisfaction. The concepts are introduced in more detail in the next section. The 2011 WERS was the first survey in the series to incorporate questions on all three dimensions, with the 2004 WERS only having included questions on job-related contentment and job satisfaction. The chapter therefore begins by examining levels of employee well-being on each of the three dimensions in 2011 and by exploring how levels of well-being vary between employees in different types of jobs. The links with the measures of job quality introduced in Chapter 6 are a primary focus. The chapter then goes on to explore how levels of job-related contentment and job satisfaction changed between 2004 and 2011. The importance of changes in job quality over the period forms a major part of the investigation, but the changes in the characteristics of employees and workplaces over the period are also considered. The chapter concludes by examining the impact of the recession on employee well-being.

CONCEPTS AND MEASURES

Psychologists often distinguish between two dimensions of employee well-being (Warr, 2007). The first relates to the pleasure or displeasure gained from work ('emotional affect' in the language of psychology). The second relates to the degree of mental arousal experienced by the individual. An employee's position along these two dimensions is measured by the use of scales which capture the interaction between them (Figure 7.1). One scale ranges from the feeling of 'depression' (low pleasure and low arousal) to the feeling of 'enthusiasm' (high pleasure and high arousal).[1] The other ranges from the feeling of 'anxiety' (low pleasure, high arousal) to 'contentment' (high pleasure, low arousal). Job satisfaction lies along the pleasure dimension and contains an implicit element of comparison with some alternative state (for example, the features of that job in a prior period, or the features of jobs held by other employees). As Figure 7.1 illustrates, job-related enthusiasm, job-related contentment and job satisfaction are positively correlated with one another. However, specific job characteristics often have different associations with each of the three scales and so it is valuable to consider them separately.

To measure job-related anxiety-contentment in the 2011 WERS, employees were asked, 'Thinking of the past few weeks, how much of the time has your job made you feel each of the following: Tense, Worried, Uneasy'. For each state employees could respond on a five-point scale from 'All of the time' to 'Never'. The 2004 WERS also included three positive items on the anxiety–contentment scale ('Calm', 'Relaxed' and 'Content') but these were omitted in 2011 to make way for three negative items

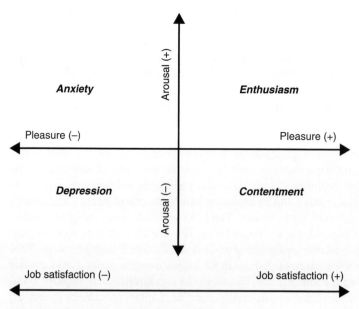

Figure 7.1 *Dimensions of employee well-being*
Source: Adapted from Warr et al. (2013).

on the depression–enthusiasm scale, namely: 'Depressed', 'Gloomy' and 'Miserable'.[2] To measure job satisfaction in the 2011 WERS, employees were asked, 'How satisfied are you with the following aspects of your job?' and rated each of nine items on a five-point scale from 'Very satisfied' to 'Very dissatisfied'. The nine items were: 'The sense of achievement you get from your work', 'The scope for using your initiative', 'The amount of influence you have over your job', 'The training you receive', 'The opportunity to develop your skills in your job', 'The amount of pay you receive', 'Your job security', 'The work itself' and 'The amount of involvement you have in decision-making at this workplace'.[3] The 2004 WERS had included the same list of items, with the exception of opportunities for skill development, which was added in 2011.

EMPLOYEE WELL-BEING IN 2011

In 2011 over half (55 per cent) of employees felt tense because of their job at least some of the time, while around a third (33 per cent) felt worried and one quarter (27 per cent) uneasy (Table 7.1). Overall 60 per cent of employees felt tense, worried or uneasy at least some of the time. The proportion of employees feeling depressed, gloomy or miserable was generally lower than the proportion showing signs of anxiety. Nevertheless, 23 per cent reported feeling depressed at least some of the time, with 24 per cent gloomy and 21 per cent miserable.

Turning to job satisfaction, employees in 2011 were most likely to report being very satisfied or satisfied with the scope for using their initiative (75 per cent), the work itself (75 per cent) and the sense of achievement they derived from work (74 per cent). While employees were least likely to be satisfied with their pay (42 per cent) and the extent of their involvement in decision-making (43 per cent) (Figure 7.2).

To explore variations in well-being between employees, we combined the individual items to form three scales. Each of the three items under the heading of 'anxiety–contentment' in Table 7.1 were scored from –2 for 'All of the time' to +2 for 'Never', and then summed together to form a scale for job-related contentment

Table 7.1 Employee well-being, 2011, row per cent

	All of the time	Most of the time	Some of the time	Occasionally	Never
Anxiety–contentment					
Tense	4	13	38	28	17
Worried	3	7	23	34	34
Uneasy	3	6	18	30	45
Depression–enthusiasm					
Depressed	2	5	16	23	53
Gloomy	2	6	16	28	47
Miserable	3	5	13	22	57

Base: All employees in workplaces with five or more employees. Figures are based on responses from at least 21,613 employees.

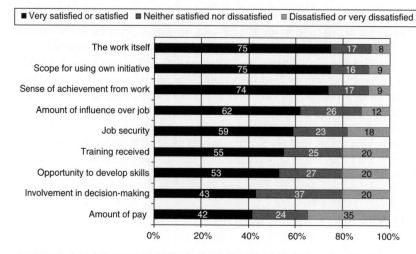

Figure 7.2 *Satisfaction with aspects of the job, 2011, row per cent*

Base: All employees in workplaces with five or more employees. Figures are based on responses from at least 21,233 employees.

which ranged from –6 to +6, thus a higher score on the resulting scale indicates greater contentment. The same approach was taken with the remaining three items in Table 7.1, forming a scale for job-related enthusiasm which also ranged from –6 to +6, and on which a higher score indicated greater enthusiasm. Finally, the nine job satisfaction items were each scored from +2 for 'Very satisfied' to –2 for 'Very dissatisfied', and summed to form an overall scale of job satisfaction which ranged from –18 to +18, with a higher score indicating greater satisfaction.

Table 7.2 shows the relationship between the three scales and employees' gender and age, and the sector in which they worked. In 2011, job-related enthusiasm and job satisfaction were higher on average among women than men (the small difference between men and women in job-related contentment is not statistically significant). In keeping with previous research (for example, Clark et al., 1996), each measure showed a U-shaped relationship with age, being highest for employees aged under 20 years and those aged 60 years and over. Job-related contentment, job-related enthusiasm and job satisfaction were each higher, on average, among private sector employees than among employees in the public sector.

Psychological theories have highlighted the importance of job quality as an influence of employee well-being (Karasek, 1979). Regression analyses confirmed this, showing that the characteristics of the job are considerably more important in influencing well-being than employee or workplace characteristics. The regressions took the three scales presented in Table 7.2 as dependent variables, and controlled for the demographic characteristics of employees (such as gender and age), as well as workplace characteristics (such as industry and workplace size) and job characteristics (including the indicators of job quality discussed in Chapter 6).[4] The workplace accounted for 9 per cent of the variance in both job-related enthusiasm and job-related contentment, and 16 per cent for overall job satisfaction. Employees'

Table 7.2 *Employees' job-related contentment and enthusiasm, and job satisfaction, 2011, mean*

	Job-related contentment	Job-related enthusiasm	Overall job satisfaction
Gender			
Male	2.34	3.38	4.44
Female	2.41	3.77	5.26
Age			
Less than 20 years	4.12	4.63	6.36
20–29 years	2.57	3.48	4.77
30–59 years	2.18	3.48	4.72
60 years or more	3.24	4.42	6.02
Sector of ownership			
Private sector	2.46	3.63	5.15
Public sector	2.13	3.42	3.98
All employees	2.38	3.58	4.86

Notes: The scales for job-related contentment and enthusiasm range from –6 (low) to +6 (high) and job satisfaction scale is from –18 (low) to +18 (high).
Base: All employees in workplaces with five or more employees. Figures are based on responses from at least 20,481 employees.

demographic characteristics explained a further 1–2 per cent of the variation in each measure of well-being. But it was the characteristics of the job – including job quality – that explained the greatest proportion of the variance, explaining almost a further quarter of the variation for job-related contentment (23 per cent) and enthusiasm (24 per cent) and around 45 per cent in the case of job satisfaction.

Table 7.3 indicates the associations (determined by the regression analysis) between the various aspects of job quality and each of the three measures of well-being at work. All items are derived from the employee survey, with the exception of the indicators of teamwork, and health and safety risks and control. To simplify the presentation, a '+' sign is used to indicate that a particular aspect of job quality was associated with higher levels of well-being, while a '–' sign is used to indicate the reverse. A '~' sign is used to identify associations that were not statistically significant after controlling for other factors.

Higher job demands, or greater work intensity, were associated with lower levels of contentment. Job-related contentment was lower among employees who agreed or strongly agreed that their job required them to work very hard, and among those who never had enough time to get their work done. Contentment was also related to hours worked, with higher levels of contentment among employees working less than 30 hours per week, and lower levels among those working 48 hours or more, compared to those working between 30 and 47 hours per week. The same patterns are observed for job-related enthusiasm. Employees who felt longer hours were required in order to progress at their workplace also reported lower levels of both job-related contentment and enthusiasm. These findings are consistent with the Karasek model and much of the other literature, including recent evidence from Understanding Society, which also found that longer working hours were associated with lower contentment (Bryan, 2012).

Table 7.3 *Job-related contentment, enthusiasm and satisfaction, 2011, multivariate analysis*

	Job-related contentment	Job-related enthusiasm	Overall job satisfaction
Work intensity			
Working hours (ref: 30–47 hours):			
Less than 30 hours	+	+	~
48 hours or more	−	~	+
My job requires that I work very hard	−	−	+
Never enough time to get work done	−	−	−
Long hours required to progress	−	−	~
Autonomy			
Employee control over work (scale)	+	+	+
Teamwork at workplace	+	+	~
Job security	+	+	+
Indicators of job support			
Any training in previous 12 months	~	+	+
Skill mismatch (ref: No mismatch):			
Over-qualified	+	−	−
Under-qualified	−	−	−
Any flexible working available	~	~	+
Work–life conflict	−	−	−
Degree of health and safety risk at workplace	~	~	~
Degree of employee control over health and safety risk	~	~	+
Supportive management (scale)	+	+	+
Pay (ref: 1st quartile)			
2nd quartile	~	~	~
3rd quartile	−	~	+
4th quartile	−	~	+
Overall model fit (R^2)	0.32	0.33	0.60

Notes: See note 4 for details of the underlying regression analysis. The scales for employee control at work and supportive management are those discussed in relation to Box 6.1.
Base: All employees in workplaces with five or more employees. Figures are based on responses from at least 20,596 employees.

Employees reporting higher levels of control over their work had higher levels of both job-related contentment and enthusiasm. The presence of any formally designated teams at the workplace was also associated with increased contentment and enthusiasm. It was also possible to identify a positive interaction between job demands and job control in more detailed specifications, suggesting that control is important in counteracting the negative effects of demands on well-being.

In accordance with the Karasek model, both job-related contentment and enthusiasm were higher where managers at the workplace were deemed to be more supportive. Provision of training was associated with higher levels of enthusiasm. While there was also a simple two-way association between receipt of training and job-related contentment, this association was no longer statistically significant after controlling for other factors. This was also the case for associations between access to flexible working arrangements and higher contentment and enthusiasm. The presence of work–life conflict did play a significant role, however, with both contentment and enthusiasm lower among employees who agreed or strongly agreed that work interfered with their ability to fulfil their commitments outside of their job.

The fit between an individual's skills and those required for the job may also affect well-being. Employees who felt their skills were lower than those required for the job reported lower levels of both contentment and enthusiasm, compared to those who felt the match between their skills and the job they did was about right. Job-related enthusiasm was also lower among those who considered themselves to be over-qualified, although the magnitude of the relationship was smaller than for those who felt under-qualified. However, for contentment this particular relationship operated in the opposite direction, with higher contentment among those who were over-qualified when compared to those who felt their skills were a good match for their job.

The regression analysis also found evidence of a relationship with well-being for some extrinsic aspects of job quality. Greater job security was associated with higher contentment and enthusiasm among employees. However, the level of health and safety risks and the control employees had over these risks, as perceived by managers, were not significantly related to either well-being measure. In keeping with earlier research using the 2004 WERS (Bryson et al., 2012), employees in the upper half of the wage distribution reported lower levels of contentment than those in the bottom half, after controlling for other factors. However, the multivariate analysis did not show any statistically significant relationships between rates of pay and job-related enthusiasm.

The relationships between specific elements of job quality and overall job satisfaction were, in some cases, different from those for job-related contentment and enthusiasm. As for contentment and enthusiasm, employees who reported never having enough time to get their work done also reported lower levels of job satisfaction. But in contrast, satisfaction was higher among those who felt their job required them to work very hard, and among those who worked 48 hours or more per week compared to those working fewer hours.

Having greater job control was also associated with higher overall job satisfaction. The presence of any teamworking at the workplace showed no significant relationship with satisfaction. In contrast, we saw previously that contentment and enthusiasm were higher where teamwork was in place and it may be that it is acting as a form of social support in terms of enthusiasm and contentment.

Supportive management was positively associated with overall job satisfaction. Further, job satisfaction was also higher where flexible working practices were available, and where the employee had received training in the year prior to the survey. Work–life conflict again appeared to play a significant role – with lower job satisfaction among employees who felt work interfered with their ability to fulfil commitments outside of work. Job satisfaction was lower among employees who felt under-qualified for their job, and among those who felt over-qualified, compared to those who felt their skills were about right.

Job satisfaction did not vary according to the degree of health and safety risks at the workplace. There was a small positive relationship between the degree of control employees were considered to have over risks and overall job satisfaction. Overall job satisfaction was higher among employees who felt their job was more secure; this result is robust to removing satisfaction with job security from the overall satisfaction measure.

Finally Table 7.3 shows that there is a relationship between earnings and job satisfaction. A U-shaped relationship is evident in descriptive analysis. This becomes less evident in the multivariate analysis, although those in the upper half of the pay distribution report higher overall satisfaction than those in the lower half of the pay distribution.

It is noteworthy that our regression analysis of overall job satisfaction is able to explain a much greater proportion of the variability in this measure between different employees (60 per cent), than is the case for the regression analyses of job-related contentment and job-related enthusiasm (32 per cent and 33 per cent, respectively). This may be because feelings of anxiety–contentment and depression–enthusiasm, even in the context of work, are more heavily influenced by other factors (perhaps non work-related) that we do not capture here. Nevertheless, the analysis has demonstrated the significant relationships between various dimensions of job quality and each of the three indicators of well-being at work, showing that job quality is a critically important factor in explaining variations in employee well-being.

CHANGES IN EMPLOYEE WELL-BEING, 2004–11

There is a sizeable literature on changes in employee well-being in Britain over time, though most of it focuses on aspects of job satisfaction. Analyses of the British Household Panel Survey (BHPS) and the General Household Survey (GHS) indicate that job satisfaction declined in Britain between the 1970s and the late 1990s. This fall was due to a reduction in job quality, notably work intensification and declining task discretion (Green and Tsitsianis, 2005). However, between 1998 and 2004 certain aspects of job satisfaction improved (one's sense of achievement) or were stable (pay and influence). Brown et al. (2007: 953) found that, in part, this was because new workplaces were generating higher job satisfaction than workplaces that had shut down. But they also emphasised the role played by the wider labour market in explaining the rise in job satisfaction between 1998 and 2004, arguing that improvements in the wider labour market 'placed greater pressure on employers to raise the quality of work' (2007: 966) which in turn led to higher job satisfaction.

There are some inconsistencies in reported trends in employee well-being since 2004. The European Social Survey indicates overall job satisfaction in Britain has stabilised and even improved a little between 2005 and 2010, despite the onset of recession (McManus and Perry, 2012). The European Quality of Life Survey also indicates a small improvement in recent years.[5] The Skills and Employment Survey, on the other hand, suggests there have been small but significant declines between 2006 and 2012 in job satisfaction, job-related enthusiasm and job-related contentment, which are partly attributed to work intensification and rising job insecurity (Green et al., 2013).

Any examination of changes in well-being over time relies on the availability of consistent measures. As noted earlier, the WERS measure of job-related enthusiasm was introduced for the first time in 2011. Accordingly, the following discussion focuses solely on job-related contentment and on job satisfaction. Furthermore, the analysis of job satisfaction relies on the eight items that are included in both the 2004 and the 2011 surveys.

As in the preceding section, the analysis begins by examining changes on each of the individual measures of job satisfaction and job-related contentment. In order to investigate some of the reasons for change over time, the descriptive analysis then gives way to multivariate analysis which relies on the use of summary scales. The summary scale of job-related contentment is identical to that used in the previous section. The summary scale of overall job satisfaction differs, however, because the new item in 2011 measuring employees' satisfaction with opportunities to develop their skills is necessarily excluded here. The analysis of job satisfaction is extended by separating satisfaction with pay from satisfaction with other, non-pecuniary aspects of the job since the determinants of satisfaction sometimes differ across these two dimensions, perhaps reflecting a need or desire for employers to compensate employees for undertaking less pleasurable jobs (Rosen, 1986).

Table 7.4 shows that average levels of job satisfaction rose significantly, on average, between 2004 and 2011 for seven of the eight job satisfaction items; the exception was satisfaction with job security which fell. The increases in job satisfaction were largely driven by change in the private sector where job satisfaction rose on seven items, remaining static on job security. In the public sector, on the other hand, only three of the eight individual job satisfaction items changed significantly between 2004 and 2011. Each of the individual items listed in the table is scored on a five-point scale. By far the largest change in the public sector was the decline in satisfaction with job security which fell by 0.42 points. Satisfaction with the scope to use one's initiative rose a little, while pay satisfaction rose quite markedly in spite of widespread pay freezes in the public sector. Nevertheless, levels of satisfaction with pay were lower in the public sector than those for any other job characteristic in both 2004 and 2011 (as they are in the private sector also; see Figure 7.3).

Levels of non-pecuniary job satisfaction were higher in the private sector than in the public sector in 2004, but the gap had widened by 2011. The divergence in satisfaction with job security is particularly stark: in 2004 the average level of satisfaction with job security was virtually identical in the two sectors (a mean of 3.59 in the public sector, compared with 3.61 in the private sector). By 2011 a highly statistically significant gap of 0.42 had opened up (the mean stood at 3.17 in the public sector in 2011, compared with 3.59 in the private sector; see Figure 7.3).

As noted earlier, many of the changes in job satisfaction shown in Table 7.4 are statistically significant; however, most are not particularly large. Figure 7.3 indicates that most items have a mean value of around 3.5 points. Yet none of the changes listed in Table 7.4 exceeds 0.2 points, with the exception of the fall in satisfaction with job security in the public sector, which fell by twice this amount (0.42 points).

In contrast to job satisfaction, there was an increase in job-related contentment between 2004 and 2011 in both the public and private sectors (Table 7.5). The increase was evident on each of the three constituent items, with the mean scores on tension, worry and unease each having fallen significantly in both sectors. In both years private sector employees were, on average, more contented in their jobs than public sector employees. In the private sector, the mean score on the overall

Table 7.4 Changes in employee job satisfaction, 2004–11, change in mean score

	Private sector	Public sector	All employees
Pay	+0.15	+0.19	+0.16
Sense of achievement	+0.10	+0.04	+0.08
Scope for using initiative	+0.08	+0.06	+0.08
Influence	+0.09	+0.03	+0.07
Training	+0.12	+0.04	+0.10
Job security	−0.02	−0.42	−0.12
Work itself	+0.09	+0.03	+0.07
Involvement in decision-making	+0.08	−0.03	+0.05
Non-pecuniary job satisfaction (excluding pay)	+0.52	−0.24	+0.33
Overall job satisfaction (all items)	+0.68	−0.05	+0.49

Notes: The eight individual job satisfaction items are scored from 1 (Very dissatisfied) to 5 (Very satisfied). The non-pecuniary job satisfaction scale combines seven items to form a scale that ranges from −14 to 14. The overall job satisfaction scale combines all eight items and ranges from −16 to 16.
Base: All employees in workplaces with five or more employees. Figures are based on responses from at least 27,148 private sector and 14,528 public sector employees.

contentment scale was 1.79 in 2004 and 2.46 in 2011. In the public sector the respective figures were 1.45 and 2.13.

These changes in mean job-related contentment are largely due to increases in the percentage of employees saying they were 'Never' uneasy, worried or tense (Figure 7.4). It is unusual to see changes of this nature and it is possible that the changes, discussed earlier, in the design of the questions on job-related contentment between the 2004 and 2011 WERS may have made some contribution.[6] However, it is also possible that the change may reflect reductions in job-related pressures due to recession-induced slack in the economy. The remainder of the chapter investigates the extent to which changes in well-being between 2004 and 2011 can be accounted for by observable changes in employee or workplace characteristics, or changes in job quality.

WHAT ACCOUNTS FOR THE CHANGES IN EMPLOYEE WELL-BEING?

What might account for the quite complex changes in job satisfaction and job-related contentment we have reported for both the private and public sector? This section explores three potential influences. The first is change between 2004 and 2011 in the characteristics of employees, jobs and workplaces. The second is the process of churn in the economy, whereby workplaces close down and new ones replace them – potentially offering a more satisfying working environment. The third is change induced by the recession.[7]

Changes in Well-being and the Characteristics of Employees, Jobs and Workplaces

Trends in employee well-being may partly reflect changes between 2004 and 2011 in the characteristics of employees, their jobs and the workplaces in which they

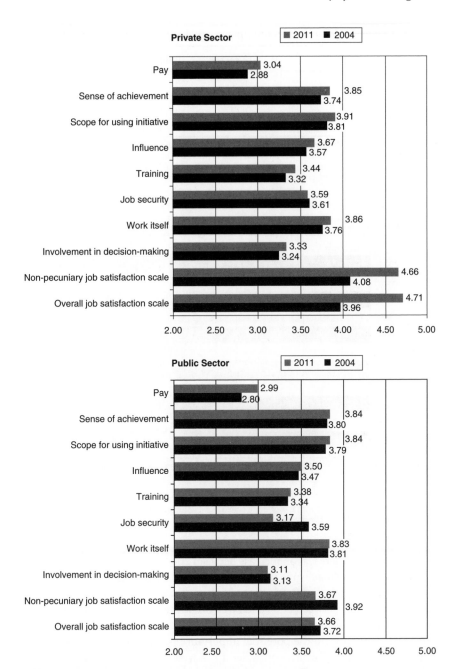

Figure 7.3 *Employee job satisfaction, 2004 and 2011, mean*

Base: All employees in workplaces with five or more employees.
Figures are based on responses from at least 14,302 (2004) and 12,846 (2011) employees in the private sector, and at least 6,724 (2004) and 7,804 (2011) employees in the public sector.

Table 7.5 *Changes in job-related contentment, 2004–11, change in mean score*

	Private sector	Public sector	All employees
Tense	−0.11	−0.11	−0.11
Worried	−0.29	−0.28	−0.29
Uneasy	−0.27	−0.28	−0.27
Job-related contentment scale	+0.67	+0.67	+0.67

Notes: Tense, Worried and Uneasy are scored from 1 (Never) to 5 (All the time). The contentment scale combines these items to form a scale that runs from −6 to 6, where 6 is high.

Base: All employees in workplaces with five or more employees. Figures are based on responses from at least 28,428 private sector and 15,168 public sector employees.

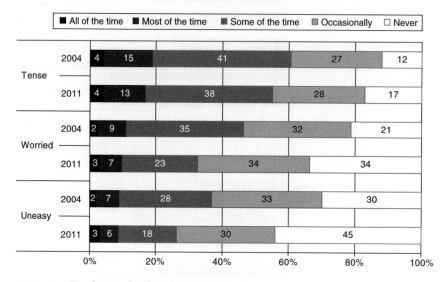

Figure 7.4 *Employee job-related contentment, 2004–11, row per cent*

Base: All employees in workplaces with five or more employees. Figures are based on responses from at least 22,109 (2004) and 21,669 (2011) employees.

work. For example, there was an increase between 2004 and 2011 in the percentage of employees that held a degree (from 26 per cent to 32 per cent) (see Table 1.2). Since those with higher qualifications tend to have lower job satisfaction than those without, this change between 2004 and 2011 would lower the aggregate level of job satisfaction, all other things being equal.

In order to investigate the potential importance of such changes, a regression analysis was conducted which controlled for a wide range of employee, job and workplace characteristics. The regression included observations from both 2004 and 2011 and served to identify the impact of changes in any of these characteristics (such as the increase in the percentage of all employees holding a degree). The analysis thus showed the extent to which levels of job satisfaction and job-related contentment would have altered had there been no change in the characteristics of employees, jobs and workplaces between 2004 and 2011.

Employee characteristics in the analysis comprised gender, age, ethnicity, disability, marital status, academic qualifications and union membership. Job characteristics comprised occupation, working hours, job tenure, contract type, hourly pay and the four scales of job quality presented in Box 6.1. Workplace characteristics comprised workplace size, workplace age, organisation size, whether any recognised union was present, industry and region. The regression was conducted using the Oaxaca-Blinder method of decomposition (see Jann, 2008).

Beginning with the change in non-pecuniary job satisfaction, Table 7.6 shows an overall increase of 0.52 points between 2004 and 2011 in the mean score for employees in the private sector. Changes in the characteristics of employees, jobs and workplaces can account for around two thirds of this increase (0.36 points). Investigating further, it was improvements in average levels of job control and in employees' perceptions of management supportiveness which brought about this element of the overall rise in non-pecuniary job satisfaction in the private sector.

In the public sector, there was a (non-significant) fall of 0.26 points in the mean score for non-pecuniary job satisfaction (this differs slightly from the reduction of 0.24 points shown in Table 7.4 because of the exclusion of a small number of employees with missing values on the variables entered into the regression analysis). Here changes in characteristics brought about a larger (and statistically significant) fall of 0.61 points. In other words, if the characteristics of employees, jobs and workplaces in the public sector had not changed at all between 2004 and 2011, the overall level of non-pecuniary job satisfaction would actually have risen, by 0.35 points. The main reason that non-pecuniary job satisfaction did not rise in the public sector was that perceived levels of job security fell substantially (see Table 6.10). Employees in insecure jobs are less satisfied than those in secure jobs and so the decrease in job security in the public sector brought levels of job satisfaction down with it, accounting for around 90 per cent of the 0.61 point reduction shown in Table 7.6. The increase of 0.35 that we estimate would have occurred in the absence of any change in characteristics is largely accounted for by an increase in ratings of job satisfaction in public sector workplaces with recognised unions, relative to those in workplaces without recognition. The statistical analysis is not able to identify why the differential in job satisfaction between recognised and non-recognised workplaces in the public sector rose between 2004 and 2011, except to indicate that it cannot be accounted for by any changes in the relative characteristics of these two types of workplace.

Employees' pay satisfaction rose significantly and by similar amounts in the public and private sectors, in spite of the prevalence of pay freezes in the public sector. In the private sector, around one third of the total 0.15 point rise in pay satisfaction could be accounted for by changes in characteristics. The main contributor was a rise in average job quality. Increased nominal hourly pay, greater job control and improvements in supportive management all served to raise pay satisfaction, although these positive influences were offset to some extent by increased job demands. The largest single effect came from the improvement in supportive management. In the public sector, changes in characteristics did not, together, have a statistically significant impact on levels of pay satisfaction between 2004 and 2011. However, the figure of −0.03 shown in Table 7.6 represents the net effect of

Table 7.6 *Changes in employee well-being and employee, job and workplace characteristics, 2004–11, multivariate analysis*

	Private sector	Public sector
Non-pecuniary job satisfaction		
Overall difference in mean scores between 2004 and 2011	+0.52	−0.26
Contribution of changes in characteristics	+0.36	−0.61
Estimated difference if no changes in employee, job or workplace characteristics between 2004 and 2011	+0.16	+0.35
Satisfaction with pay		
Overall difference in mean scores between 2004 and 2011	+0.15	+0.20
Contribution of changes in characteristics	+0.05	-0.03
Estimated difference if no changes in employee, job or workplace characteristics between 2004 and 2011	+0.11	+0.22
Job-related contentment		
Overall difference in mean scores between 2004 and 2011	+0.69	+0.73
Contribution of changes in characteristics	−0.15	−0.17
Estimated difference if no changes in employee, job or workplace characteristics between 2004 and 2011	+0.84	+0.90

Notes: Oaxaca-Blinder decomposition using pooled regression models containing the full set of control variables described in the text.
Base: All employees in workplaces with five or more employees. Figures are based on responses from at least 32,796 employees.

all of the individual influences. Increases in nominal hourly pay would have raised pay satisfaction, all other things being equal, but increases in job insecurity entirely offset this effect.

Job-related contentment rose in both sectors between 2004 and 2011 despite significant compositional changes which would have reduced it, all other things being equal. In the private sector changes in job characteristics and in job quality would have led to a reduction of 0.15 points in job contentment.[8] However, these compositional effects were more than offset by other factors that led to improvements in job contentment. One of these was an increase in contentment ratings among employees with high levels of supportive management, relative to the ratings given by employees with low levels of supportive management. In other words, the returns for having high levels of supportive management increased between 2004 and 2011 in the private sector.

In the public sector compositional change by itself would have resulted in a reduction in job contentment by 0.17 points. This was largely due to a rise in perceived job insecurity. Changes in employee demographic characteristics had a significant offsetting effect contributing to the rise in job contentment. As in the private sector the total effect of compositional changes was more than offset by other factors that led to improvements in job contentment. The largest of these was an increase in ratings of job contentment among white employees, relative to those from minority ethnic groups.

These decompositions of the changes in employee well-being between 2004 and 2011 indicate that compositional change was the main factor behind the rise in non-pecuniary job satisfaction in the private sector, and the small fall seen in the public sector, with changes in job quality being the most influential component. However, most of the improvements in pay satisfaction and job contentment cannot be accounted for by compositional changes. The improvements in pay satisfaction and job contentment that were seen between 2004 and 2011 are, then, largely unexplained. However, changes in job quality played the dominant role in those compositional effects that were observed. In the public sector the dominant feature was the reduction in perceived job security – its decline had the effect of reducing all three measures of employee well-being.

Changes in Employee Well-being Across and Within Workplaces

So far the analysis has focused solely on changes in employees' well-being in all workplaces surveyed in either 2004 or 2011. However, the aggregate changes in well-being in the full population represent the combined effect of any changes within workplaces that continued to operate between 2004 and 2011, and any differences in well-being between workplaces that closed and the new ones that replaced them in the economy. In a prior analysis of the 1998 and 2004 WERS, Brown et al. (2007) found that the replacement of old workplaces with new ones made a notable contribution to the overall increases in employees' levels of satisfaction with pay and influence over their work, which did not rise within workplaces that continued to exist over that period. These results suggest that satisfaction may have risen between 1998 and 2004 because of differences in the way that old and new workplaces were managed, rather than as a result of improvements in the management of continuing workplaces.

We approached this issue by calculating the average workplace score on each well-being measure and then examining how this score changed between 2004 and 2011 in the panel of workplaces surveyed in both years, and how it differed between workplaces that left the population and those that joined it. Workplaces that were surveyed in 2004 and then closed down or no longer had five or more employees by 2011 will be referred to as 'leavers', and workplaces that came into existence or reached five or more employees by 2011 will be referred to as 'joiners'. Between 2004 and 2011, levels of non-pecuniary job satisfaction were virtually unchanged in panel workplaces (Table 7.7, Panel A). Instead it was the replacement of leavers by joiners that led to the sizeable overall increase in the private sector and the smaller fall in the public sector seen in Table 7.4, although the differences between leavers and joiners were not in fact statistically significant because of the smaller sample sizes (Table 7.7, Panel B). In contrast, levels of job-related contentment rose to a statistically significant extent within continuing workplaces in both the public and private sectors. The replacement of leavers by joiners also contributed to the overall increases in pay satisfaction and job contentment seen in Table 7.4 although, again, the small samples of leavers and joiners mean that the differences were not statistically significant. The pattern of changes in satisfaction with pay was more complex. In the private sector, levels of satisfaction with pay remained virtually unchanged in continuing workplaces. Consequently, it was the replacement of leavers by joiners that resulted in the overall rise in satisfaction with pay observed in the private sector in Table 7.4. In the public sector on the other hand, levels of satisfaction with

Table 7.7 *Mean employee well-being within continuing workplaces, joiners and leavers, 2004–11*

	Private sector	Public sector	All employees
Panel A: Change in mean employee well-being within continuing workplaces			
Non-pecuniary job satisfaction	-0.66	+0.86	-0.32
Satisfaction with pay	-0.01	+0.23	+0.04
Job contentment	+0.60	+0.71	+0.62
Panel B: Difference in mean employee well-being between workplaces leaving the population and those joining it (joiners–leavers)			
Non-pecuniary job satisfaction	+0.72	-0.18	+0.65
Satisfaction with pay	+0.18	+0.42	+0.20
Job contentment	+0.33	+1.30	+0.39

Notes: Continuing workplaces are those that were surveyed in both 2004 and 2011. The continuing workplaces included in this table all returned at least one response to the Survey of Employees. Leavers are workplaces that since 2004 closed or had shrunk below five employees by 2011. Joiners are workplaces that since 2004 were born or had grown above four employees by 2011.

Base: Employees in workplaces that were surveyed in both 2004 and 2011, or workplaces that 'joined' or 'left' the population between 2004 and 2011. Figures are based on employee responses from 600 (Panel A) and at least 509 (Panel B) workplaces.

pay rose in continuing workplaces. This increase, together with the replacement of leavers by joiners, not only contributed to the rise in satisfaction with pay in the public sector but also prompted the overall increase in satisfaction with pay seen in Table 7.4.

The Effects of Recession on Employee Well-being

In the final part of the chapter we consider the effect of recession on employees' well-being. There are at least three ways in which recession may affect employees' well-being. First, knowing that others have lost their jobs, employees may downwardly adjust their expectations about what they can get from employment such that they express greater satisfaction about their jobs than they might have done previously. Second, the recession may improve some employees' well-being if declining consumer demand for goods and services leads to slack in the production process in certain workplaces, as is suggested by the declining rates of labour productivity documented by Patterson (2012) and others. However, recessionary pressures are likely to have deleterious effects on the well-being of some employees too, through the generation of job insecurity and increased work pressure in workplaces where employment levels have been reduced.

Previous research finds complex relationships between facets of employee well-being and levels of economic activity. Clark (2011) found that in the period 1992–2007 overall job satisfaction and satisfaction with 'the work itself' were positively correlated with levels of unemployment, while satisfaction with pay and job security were negatively correlated with it. Satisfaction with hours worked was unrelated to the level of unemployment. The negative correlation between unemployment and satisfaction with job security is hardly surprising. But the link between unemployment and feelings about one's pay is less intuitive. Indeed, Bryson and Forth

(2010a) showed that over the period 1983–2009 employees were more likely to perceive their wages as 'reasonable' or 'on the high side' when unemployment was rising. They suggested that 'those employees who remain in work during these sorts of periods [may be] glad still to be receiving some kind of wage when the aggregate risk of job loss is rising, and their views about their wage levels reflect this' (2010: 109). Clark (2011: 134) offers a similar explanation for the positive correlation between overall job satisfaction and unemployment.

In light of these findings it is perhaps not surprising to find non-pecuniary job satisfaction and satisfaction with pay rose between 2004 and 2011, while satisfaction with job security fell, at least in the public sector. To examine the potential role of recession more directly, however, we look at the association between employee experiences of the recession and their job satisfaction and job contentment in 2011.

Employees' experiences of the recession are characterised using two survey measures, both of which were discussed in Chapter 2. The first is how adversely the workplace had been affected by the recession, as reported by workplace managers; in the regression models 1 indicates 'No adverse affect' and 5 indicates 'A great deal'. The second is the number of changes employees say have been made to their working conditions as a result of the most recent recession, which ranges from zero to nine. The effects of recession may be uneven across employees within the same workplace, even where the workplace has been severely affected. Therefore both measures are included in the following analyses.

To investigate the association between employee experiences of the recession and their job satisfaction and job contentment, the two survey measures mentioned previously were both entered together in the regression analyses of each of the three measures of well-being. The analysis was confined to the 88 per cent of employees who had been working at their current workplace during the recession. The regressions controlled for the full set of employee, job and workplace characteristics discussed earlier in respect of Table 7.6.[9] In particular the regressions controlled for the level of job quality experienced by the employee. This ensured that the analysis identified the impact of *recession-related changes* in employees' working conditions, rather than merely identifying the impact of low job quality per se.

Employees' well-being in the private sector was unaffected by the extent to which recession impacted on the workplace as a whole (Table 7.8). The same was true in the public sector for pay satisfaction and job-related contentment, but not for non-pecuniary job satisfaction, where the association was unexpectedly positive. Generally, then, it was the direct impact of the recession on the employee themselves that affected their well-being. For each of the three well-being measures, and in both the private and public sectors, employee well-being fell with the number of changes that the recession had brought to their working conditions.

Which recessionary changes were most salient in explaining the impact of the recession on employees' well-being? In both the private and public sectors job contentment was adversely affected by increases in workload and work reorganisation. Pay satisfaction in both sectors was adversely affected by wage freezes and cuts, and by restricted access to overtime. In the public sector, pay satisfaction was also adversely affected by increases in workload and by reductions in contractual hours. Work reorganisation was associated with *higher* pay satisfaction in the public

Table 7.8 *Employee well-being and the recession, 2011, multivariate analysis*

	Private sector	Public sector	All employees
Panel A: Non-pecuniary job satisfaction			
Overall impact of recession on the workplace	+0.01	+0.09	+0.03
Number of changes reported by employee	−0.17	−0.17	−0.17
Panel B: Satisfaction with pay			
Overall impact of recession on the workplace	−0.03	−0.01	−0.02
Number of changes reported by employee	−0.10	−0.06	−0.09
Panel C: Job-related contentment			
Overall impact of recession on the workplace	−0.03	−0.01	−0.03
Number of changes reported by employee	−0.12	−0.17	−0.13

Notes: Regression analyses containing the full set of control variables described in the text surrounding Table 7.6. The recession measures are discussed in the text surrounding this table.
Base: Employees who were present in the workplace (with five or more employees) at the time of the recession. Figures based on responses from at least 8,452 private sector and 5,559 public sector employees.

sector, perhaps because employees received some form of pay compensation for agreeing to work reorganisation. The only recession-induced change to affect private sector employees' non-pecuniary job satisfaction was a reduction in contractual hours, which lowered this measure of job satisfaction. Public sector employees' non-pecuniary job satisfaction was lowered if their access to training had been restricted or if they had been moved to another job within the workplace.

CONCLUSION

This chapter has investigated employee well-being along three dimensions: job-related contentment, job-related enthusiasm and job satisfaction. The 2011 WERS was the first in the series to measure all three of these dimensions and it has provided further confirmation for the significant relationship between various dimensions of job quality and well-being at work. Job characteristics remain key in explaining variation in employee well-being, whether considering contentment, enthusiasm or job satisfaction. It is clear that any policy aimed at improving employee well-being needs to take account of the important role of job quality.

The associations between job-related enthusiasm and job quality bore many similarities to those apparent in respect of job-related contentment, but there were also some differences. For instance, employees who had received training in the year prior to the survey were more likely to report job-related enthusiasm, but such an association was not apparent for contentment. And while higher earnings were associated with lower contentment, the same relationship was not apparent for enthusiasm. Consideration of both dimensions of well-being, as well as job satisfaction, is therefore important in order to gain a more rounded picture of how job quality contributes to well-being at work.

The chapter has also identified how non-pecuniary job satisfaction, pay satisfaction and job contentment changed between 2004 and 2011. There were a number of statistically significant changes in employee well-being over the period. Many of them were quite small, but there was a substantial increase in job contentment. This was apparent in the private and the public sectors, and among workplaces that had been in operation throughout the period.

The public and private sectors experienced very different trends in employee job satisfaction. In the private sector all aspects of job satisfaction measured in 2004 and 2011 rose significantly, with the exception of satisfaction with job security, which remained constant. In the public sector, on the other hand, non-pecuniary job satisfaction remained stable despite a small rise in satisfaction with scope to use initiative and a large decline in satisfaction with job security. Pay satisfaction rose significantly in both sectors, despite widespread pay freezes.

Compositional change in employees' jobs was the chief factor behind the small fall in non-pecuniary job satisfaction in the public sector and its rise in the private sector, with changes in job quality being key. Changes in pay satisfaction and job contentment remained largely unexplained by compositional changes, although that part which could be attributed to compositional change was largely due to changes in job quality. In the public sector the dominant feature was the decline in perceived job security, which had the effect of reducing employee well-being.

Behavioural changes within continuing workplaces and the replacement of old workplaces with new ones both contributed to changes in aggregate employee well-being. Pay satisfaction and job contentment rose significantly among continuing workplaces, although non-pecuniary job satisfaction was stable. Workplace churn led to a significant rise in pay satisfaction and increases in non-pecuniary job satisfaction and job contentment, though the latter were not statistically significant.

Finally, although the onset of recession has theoretically ambiguous consequences for the job-related well-being of those who remain in employment, the impact of the recession was associated with lower employee well-being. The overall impact of recession on the workplace had small, usually non-significant, effects on employee well-being. Instead it was the recession-induced changes that employees said had been made to their jobs which significantly reduced employees' well-being.

8 The Quality of Employment Relations

INTRODUCTION

In the late 1990s and early 2000s the quality of employment relations in British workplaces was broadly stable, if not improving (Kersley et al., 2006: 277; Brown et al., 2009: 145). However, the last few years have been challenging as managers and employees have navigated a difficult economic environment. Workplaces have, among other things, reorganised, restructured and resized, all of which have the potential to give rise to conflict at a collective or individual level. Yet, perhaps contrary to expectations, the last two chapters have shown that there have been some positive developments since 2004. More managers are displaying 'supportive' behaviours such as extending the provision of training to more employees; more employees consider managers to be acting with honesty and integrity; and more employees are satisfied in their jobs. So to what extent is conflict a feature of the modern workplace, and has the uncertainty created by the recession had an impact on the climate at work, both in terms of the incidence of conflict and more widely, the quality of employment relations?

This chapter begins by exploring the trends in both collective and individual disputes measured through the incidence of industrial action and Employment Tribunals. It then turns to other measures of discontent within the workplace, including the level of grievance and disciplinary events. These are the most visible indicators of discontent. Other conflict remains less apparent and may manifest in different forms such as employees choosing to leave the workplace, either by resigning or being absent from work, though clearly not all instances of either voluntary exits or absenteeism are rooted in conflict. However, taken together the aforesaid measures help to build a picture of the climate in the workplace. WERS also gauges the overall climate with a summary measure.

What role has the recession played in the employment relationship? We know that the recessionary environment has brought about a spate of industrial action in the public sector and in some parts of the private sector, indicating that the employment relationship inside the workplace may have deteriorated in recent years. On the other hand, the recession may have had the effect of suppressing the expression of discontent at an individual level. In a tough economic environment, employees – faced with the prospect of reduced job security and fewer options in the labour market – may be less inclined to speak out about their concerns or unhappiness at work.

These factors are considered and the chapter then concludes by examining the extent to which instances of conflict impact on the general state of relations at the workplace. Not all conflict results in long-term damage to workplaces or to individual relationships. Formal and informal approaches to dispute resolution can offer important mechanisms for managing conflict, and provide 'voice practices', whether it be through direct representation or procedures (Freeman, 1980). Indeed, the 'voice-exit' dichotomy (Hirschman, 1970; Freeman and Medoff, 1984) asserts that employers can benefit from employees 'voicing' their discontent, as they are given the opportunity to redress the matter before the employee decides whether to exit the workplace altogether. The chapter explores the mechanisms in place for disputes resolution, and also delves a little deeper into the notion of the workplace climate to examine whether conflict impacts on employees' commitment to their workplace and their engagement with their work.

INCIDENCE OF CONFLICT

Conflict arising in the employment relationship can most easily be measured when it results in overt manifestations. Indeed official statistics focus only on events that take place in the public sphere, namely strikes and Employment Tribunal claims. The raising of individual grievances within the workplace, and the disciplining of individual employees, also serve as indicators of the quality of employment relations within the workplace, however. This section examines what official statistics can tell us about the annual incidence of collective and individual conflict, and then what WERS can add to this picture.

The decline in industrial action over the last three decades has been well-documented (Dix et al., 2009). Between 1979 and 1980, the point at which the WERS series began, there were 3,380 stoppages in which 32 million working days were lost. Twenty years later in 2004–05 (at the time of the last WERS), 158 stoppages were recorded accounting for 535,000 days lost. While there was a relatively small increase in the number of stoppages in 2011–12, rising to 184, the days lost amounted to 1.38 million. This recent spike in the series (see Figure 8.1) can be attributed to the large-scale strikes in the public sector in response to changes to pensions and ongoing pay freezes that were prescribed by the Government. These public sector strikes together accounted for almost 1.29 million days lost in 2011–12.[1] While strikes in the private sector account for a small proportion of the overall figure, these have also increased since 2009 compared to the two previous years. This is primarily a result of industrial action in parts of the Transport and communications industry that were historically part of the public sector, and reflects longer-term patterns in industrial relations which are thought to have been exacerbated by the economic crisis (Podro, 2010).

At the same time, individual disputes as measured through Employment Tribunal (ET) claims have been increasing rapidly over recent decades (Figure 8.1).

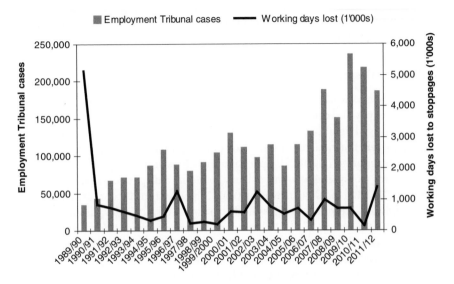

Figure 8.1 *Days lost to stoppages and Employment Tribunals applications, 1989–90 to 2011–12*

Sources: 1980–98: Hawes (2000); 1998–2010: Ministry of Justice (2012), and Office for National Statistics (2012b) LABD01: 'Labour Disputes in Labour Market Statistics Data Tables', November 2012 release.

From the same starting point, in 1979–80, there were just over 41,000 ET cases and for the remainder of the decade the figure remained well below 50,000. The 1990s saw a steady incline reaching to more than 91,000 cases in 1998–99 so that by the following decade cases were well above 100,000 in most years, albeit with considerable year-on-year variation. By 2009–10 cases had reached in excess of 200,000. However, a good deal of this growth in ET cases can be attributed to large-scale multiple claims on issues such as equal pay, working time and redundancy (Saundry and Dix, 2014).[2] For instance, if we examine the time points covered by the last two WERS, in 2004–05 ET cases totalled 86,161 and in 2011–12 it was 186,300; however, the increase in single claims has been relatively minor – from around 55,000 to almost 60,000. A common proposition is that ET claims, including multiple claims, have substituted for more traditional forms of collective disputes but Saundry and Dix (2014) dismiss this as an over-simplification of a complex interplay of factors including the decline in union density, as well as a changing economic and legal context (see also Dix et al., 2009).

WERS can enrich this picture to provide more information about the workplaces that have been affected by collective disputes, the various types of industrial action that have been threatened and taken place, and the incidence and type of individualised conflict. While ET statistics tell us about disputes that have escalated to the tribunal process, WERS tells us about individual disputes that have been raised inside the workplace, how they are handled and the matters concerned. Has the economic downturn created more conflict inside the workplace or are employers and employees choosing to overlook their differences in order to survive the challenging economic circumstances? And has an increased policy emphasis on internal dispute resolution altered the picture?

Collective Disputes

Five per cent of workplace managers reported that there had been a collective dispute over pay and conditions in the 12 months prior to the survey, a figure that had not changed significantly from the 4 per cent in 2004. Public administration and Education were the industries in which disputes over pay and conditions were most commonly reported in 2011 (21 per cent and 18 per cent, respectively). Overall, public sector workplaces were more likely to report a dispute over pay and conditions in 2011 than in 2004, increasing from 13 per cent to 20 per cent. Workplaces in large private enterprises were less likely to report a dispute, falling from 6 per cent in 2004 to 2 per cent in 2011. Where a dispute did arise the majority (87 per cent) of workplaces had a collective disputes procedure in place to deal with it; however, it was not always used – only two thirds (66 per cent) of workplaces with a procedure actually used it for the last dispute that had occurred.

Where a dispute does not appear to be moving towards a resolution, a union, if present, may conduct a ballot for industrial action. In the 12 months prior to the survey, ballots for industrial action were conducted in 7 per cent of workplaces, an increase from 3 per cent in 2004. Ballots had taken in place in only 1 per cent of private sector workplaces, reflecting both the scarcity of collective disputes but also the relatively scarce presence of unions in these workplaces (see Chapter 4). The incidence of ballots in public sector workplaces increased from 19 per cent in 2004 to 51 per cent in 2011. It is notable that the increase in disputes over pay and conditions reported by managers in the public sector was much lower than the rise in reported ballots. This may reflect the nature of the public sector trade unions' industrial action campaign, which was run at a national level rather than organisational or workplace level, with many workplaces being balloted even though the dispute was not organised locally.

Against the backdrop of increased balloting, some employer groups and politicians have raised questions about the legitimacy of the process (Mullholland and Gabbatt, 2010). In particular, questions have been raised as to the proportion of members that typically cast a vote. If a ballot took place in the 12 months prior to the survey, workplace managers were asked the proportion of eligible employees who voted in the last ballot. Two thirds (67 per cent) did not know, illustrating the general paucity of knowledge in this area. Of those managers who did know, 62 per cent reported that half or more of eligible employees voted.

Even if a majority of voters are in favour of industrial action, it may not take place. For instance, unions may use the balloting process, or ballot results, as part of their strategy to threaten action, or to increase their bargaining power without their members having to endure the consequences of action (such as losing a day's pay) (Heery and Nash, 2011).

The proportion of public sector workplaces where industrial action was threatened doubled from 11 per cent in 2004 to 22 per cent in 2011 (Table 8.1). This did not translate into a rise across all workplaces – where threats remained stable at

Table 8.1 *Industrial action by sector of ownership, 2004 and 2011, cell per cent*

	Public sector		Private sector		All workplaces	
	2004	**2011**	**2004**	**2011**	**2004**	**2011**
Any industrial action (threatened or taken)	15	<u>36</u>	3	2	5	6
Threatened action	11	<u>22</u>	3	2	4	4
Industrial action taken	9	<u>32</u>	1	1	2	<u>5</u>
Of which:						
Strike action	6	<u>29</u>	(0)	1	1	<u>4</u>
Non-strike action	(4)	6	1	(1)	1	1

Base: All workplaces with five or more employees. Figures are based on responses from 2,110 (2004) and 2,659 (2011) workplace managers.

4 per cent of workplaces – as the figures are dominated by what happened in the private sector. There was an increase in the proportion of all workplaces that experienced strikes (from 1 per cent to 4 per cent) but, again, the increase can primarily be attributed to the public sector. In 2004, 6 per cent of public sector workplaces experienced strike action in the 12 months prior to the survey, and this more than quadrupled to 29 per cent in 2011. The proportion of workplaces experiencing non-strike action such as overtime bans or go slows remained low at 1 per cent in either year. Some 6 per cent of all workplaces experienced industrial action – or the threat of it – in the 12 months prior to the survey. While industrial action was relatively rare among private sector workplaces, it was four times more likely to take place in workplaces that recognised a union (4 per cent compared to 1 per cent of private sector workplaces that did not recognise a union).

Collective disputes in the recession
Overall, there was some indication of a relationship between the incidence of industrial action and the degree to which the workplace had been adversely affected by the recession. While not statistically significant, there appeared to be some association in the public sector – industrial action took place in 35 per cent of public sector workplaces that were adversely affected 'A great deal' or 'Quite a lot' compared with 32 per cent that were affected 'A moderate amount' and 28 per cent that experienced little or no effect.

Further in the public sector, there was a relationship between whether industrial action was taken and whether the workplaces had made employment-related changes in response to the recession. Among public sector workplaces that had instituted at least one of the measures listed in Chapter 2 (Table 2.4), 34 per cent experienced industrial action in the year prior to the 2011 WERS; this compared with 15 per cent of those where no changes had been made. Industrial action in the public sector tended to be associated with particular types of responses to the recession too – with a higher incidence in workplaces that underwent a wage freeze or cut in response to the recession (39 per cent compared with 20 per cent of workplaces that did not have a wage freeze or cut).

Turning to the panel of public sector workplaces surveyed in 2004 and 2011, the incidence of industrial action doubled between 2004 and 2011 (from 19 per cent to 44 per cent) among those workplaces that had made changes in response to the recession, whereas it was stable in workplaces where no actions were taken in response to the recession (30 per cent had experienced industrial action in 2004, compared with 27 per cent in 2011).

Individual Disputes

Increasingly, conflict at work is manifested through individual rather than collective disputes. Employers may take disciplinary action against an employee or decide to dismiss them, and employees may raise a grievance with their employer or seek legal redress on the issue via an external body, in the form of the Employment Tribunal.

Beginning with grievances, WERS has two ways of identifying whether a grievance has been raised within a workplace. The first indicator is derived from a question in which workplace managers are asked whether any grievances have been formally raised by an employee through a grievance procedure in the past year. The second indicator is derived from a question in which workplace managers are asked to report on the types of grievances that have been raised at the workplace in the past year (with one response option being 'No grievances raised'). The advantage of the latter measure is that it does not rely on a procedure being in place to determine whether an individual dispute has occurred, although changes in the lead-in to this question between the 2004 and 2011 surveys may have impaired comparability on this particular measure over time, and so both measures are presented in Table 8.2.[3]

The second of the two measures discussed previously suggests that there was a drop in the proportion of workplaces in which at least one employee raised a grievance in the year prior to the survey, from 38 per cent of workplaces in 2004 to 29 per cent in 2011. While the decline appeared across all sectors, significant falls were observed in the private services sector (from 37 per cent to 28 per cent) and, in particular, Other business services (41 per cent to 25 per cent).[4] However, the first measure which focuses only on grievances raised through formal procedures, shows stability, with 18 per cent of workplaces that have a grievance procedure having had an employee use it in 2004 compared with 19 per cent in 2011. The results for the second measure show a marked decline in grievance-raising, in general, by employees. However, the uncertainties noted earlier imply that there is a sounder basis for judging what happened to formal grievances, and there we see no change. The presence of procedures for handling conflict will be explored further in the following section.

The aggregate number of employees that raised a grievance through a formal procedure was a mean of 1.5 per 100 employees in the 12 months prior to the 2011 survey.[5] Larger workplaces are more likely than smaller ones to experience at least one grievance in a year but, if one expresses the likelihood of grievances in terms of the mean number of grievances per 100 employees, there is no difference in grievance rates by workplace size. The average number of grievances per 100 employees is 1.4 in workplaces with five to nine employees, which is not statistically different from the average of 1.2 in workplaces with 500 or more employees. The average

Table 8.2 *Individual disputes by sector of ownership, 2004 and 2011, cell per cent*

	Any formal grievance	Any grievance	Employment Tribunal claim	Disciplinary sanction	Dismissal
Public sector					
2004	25	44	6	30	8
2011	23	35	7	32	12
Private manufacturing					
2004	21	41	11	58	19
2011	11	31	4	41	15
Private services					
2004	16	37	5	43	21
2011	20	28	4	42	19
All Workplaces					
2004	18	38	6	44	19
2011	19	29	4	41	18

Notes: A 'formal grievance' is one that is raised through the grievance procedure and 'any grievances' are those either raised through a procedure or not. Disciplinary sanction includes dismissals.
Base: All workplaces with five or more employees, except column for 'Any formal grievance' where it is those workplaces with five or more employees who have a grievance procedure in place. Figures are based on responses from at least 2,173 (2004) and 2,562 (2011) workplace managers.

number of grievances per 100 employees was also similar between workplaces with a recognised union (1.5 per 100 employees) and those without (1.4 per 100 employees). The rate of grievances did vary by sector in 2011, however, with higher average rates in private services and public sector workplaces (1.5 and 1.3 per 100 employees, respectively) than in private manufacturing workplaces (an average of 1.0 per 100 employees).

As noted earlier, workplace managers in the 2011 WERS were asked about the types of grievances that had been raised at the workplace in the 12 months prior to the survey. The most commonly cited was 'Unfair treatment by managers or supervisors', which could include a variety of aspects of relations between employees and their superiors, including perceived victimisation or concerns relating to treatment during performance appraisals. Two fifths (39 per cent) of workplace managers who reported a grievance said this was one of the reasons. The next most common type of grievance related to pay, terms and conditions (30 per cent), followed by bullying and harassment at work from colleagues or managers (23 per cent of workplaces in which a grievance had been raised), confirming the work of Fevre et al. (2012) on the significance of ill treatment at work. While comparisons with 2004 are limited due to changes to the questions (mentioned previously), it is of note that grievances regarding the selection for redundancy doubled since 2004 to 9 per cent in 2011. There were some differences between the public and private sectors in 2011, with public sector workplaces more likely to have had grievances relating to behavioural issues as opposed to those relating to the terms and conditions of work. The two most common reasons for grievances cited by public sector workplace managers were: unfair treatment – a reason in 52 per cent of workplaces reporting grievances compared with 37 per cent in private sector workplaces, and bullying or harassment – 39 per cent compared with 20 per cent in the private sector.

The proportion of workplaces where one or more employee made an application to an Employment Tribunal did not change to a statistically significant extent, standing at 6 per cent in 2004 and 4 per cent in 2011 (Table 8.2). However, there were statistically significant changes in some industries: the proportion of workplaces that reported an ET application fell in Manufacturing (from 11 per cent in 2004 to 4 per cent in 2011) and Other business services (from 9 per cent to 3 per cent), while workplaces in Education faced an increase from 3 per cent in 2004 to 8 per cent in 2011.

Turning to employer-led sanctions, there was no change between 2004 and 2011 in the proportion of workplaces where a manager had taken disciplinary action against an employee in the 12 months preceding the survey interview. This had occurred in 41 per cent of workplaces in 2011, which was not a significant difference from the 44 per cent of workplaces in 2004 (Table 8.2). Controlling for workplace size and a variety of other workplace and workforce characteristics confirms the findings of earlier research which indicate that the characteristics of the workforce influence whether a disciplinary sanction has been applied at the workplace (see Knight and Latreille, 2000; Saundry and Dix, 2014).[6] In 2011, disciplinary sanctions were less likely to have been applied in workplaces with higher proportions of female employees, in those with higher proportions of older workers (those aged 50 years and above) and in those with lower proportions of higher-skilled workers. The same associations were not all apparent in the case of grievances – the only workforce characteristic that had some influence on the likelihood that a grievance had been raised (either formally or informally) was the proportion of older employees, which decreased the likelihood of a grievance.

Across all workplaces, for every 100 employees a mean of 4.8 disciplinary sanctions had been applied in the 12 months prior to the survey. This had not changed significantly from 2004. Among those workplaces where disciplinary sanctions were applied, the majority (66 per cent) applied only one or two different types of sanctions, the most common being formal verbal warnings (66 per cent) or formal written warnings (63 per cent). This marks a change from 2004 where a wider variety of sanctions had been applied – one or two different types of sanctions were applied in 58 per cent of workplaces that undertook disciplinary action. In 2004, formal verbal warnings were more common and were applied in 82 per cent of workplaces. Further, suspension with or without pay was also more likely, having been applied in 32 per cent of workplaces in 2004 (24 per cent in 2011), as were internal transfers (11 per cent in 2004 and 6 per cent in 2011).

The most common reason for an employer taking disciplinary action in 2011 was poor performance – this reason was mentioned by 59 per cent of workplaces in which sanctions were applied and there was an increase from 47 per cent in 2004. In 2004 the most common sanctions were concerned with poor timekeeping or unauthorised absence, being cited in 52 per cent of workplaces taking disciplinary action and decreasing to 44 per cent in 2011. The other change was a decline in workplaces taking disciplinary action for alcohol or drug use which declined from 10 per cent in 2004 to 6 per cent in 2011. Other reasons for applying a disciplinary sanction were theft or dishonesty (which was at least one of the reasons in 24 per cent of workplaces applying sanctions in 2011), abusive behaviour or bullying and harassment (21 per cent), disobedience (18 per cent) or health and safety breaches (13 per cent).

Chapter 5 noted the large increase between 2004 and 2011 in workplaces where the performance of non-managerial employees is formally appraised and this would seem to be associated with the increase in poor performance sanctions. In 2004, there was no significant difference in the incidence of these types of sanctions between workplaces that conducted appraisals and those that did not. But by 2011, there was a clear difference. Some 63 per cent of workplaces that appraised performance had issued a poor performance sanction in the previous 12 months, compared with just 48 per cent of workplaces that did not conduct appraisals.

In keeping with the stability in the incidence of disciplinary sanctions between 2004 and 2011, the rate of workplaces conducting dismissals reduced by only one percentage point to 18 per cent in 2011, which is not statistically significant.

The role of representatives in individual disputes

Where present, employee representatives, particularly union representatives, tend to have a role in individual disputes at the workplace. In 2011, almost two thirds (66 per cent) of all representatives said that they had spent time on disciplinary matters and grievances in the 12 months prior to the survey. This appeared to have increased since 2004, when the figure stood at 59 per cent, but the difference was not statistically significant. Union representatives were more likely to have spent time on disciplinary and grievance matters at the workplace than non-union representatives (78 per cent and 44 per cent, respectively, in 2011).

A relatively high proportion of representatives reported involvement here in the formal grievance process. Almost half (45 per cent) of representatives reported that they were automatically notified by management if an employee they represented raised a matter through the grievance procedure. This had not changed significantly since 2004 (when it stood at 50 per cent). Furthermore, 33 per cent said that at least one employee that they represented had formally raised a grievance through the procedure in the 12 months prior to the survey. This figure of 33 per cent is higher than the 19 per cent of workplace managers who reported a formal grievance, but the difference is explained by the fact that grievances were more likely to be raised in workplaces where representatives were present: workplace managers reported formal grievances in 27 per cent of all workplaces with arrangements for employee representation, compared with just 15 per cent of workplaces with no representative structures.[7]

Turning to procedures for handling disciplinary sanctions, many employees were supportive of the involvement of employee representatives. When asked, 'Ideally, who do you think would best represent you in dealing with managers here ... if a manager wanted to discipline you?', almost half (47 per cent) of employees in workplaces that had some form of representation chose a union or non-union representative. In particular, union members were even more likely to choose representation – 73 per cent said a trade union representative would ideally represent them in a disciplinary matter. This had not changed significantly from 2004.

Individual disputes in the recession

The economic downturn may have impacted on the level of individual disputes, but in different ways. While workplace changes may have resulted in employees being aggrieved, it is also possible that both employers and employees may have felt reluctant to formally escalate their concerns in the context of other pressures inside and outside the workplace.

The incidence of grievances and disciplinary actions were both related to workplace experiences of recession. Grievances were more common in workplaces where managers had made changes in response to the recession (32 per cent compared with 21 per cent where no changes had been made). Further, a grievance was raised in 44 per cent of workplaces where four or more actions in response to the recession had taken place, compared with 24 per cent of workplaces where only one change was made. This same pattern was observed for the incidence of disciplinary action, but to a lesser extent. Disciplinary sanctions had been applied in 43 per cent of workplaces that had taken action in response to the recession, compared with 34 per cent of workplaces where no such change had taken place. In a multivariate regression analysis, the workplace manager's assessment of the extent to which the workplace had been adversely affected by the recession, the number of actions they reported had been taken as a result of the recession, and whether the workplace undertook any redundancies in the 12 months prior to the survey were all significant factors in whether grievances were raised at the workplace. This was also the case in an equivalent regression analysis of whether any disciplinary sanctions had been applied in the workplace in the 12 months prior to the survey.[8]

RESOLVING WORKPLACE DISPUTES

One feature mitigating the incidence and experience of conflict in the workplace is the strategies that are in place to help resolve disputes. Dix et al. (2009: 195) found that the presence of procedures does not prevent disputes from arising but in fact 'provide[s] a means through which discontent can be articulated and the resulting conflict addressed'. Structures for representative voice are an important factor in whether an employee will raise a grievance within the workplace and this relationship is further bolstered with the presence of grievance procedures (Freeman, 1980). Procedures can help ensure that all parties to the conflict are treated fairly and given an opportunity to air their concerns. The opportunities they provide for resolution can mean that formal grievance arrangements prevent conflict from escalating further.

The formalising of procedures to handle workplace disputes has been one of the defining features of the changing employment relations landscape in the last three decades (Kersley et al., 2006: 211–15). At the same time, as the number of ET applications has risen, so have concerns in the policy and employer communities about cost and detrimental impacts on the state and parties (Gibbons, 2007; Department for Business, Innovation and Skills, 2011b). One consequence has been an increased policy focus on resolving disputes with a growing emphasis on the value of addressing disputes *early* and *inside* the workplace, via discipline and griev-ance arrangements, early conciliation and other routes such as mediation.

Between 1998 and 2004 there was no significant growth in the presence of procedures for handling collective disputes and individual grievances, but there was an increase in disciplinary procedures (Kersley et al., 2006: 212–16). During the 2004 WERS fieldwork period, the Dispute Resolution Regulations 2004 were implemented with the introduction of the statutory three-step procedure for resolving disputes. However, in 2007 the Gibbons Review recom-mended the repeal of the statutory three steps in favour of a more flexible and simplified arrangement. In 2009 a new principles-based Acas Statutory Code on discipline and grievance was published. One question is whether the shift from a prescribed to a principles-based Code has altered parties' approach to handling disputes.

This section examines first whether there has been an increase in the inci-dence of procedures for handling individual disputes between 2004 and 2011 and then goes on to look more closely at the content and development of these procedures. Finally, the incidence and content of collective dispute procedures is also discussed.

Individual Dispute Procedures

The proportion of workplaces that have procedures in place for handling discipline or dismissal, and individual grievances has increased since 2004, so too has the proportion of employees that these procedures cover (Table 8.3). In 2011, 97 per

Table 8.3 *Presence of procedures for handling individual disputes, 2004 and 2011, cell per cent*

	Discipline or dismissal		Individual grievance	
	2004	**2011**	**2004**	**2011**
Proportion of employment	95	97	93	97
Proportion of workplaces	84	89	82	89
Workplace size				
5–9 employees	76	82	74	82
10–19 employees	83	92	81	90
20–49 employees	95	96	91	97
50–99 employees	98	98	99	100
100–499 employees	99	100	99	100
500 or more	100	100	100	100
Union recognition				
No recognised union	80	87	77	86
Recognised union	99	99	99	99

Base: All workplaces with five or more employees. Figures are based on responses from at least 2,291 (2004) and 2,676 (2011) workplace managers.

cent of all employees worked in an establishment with a formal disciplinary procedure and the same proportion worked in an establishment with a formal grievance procedure. All workplaces with 100 or more employees had both discipline and grievance procedures in place. The increase in individual dispute procedures is evident in workplaces without a recognised union, with the presence of discipline or dismissal procedures increasing by seven percentage points since 2004, and individual grievance procedures rising by nine percentage points. This upward trend was also noted in 2004 when it was tentatively attributed to the increasing scope of individual employment rights and tribunal cases (Kersley et al., 2006: 216).

Individual dispute procedures: Development and practice

In developing and refining the procedures, managers may wish to consult the parties who will inevitably use the procedures, that is, representatives of employees. This process of consultation may be especially important in securing and embedding procedures as effective voice mechanisms in the workplace (Eigen and Litwin, 2011).

Chapter 5 found that there had been a decline in the proportion of workplace managers reporting that collective bargaining covered grievance procedures, from 31 per cent in 2004 to 19 per cent in 2011. Some part of this fall could be attributable to a change in the questionnaire: in 2004 one question asked managers about negotiations over disciplinary procedures and another asked about negotiations over grievance procedures, in 2011 there was a single question asking about negotiations over 'grievance and disciplinary procedures'. We do not expect this to have had a major effect, however, as the majority of managers in 2004 (96 per cent) reported the same approach to both grievance and disciplinary procedures.

It is useful to turn to the accounts of the representatives themselves to determine how embedded they are in the process. Again, similar changes were made to the question wording so that in 2011 the most senior representative at the workplace was asked, 'Does management normally negotiate with union / employee representatives ... over the development of disciplinary and grievance procedures?' Union representatives reported no change between 2004 and 2011 in whether managers involve them in the development of these procedures.[9] In 2011, 37 per cent of union representatives said that management negotiated over the development of individual dispute procedures and a further 36 per cent said they were consulted.

WERS explores what practice parties actually follow in handling discipline and grievance situations, using the framework of the principles-based Acas Code as a benchmark for assessment. The principles include: setting out the issue of concern in writing, holding a meeting to discuss the matter and providing employees with an opportunity to appeal the decision. Managers were asked whether these principles were practiced regardless of whether there was a procedure in place. Table 8.4 shows that workplaces were more likely to report that their practices reflected the three principles set out in the Code when handling disciplinary situations, than in grievance situations. In disciplinary situations, all three elements were carried out all of the time in 81 per cent of workplaces in 2011, but in the case of grievances they were carried out all of the time in only 46 per cent of workplaces. Reporting on the 2004 WERS, Kersley et al. (2006: 219) found the same disjuncture, which may in part reflect the fact that managers, whose accounts are reported here, have less

Table 8.4 *Practice of the three principles for handling individual disputes, 2004 and 2011, column per cent*

	Discipline or dismissal		Individual grievance	
	2004	**2011**	**2004**	**2011**
All three, all of the time	69	81	37	46
All three, but not all of the time	15	11	28	36
One or two, all or some of the time	15	5	32	16
None of the principles	2	2	3	2

Notes: The three principles are: (i) setting out the issue of concern in writing, (ii) holding a meeting to discuss the matter and (iii) providing employees with an opportunity to appeal the decision.
Base: All workplaces with five or more employees. Figures are based on responses from 2,259 (2004) and 2,660 (2011) workplace managers.

control over whether employees bringing grievances follow certain aspects of the procedure – for instance, always setting out concerns in writing.

The principles set out in the 2009 Code largely mirror the statutory three steps of the preceding Code but it is noteworthy that, overall, more workplaces are putting the principles in practice since 2004. For grievances, there has been a 17 percentage point increase in the percentage of workplaces using all three aspects at least some of the time, from 65 per cent to 72 per cent; and for disciplinary matters it has increased by nine percentage points from 84 per cent in 2004 to 93 per cent in 2011. Kersley et al. (2006: 219) made tentative conclusions about the positive impact of the Dispute Resolution Regulations by determining that there had been small increases (of four to six percentage points) in the use of the three steps by examining the 2004 WERS data pre- and post-1 October 2004 – the date of implementation. Disentangling the impact of the Dispute Resolution Regulations from the 2009 Code is problematic, but the increase in arrangements suggests that the Regulations, and the subsequent Acas Code, have influenced the approach to handling individual disputes inside the workplace (see also Rahim et al., 2011).

Collective Dispute Procedures

In contrast to individual dispute procedures, the proportion of workplaces with a collective dispute procedure fell from 40 per cent in 2004 to 35 per cent in 2011, perhaps reflecting the general downward trend in the presence of unions and days lost to stoppages since the 1990s. Collective dispute procedures are primarily relevant in workplaces where this type of conflict is most likely to occur, that is, where unions are present. The reduction in procedures among workplaces without a recognised union was statistically significant – from 29 per cent in 2004 to 24 per cent in 2011. However, there was no such reduction among workplaces with a recognised union, where the decline from 78 per cent to 75 per cent was not statistically significant.

Two thirds (68 per cent) of collective dispute procedures in 2011 included a provision for the issue to be referred to a body outside the workplace. This figure had not changed notably since 2004. The most common outside body cited in these procedures was Acas conciliation (37 per cent) and the next most common was Acas arbitration (25 per cent of referral provisions). There were increases in the proportion of procedures that referred to an independent mediator (from 4 per cent in 2004 to 11 per cent in 2011), a union (from 28 per cent to 38 per cent) and an employers' association (from 7 per cent to 13 per cent). In 2011, around half (54 per cent) of the procedures that referred disputes to an outside body prohibited industrial action from taking place before the matter was referred outside the workplace.

OTHER POTENTIAL INDICATORS OF DISCONTENT

The increasing prevalence of procedures for handling disputes in the workplace confirms the trend of the increasing formalisation of dispute resolution in Britain. So far, the focus has been on more overt forms of conflict. However, there are many reasons why an employee may not feel inclined to raise a grievance formally – it could be that there are no procedures in place, or that the employee is not aware of procedures or that they fear the repercussions of raising a concern. Therefore, relying solely on the incidence of grievances raised is unlikely to give the full picture of discontent in the workplace, and it can be useful to explore other indicators.

Chapter 7 indicated that employees' job satisfaction increased between 2004 and 2011. Table 8.5 provides a summary, showing the proportion of employees who were satisfied with all seven aspects of their job. One fifth (20 per cent) of all employees were satisfied with all aspects of their job in 2011. There were significant increases in the proportions of employees in private manufacturing and private services that reported satisfaction with all aspects of their job; however, there was no such increase among public sector employees.

One might also look at rates of resignations or absenteeism as indicators of whether employees are content in their jobs (see Dix et al., 2009: 194). When an employee is discontented at work and does not feel their concerns will be adequately addressed, they may decide to leave by voluntarily resigning. However, during the recession and periods of high unemployment, employees may be less willing to exit the workplace as result of limited prospects elsewhere in the labour market (Faggio et al., 2011: 98). Thus, an employee may alternatively resort to temporary leave from the workplace in the form of absence. Of course, there are many other reasons why employees resign or are absent from their work, such as relocation, career progression or poor health; and therefore resignation and absence as measures of discontent are informative only to some degree.

WERS asks managers for the number of employees who left or resigned voluntarily in the past 12 months and this is used along with the number of employees that were at the workplace 12 months prior, to produce a resignation rate. Across all workplaces the mean voluntary resignation rate was 9 per 100 employees in 2011 (see Table 8.5). There was considerable variation across industries, with the highest resignation rate, by far, in Hotels and restaurants at an average of 20 per 100 employees and the lowest in Public administration and Electricity, gas and

Table 8.5 *Employee job satisfaction, average voluntary resignation rates and absence rates, 2004 and 2011, cell per cent and mean*

	Overall job satisfaction		Voluntary resi gnations		Absence	
	% of employees satisfied with all aspects of job		Resignations per 100 employees		% of working days lost (workplace average)	
	2004	**2011**	**2004**	**2011**	**2004**	**2011**
All workplaces	16	<u>20</u>	13.8	<u>9.1</u>	3.7	3.4
Private manufacturing	13	<u>18</u>	9.4	<u>4.9</u>	3.2	3.4
Private services	17	<u>22</u>	17.3	<u>11.3</u>	3.6	3.2
Public sector	14	15	7.4	<u>4.9</u>	4.9	4.7

Base: All employees and workplaces with five or more employees.
Figures are based on responses from 21,148 employees and at least 2,116 workplace managers (2004), and 20,720 employees and at least 2,491 workplace managers (2011).

water, both at 4 per 100 employees. Other industries that had higher than average resignation levels were Wholesale and retail trade (12 per 100 employees), Other community services (11 per 100 employees), Other business services and Health (both 10 per 100 employees).

Notably, the average rate of resignations fell from 14 per 100 employees in 2004. Particularly notable falls occurred in Construction (from 15 to 7 per 100 employees) and Wholesale and retail trade (from 20 to 12 per 100 employees). In a steady economic environment, a change in the resignation rate may signal some change in worker discontent. In a more unstable environment, however, resignations also signal the availability of outside options, as a fall in resignations is typical of a depressed economic climate (Faggio et al., 2011). Looking at the panel survey of workplaces that were interviewed in 2004 and 2011, we found that, where managers reported that their workplace was adversely affected 'A great deal' by the recession, the mean resignation rate had stood at 17 per 100 employees in 2004 but fell to 6 per 100 employees in 2011. In comparison, for workplaces that experienced 'No adverse effect' from the recession, the mean resignation rate was 17 per 100 employees in 2004 but only decreased to 12 per 100 employees in 2011.This indicates that the overall decline in the resignation rate can at least partly be attributed to the changed economic conditions, and so it would not be safe to infer anything more broadly from it about changes in levels of discontent.

In respect of absenteeism, workplace managers were asked about the percentage of days lost to sickness or absence over the last 12 months prior to the survey. There was less movement in the average rates of absence between 2004 and 2011 than was seen in resignation rates. In 2011 the workplace absence rate was 3.4 per cent – not a statistically significant difference from the 3.7 per cent in 2004. In contrast to the resignation rate, the absence rate was higher in the public sector than in the private sector, standing at 4.7 per cent compared with 3.3 per cent. One would not expect absence rates to be as heavily influenced by economic conditions and so the stability in the absence rate between 2004 and 2011 may be taken as a further indicator that individual expressions of discontent did not rise substantially between 2004 and 2011.

EMPLOYMENT RELATIONS AND DISCONTENT

This final section of the chapter goes on to consider summary evaluations of the climate of employment relations at the workplace, provided by managers, employees and employee representatives. Comparisons are made between the evaluations given in 2004 and 2011, before going on to consider the extent to which instances of conflict impact on the general state of relations at the workplace. The section ends by looking at employees' levels of engagement and commitment and, again, at the extent to which these are affected by disputes in the workplace.

Managers' and Employees' Evaluations of the Employment Relations Climate

Workplace managers are asked, 'How would you rate the relationship between management and employees generally at this workplace?', and employees are asked, 'In general, how would you describe relations between managers and employees here?', with each being given five response options from 'Very good' to 'Very poor'. Previous interrogation of these measures has found them to correlate positively with other indicators of discontent, such that they can be considered to provide a reliable summary of the general 'climate' in the workplace (Cully et al., 1999; Kersley et al., 2006).

WERS established that the climate deteriorated notably between 1984 and 1990, and then improved and stabilised up until 2004 (Blanchflower and Bryson, 2009: 69). Given official statistics on days lost to stoppages and ET cases, it would not be unreasonable to expect a decline between 2004 and 2011. The British Social Attitudes Survey has a similar question asking employees to describe relations between management and other employees at their workplace. Overall, the annual data show a similar pattern to WERS with a deterioration in climate in the 1990s and then an improvement in the early 2000s (Bryson and Forth, 2010a). More recent data than that provided by Bryson and Forth indicate little difference between 2004 and 2010. In 2004, 84 per cent of employees rated the relationship between managers and employees 'Very good' or 'Quite good' and in 2010 it was 82 per cent.[10] The following sections present the equivalent data from WERS.

Managers' and Employees' Evaluations

Overall, managers and employees perceive there to be good relations in British workplaces. Almost two thirds (64 per cent) of employees in 2011 described relations between managers and employees at the workplace to be 'Very good' or 'Good' (Figure 8.2). This is a small but significant increase from 2004 when 62 per cent

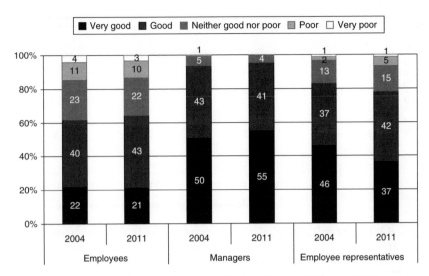

Figure 8.2 *Perceptions of the employment relations climate, 2004 and 2011, column per cent*

Base: All workplaces with five or more employees: columns one and two all employees, columns three and four all managers, and columns five and six all employee representatives, where present. Figures are based on responses from 2,278 workplace managers in 2004 and 2,672 in 2011 (columns three and four), 981 employee representatives in 2004 and 995 in 2011 (columns five and six), 22,061 employees in 2004 and 21,834 in 2011 (columns one and two).

of employees gave the same description. The increase can be attributed to the rise in the proportion of employees who said that relations were 'Good', which rose from 40 per cent to 43 per cent. From the workplace manager's perspective, the vast majority reported good relations with their employees in 2011 (96 per cent provided a rating of 'Very good' or 'Good'). There was an increase in the proportion of workplaces in which managers who reported 'Very good' relations with their employees, from 50 per cent in 2004 to 55 per cent in 2011, although this was not statistically significant.

Including managerial employees in the results for all employees has in the past skewed the results to a more positive view (Cully, 1999: 280). While managerial employees were more likely to describe the relationship with managers positively than non-managerial employees in 2011, with 76 per cent reporting 'Very good' or 'Good' relations, removing them did not change the overall average after rounding. The proportion of non-managerial employees providing a positive response was equal to the overall employee average of 62 per cent.

There is an obvious incongruence between managers' and employees' views. Figure 8.3 shows employees' reports of relations at the workplace cross-tabulated with their workplace managers' reports. Three out of five employees provided accounts corresponding with their managers of 'Very good' or 'Good' relations. One in ten employees (11 per cent) considered relations to be 'Very poor' or 'Poor' while their workplace managers thought they were good. There has been little change since 2004, when 58 per cent of employees rated relations as 'Very good' or 'Good' along with their manager.

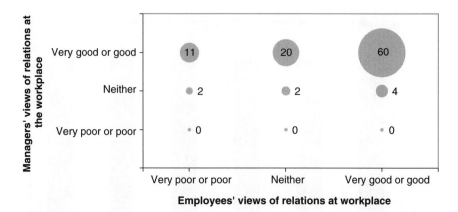

Figure 8.3 *Employees' views of relations at the workplace by managers' views, 2011, per cent*

Base: All employees in workplaces with five or more employees. Figures are based on responses from 21,816 employees.

The manufacturing sector saw a significant improvement in the employment relations climate between 2004 and 2011. The proportion of managers in manufacturing who rated relations with employees as 'Very good' or 'Good' increased from 85 per cent in 2004 to 98 per cent in 2011. More employees in this sector also rated relations with managers as positive, increasing from 50 per cent to 57 per cent. The climate was also more likely to be viewed positively by employees in 2011 in Wholesale and retail (72 per cent of employees gave a positive rating compared to 67 per cent in 2004). More generally, there were improved relations from the employees' perspective in medium and large private enterprises. In medium private enterprises 71 per cent of employees had a positive view of relations with managers in 2011, an increase from 64 per cent in 2004; and in large private enterprises there was a rise from 58 per cent to 63 per cent. There was no significant change from the employees' perspective in small workplaces, but a consistent WERS finding is that the smaller the workplace, the greater the proportion of employees who have a positive view (Kersley et al., 2006: 280). In 2011, 82 per cent of employees in workplaces with five to nine employees provided a positive rating.

Despite the increase in industrial action in the public sector between 2004 and 2011, there was no difference between these discrete time points in managers' and employees' ratings in these workplaces. The proportion of public sector employees that viewed relations with managers positively remained stable at 57 per cent in 2004 and 2011. However, the proportion of private sector employees who rated positive relations with managers increased from 64 per cent to 67 per cent. Among union members, there was a slight increase from 50 per cent in 2004 to 52 per cent in 2011 but this was not significant; in contrast, among non-members there was a significant increase in those reporting good relations from 67 per cent to 70 per cent.

Managers' and Employee Representatives' Relations

In those workplaces where there were union or non-union representatives present, the most senior representatives were asked to rate the relationship with managers. In 2011, 79 per cent of employee representatives described relations with managers as 'Very good' or 'Good', with little change since 2004 (see Figure 8.2). Non-union representatives were more likely to be positive than union representatives, 89 per cent described relations as 'Very good' compared with 72 per cent of their union counterparts. This has been a consistent finding in the WERS series (Kersley et al., 2006: 168). However, non-union representatives' views have worsened a little over time, as in 2004 95 per cent viewed relations with managers as positive.

We may expect the workplace relations climate to differ between workplaces with employee representatives and those without. Using the 1998 WERS Bryson (2005) found no adverse union effect on managers' perceptions of the climate but poorer perceptions among employees where a lay union representative was present; and considered that one possible explanation of poorer employee views was 'a by-product of union effectiveness in holding employers to account' (2005: 1129). This no longer appears to be the case for managers. In 2011 managers in workplaces without on-site representatives were more likely to describe the climate as 'Very good' or 'Good' – 97 per cent compared with 90 per cent of managers in workplaces with on-site representatives (Figure 8.4).

In common with the findings of Bryson (2005), we find that in workplaces where employee representatives are present, employees were less likely to report positive perceptions of the climate: only 57 per cent of employees in workplaces with an on-site representative described relations with managers as 'Very good' or 'Good' compared with 72 per cent of employees who do not have a representative on site. Representatives on the other hand, tend to be generally more positive than the average employee. This may be because they are influenced by their 'insider's view' of their working relationship with management and understand the constraints management are working under; or they feel inclined to rate the climate more positively (as do managers) because they are partly responsible for it.

Trust between managers and employee representatives

The quality of the relationship between managers and employee representatives can determine the legitimacy of the representative's role in the workplace (Kersley et al., 2006: 168–75). Collaborative working is one important element of the relationship and Chapter 4 examined the extent to which managers involve employee representatives with change at the workplace. The level of trust between managers and representatives is an important foundation for collaborative working and, ultimately, the quality of the relationship. Both managers and employee representatives were asked for their level of agreement as to whether the other party 'Can be trusted to act with honesty and integrity in dealings' with them – managers were asked separately for union and non-union representatives.

In 2011, four in five (80 per cent) workplace managers either strongly agreed or agreed that union representatives at their workplace could be trusted to act with honesty and integrity. On the other hand, only two thirds (66 per cent) of senior

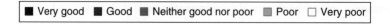

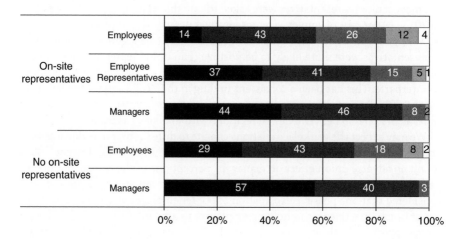

Figure 8.4 *The employee relations climate by the presence of on-site employee representatives, 2011, row per cent*

Note: The figures for employee representatives include 72 who were not on site.

Base: All workplaces with five or more employees. Figures are based on responses from 12,329 employees in row one and 9,405 in row four; 990 employee representatives in row two; and 1,218 workplace managers in row three and 1,440 in row five.

union representatives judged that they could trust managers at their workplace. Furthermore, 7 per cent of managers and 15 per cent of union representatives did not agree that the other party could be trusted to act with honesty and integrity. Levels of trust were higher between managers and non-union representatives. The vast majority – 92 per cent of managers and 93 per cent of senior non-union representatives – trusted the other to act with honesty and integrity in their dealings.

Comparing viewpoints within the same workplace we found that, in 55 per cent of workplaces where union representatives were present, both the manager and representative trusted each other. In a further 12 per cent the manager trusted the union representative but the feeling was not mutual. In contrast, in 85 per cent of workplaces with non-union representatives, there was mutual trust between the representative and manager. The situation was not significantly different from 2004, when mutual trust among union representatives and managers existed in 58 per cent of workplaces and in 81 per cent of workplaces with non-union representatives.

Engagement in the Workplace

For some time employment relations commentators and practitioners have been occupied with the idea of managerial practices that increase employees' involvement not only in their jobs but the wider workplace. The concept, widely defined,

Table 8.6 *Employees' organisational commitment and engagement, 2004 and 2011, cell per cent*

	Public sector	Private manufacturing	Private services	All employees
Agree: 'I feel loyal to my organisation'				
2004	70	66	72	71
2011	72	72	77	75
Agree: 'I share many of the values of my organisation'				
2004	60	44	57	55
2011	65	56	67	65
Agree: 'I am proud to tell people who I work for'				
2004	59	53	63	61
2011	65	63	70	68
Agree: 'Using my own initiative I carry out tasks that are not required as part of my job'				
2011	70	68	72	71

Base: All employees from workplaces with five or more employees. Figures are based on responses from at least 21,515 (2004) and 21,570 (2011) employees.

encompasses discussion of 'high involvement management' (HIM) and somewhat more recently 'employee engagement' (see MacLeod and Clarke, 2009; Rayton et al., 2012). The expected outcome of such practices is better employee performance. This leads us to ask whether the quality of employment relations at the workplace, including the level of discontent, impact on employees' levels of commitment and engagement at work.

Since the first employee survey in the 1998 WERS, employees' commitment to their organisation has been measured by asking their level of agreement with the following statements: 'I feel loyal to the organisation', 'I share many of the values of my organisation' and 'I am proud to tell people who I work for'. However, in an attempt to assess the tangible outcomes of an employee's attachment to the workplace, a new question was added in 2011 asking employees whether they agreed or disagreed with the statement, 'Using my own initiative I carry out tasks that are not required as part of my job' – almost three quarters (71 per cent) of employees agreed with this statement (Table 8.6). In the following we refer to the first three items as measures of commitment and the fourth as the engagement measure.

Between 2004 and 2011 there were increases in the proportions of employees reporting organisational commitment across all three measures. In 2011 three quarters of employees strongly agreed or agreed that they feel loyal to their organisation, a rise from 71 per cent in 2004 (Table 8.6). Loyalty is the aspect most commonly reported by employees, but there were larger rises in the other two measures. The proportion of employees who shared the values of their organisation rose from 55 per cent to 65 per cent and the proportion who were proud to tell people who they work for rose from 61 per cent to 68 per cent.

Increases in commitment between 2004 and 2011 were observed across the board, with the exception of the minor increase in public sector employees reporting loyalty to their organisation where the change was not statistically significant (Table 8.6). In terms of levels of organisational pride and loyalty, manufacturing employees were below public sector employees in 2004, but by 2011 employee commitment in the manufacturing sector as measured by these indicators, was on a par with the public sector. However, commitment was highest of all in 2011 among employees in private services.

A regression analysis was undertaken in 2011 for each of the three measures of commitment in order to determine the workplace and employee characteristics that influenced levels of commitment among employees.[11] Commitment tended to be higher in smaller workplaces. It was also higher in smaller organisations: for instance, in small private enterprises (with fewer than 50 employees) 84 per cent of employees felt loyal to their organisation; in medium enterprises (50–249 employees) it was 77 per cent; and in large private enterprises (with 250 or more employees) only 73 per cent.

Commitment was also higher among women than men, and higher among older employees than among younger workers, after other personal, job and workplace characteristics had been controlled for. For example, in 2011, 78 per cent of female employees agreed that they felt loyal to their organisation compared with 71 per cent of male employees. Tenure had a separate positive association with levels of commitment, after accounting for the age of the worker. Commitment was lower among employees with higher academic qualifications.

An equivalent regression analysis was conducted for the measure of initiative and, here, there was also a positive association with the age of the employee but, in contrast to the aforementioned findings on commitment, there was also a positive association between initiative and the employees' academic qualification level.[12] Finally, there was a positive association with working hours, such that those working less than 40 hours per week were least likely to say they initiated additional tasks and those working 48 hours per week were most likely to do so.

There was a strong indication that employees' experience of the recession may have affected levels of commitment. For all three measures of commitment, there was a negative relationship with the number of recession-related changes that the employee had personally experienced (see Table 2.5 for the list of items).[13] To illustrate, in 2011, 59 per cent of employees who experienced four or more changes as a result of the recession 'Strongly agreed' or 'Agreed' that they felt loyal to their organisation, compared with 82 per cent of employees who experienced no changes. The association with the engagement measure was weaker, but positive, such that employees who had experienced some change to their employment in response to the recession were more likely to agree that they used their initiative to undertake extra tasks. It is possible that the change that employees experienced as a result of the recession engendered them to look beyond their roles to respond to the challenges faced by the workplace. There could be several motivations here, one being a concern for their job security and a desire to make themselves indispensable to the workplace.

A key concern, given the content of the chapter, is whether the level of conflict or levels of discontent in the workplace, and the overall climate of relations have an impact on employees' commitment and engagement. Table 8.7 shows that, in general in 2011, commitment was lower in workplaces where conflict had been manifest. One exception was the proportion of employees who agreed that they

Table 8.7 *Factors influencing employee commitment and engagement, 2011, cell per cent*

	Industrial action		Individual grievance		Disciplinary sanctions		Employees' views of relations with managers	
	Yes	No	Yes	No	Yes	No	Poor	Good
'I feel loyal to my organisation'								
Agree	69	76	73	79	73	80	41	88
Disagree	11	7	9	6	9	5	31	2
'I share many of the values of my organisation'								
Agree	65	65	64	67	63	70	34	78
Disagree	8	8	8	7	8	6	28	3
'I am proud to tell people who I work for'								
Agree	63	69	67	70	66	73	30	83
Disagree	12	9	10	8	10	6	36	2
'Using my own initiative I carry out tasks that are not required as part of my job'								
Agree	71	71	70	73	70	74	65	74
Disagree	9	9	10	8	10	6	14	8

Notes: The measure of individual grievances is those raised through a procedure or not.
Base: All employees in workplaces with five or more employees. Figures are based on responses from at least 21,055 employees.

shared the values of their organisation, which did not differ depending on whether or not industrial action had taken place.

When measures of conflict and the employee's own rating of climate were added to the regression models of commitment discussed earlier, the occurrence of industrial action at the workplace within the previous 12 months had a significant and negative influence on employees' loyalty to their organisation and whether they were proud to say whom they worked for, though not on whether they shared the values of their organisation. It is possible that this last measure of commitment is more heavily influenced by the type of industry that the employee is working in, rather than by the local situation in which they are carrying out their work. Employees in Education, Health and Other community services were the most likely to report sharing the values of their organisation after controlling for other factors.[14]

Table 8.7 also shows the value of moving beyond indicators of conflict to consider employees' overall evaluation of the climate of employment relations at the workplace, as this has the strongest association with levels of commitment. As Table 8.7 shows, among employees who rated relations with managers poorly, around one third disagreed with each of the three commitment measures, compared with fewer than 1 in 20 employees who thought relations were good.

The relationships between indicators of conflict and the measure of engagement are weaker. Two thirds (65 per cent) of employees who rated their workplace climate as poor agreed that they used their initiative to carry out tasks that were not required as part of their job; this compared with three quarters (74 per cent) of employees who rated it as good. When the various indicators of conflict were entered into a regression model of the engagement measure, the indicators of industrial action, grievances and disciplinary actions were not statistically significant. The climate indicator was statistically significant, but the association was weaker than in the regression models of the three commitment measures. The quality of relations between managers and employees in the workplace does therefore appear to influence an employee's attachment to their employer and to their job, but the impact varies depending on how that attachment is measured. In particular, the results discussed here suggest that, while the quality of employment relations may strongly affect the employee's feelings towards their employing organisation, and their willingness to stay with it, there may be a much less negative influence on employees' job performance.

CONCLUSION

The quality of employment relations in the workplace is interconnected with the employee's experience at work and how the workplace functions as a whole. Conflict and discontent is an important aspect of this relationship. Over the last three decades Britain has seen a rapid decline in collective conflict and a similarly rapid increase in individual disputes. However, despite the challenging circumstances that have faced employers and employees more recently, there has not been a widespread deterioration in the quality of employment relations. This chapter has explored the state of conflict in the workplace and the extent to which the recessionary climate may or may not have spurred a rise in workplace discontent.

The most notable change in conflict between 2004 and 2011 was the increase in industrial action, and in balloting, in the public sector. The incidence of industrial action was greater in the public sector than in the private sector in 2011, and more widespread in workplaces where managers had taken actions in response to the recession, particularly where the latter related to wage restraints. Grievances and disciplinary sanctions were also more widespread in workplaces where more negative impacts of the recession were reported. This indicates that, at least on some measures, the recession did bring about a heightened state of conflict in Britain's workplaces. Other measures, such as absence and voluntary resignations, can only be taken as a partial reflection of discontent at work. It is interesting to note that the level of workplaces reporting such resignations fell when comparing 2004 and 2011. This may reflect reluctance among some employees to leave their jobs in an uncertain economic climate.

While it is possible that some expressions of conflict may have been suppressed by economic conditions, overall employees' summary ratings of the climate of employment relations at the workplace maintained the stable and high rates established in the 1990s. The proportion of employees reporting organisational commitment also rose. There were some caveats. Again where the recession had impacted negatively on the workplace, this rise in commitment was less pronounced, and was also notably lower where employees viewed the relations with managers as poor. And in the public sector, improvements in levels of commitment were smaller than those seen in the private sector, and there was no improvement in the proportion of all employees rating the climate of the workplace positively. Equally, this overall picture of stability in relations at work should not disguise the fact that there were some signs of increased conflict beyond the rise in public sector strikes. One notable change was the increase in the proportion of workplaces issuing disciplinary sanctions for poor performance.

At the same time, the further extension of workplace dispute resolution procedures are likely to have prevented some instances of conflict from escalating further than they did. The 2011 WERS observed a decline in the proportion of all workplaces with collective disputes procedures, but increases in the proportions with grievance and disciplinary procedures. The formalisation of individual disputes has been a key feature of the employment relations landscape over the past decade and the period between 2004 and 2011 saw a continuation of this trend. Moreover, there were increases in the proportions of workplaces following the three steps laid out in the Acas Code of Practice on Disciplinary and Grievance Procedures. Further analysis is needed to establish the extent to which this approach is helping to resolve conflict within the workplace; in particular, to understand the role that such procedures may play in giving proper expression to discontent at work so that the employment relationship is not permanently impaired for either party when disputes arise.

9 The Impact of Recession

INTRODUCTION

The impact of the recession has been a prominent theme in each of the preceding chapters. Chapter 2 began by assessing what it means for workplaces to be in the 'shadow of recession'. It identified the types of workplaces that were affected by recessionary pressures, and presented descriptive analysis of the actions managers said they had taken in response. Chapters 3–8 then drew back from this concerted focus on the recession to consider changes in various features of employment relations between 2004 and 2011. In doing so, these chapters made explicit attempts to investigate whether the recession had played a part in influencing employers' practices or employees' experiences over this period, but only as part of a broader narrative. The present chapter draws the focus in again to further explore the direct impact of the recession on workplaces and their employees.

The chapter first seeks to identify the types of employees who were most likely to have their employment conditions altered when managers sought to respond to recessionary pressures. Chapter 2 identified the overall proportions of employees who reported that their employment conditions had changed because of the recession, and also pointed to some differences in exposure between groups of employees – men were more likely to have seen changes to their employment conditions than women for example (see Tables 2.4 and 2.5). Subsequent chapters then explored employees' experiences of specific changes (see, for example, the discussion of pay freezes and cuts in Chapter 5, or the discussion of work intensification in Chapter 6). The present chapter goes further by looking cumulatively at the number of changes that employees experienced as a result of the recession. It also examines the extent to which employees' experiences were determined by the workplace (or industry or region) in which they were located or by factors which differentiated employees within the same workplace, such as the job they were doing.

The second broad question covered in this chapter is whether there were specific aspects of a workplace's approach to employment relations that improved its ability to cope with the recession. Chapter 2 showed that, among those workplaces that were similarly affected by recessionary pressures, there were often divergent outcomes, with some workplace managers saying that the workplace had been weakened by the recession and others saying that it had not (see p. 23). The industry and market in which the employer operated can be expected to have played some role in determining the fate of the workplace, as some industries recovered better than others. But the actions taken by workplace managers may also have played an important role, as might the employment relations structures and practices present at the workplace. In fact, the chapter goes on to show that both were influential in determining how well the workplace coped with recession, although the particular actions and practices that were important varied between the private and public sectors.

EMPLOYEES' EXPERIENCE OF RECESSION

As noted in Chapter 2, respondents to the 2011 employee survey were asked whether they had experienced any of a list of nine changes to their employment conditions as a result of the recent recession while at their current workplace.[1] Three fifths (60 per cent) of those employees who were present at their current workplace at the time identified at least one change to their job which they attributed to the recession. Common changes included a wage cut or freeze (32 per cent), an increase in workload (28 per cent) or some reorganisation of their work (19 per cent). As these figures begin to imply, a substantial minority of employees had experienced more than one change to their employment conditions. Indeed, over one third (35 per cent) of employees had experienced two or more of the changes listed on the questionnaire, with 8 per cent experiencing four or more (Table 9.1). The average number of changes experienced by an individual employee was 1.3. Public sector employees were significantly more likely to report such changes than their private sector counterparts. Overall 73 per cent of public sector employees reported at least one change, 47 per cent reported two or more and 14 per cent reported four or more changes. In contrast, 55 per cent of private sector employees reported at least one change, 31 per cent reported two or more and 6 per cent reported four or more. The average number of changes experienced by a private sector employee was 1.1, compared with 1.7 in the public sector.

Table 9.1 *Number of changes to employees' working conditions as a result of recession, 2011, mean and column per cent*

	Private sector	Public sector	All employees
Number of changes (%)			
None	45	27	40
One	24	26	24
Two	16	19	17
Three	9	14	10
Four or more	6	14	8
Mean (from a possible nine)	1.1	1.7	1.3

Notes: See Table 2.5 for the frequency of specific changes.
Base: Employees who were present in the workplace (with five or more employees) at the time of the recession. Figures are based on responses from 11,470 private sector and 7,598 public sector employees.

This variation in employees' experiences could have a variety of different causes. They may be explained by the workplace in which the employee was located. One obvious reason is that workplaces that were more severely affected by the recession could be expected to have made more drastic changes to employment conditions than workplaces that were less affected. However, there may also be other reasons to expect variations. Terms and conditions vary a great deal across workplaces, leading employees to report very different problems with their working arrangements (Bryson and Freeman, 2013). This may reflect the fact that workplaces are managed in different ways (Bloom et al., 2011a). Accordingly, one might expect some workplace managers to seek to respond to recessionary pressures by bearing down on labour costs, while others seek alternative solutions.

A further possible reason for variation between employees could be that those within the same workplace were treated differently. For example, employees paid on an hourly basis may have seen their access to paid overtime restricted while those in salaried positions may have received an increase in workload. Equally, employees' own characteristics may have been important, with some groups of employees being better able to resist unwelcome changes to their terms and conditions if, for example, they were protected by a trade union or had greater bargaining power than other employees by virtue of attributes such as high skills or education.

In order to identify the importance of these various factors, multivariate models were estimated separately for employees in the private and public sectors to explore the independent associations between employee, job and workplace characteristics, and the number of changes that each employee experienced to their employment conditions as a result of the recession. In summary, the workplace in which the employee was located was an important factor in determining employees' experiences; however, there was also variation within the workplace. Some of this could be explained by the type of job the employee was doing; in the public sector, for example, those in managerial occupations experienced more changes to their employment conditions than those in non-managerial jobs. However, some variations could not be explained by observable features of the job or workplace. Employees with a disability experienced more changes than non-disabled employees, after controlling for other factors.[2] Men also experienced more changes than women: a finding which complements research on the state of the external labour market showing that men have seen weaker net employment growth than women since the onset of recession (Philpott, 2012).

The regression analysis was based on employees who were employed at the sampled workplace at the time of the recession (as in Table 9.1) and controlled for a wide range of factors. In terms of employees' demographic characteristics, the analysis included variables to identify the employee's gender, age, ethnicity, marital status, disability, academic qualifications and union membership status. In terms of their job characteristics, it included their occupation, usual hours, hourly pay, contract type, and the indices of job demands, job control and supportive management outlined in Box 6.1. In respect of the workplace, it included workplace size (number of employees), age, whether the workplace was part of a larger organisation, whether it recognised trade unions, the region in which it was located, its industry sector and how adversely the workplace manager said the workplace had been affected by recession.[3] With one or two exceptions, associations between employee, job and workplace characteristics and the number of enforced changes to working conditions were similar across the public and private sectors, although the exceptions are notable and are discussed further.

The analysis was first conducted using the standard method of ordinary least squares regression which enabled us, in particular, to examine the importance of workplace characteristics. The models performed well, accounting for one fifth (21 per cent) of the variability in employee responses in the private sector and one quarter (27 per cent) of the variability in employee responses in the public sector.

The number of changes that an employee experienced was positively associated with the extent to which the workplace manager said the workplace had been adversely affected by the recession, after controlling for other factors. This was the case in both the public and private sectors. However, the relationship between employee experiences and whether the manager thought the workplace was weaker as a result of the recession were quite different in the public and private sectors. In the private sector, employees reported more changes to their terms and conditions where the workplace was weaker as a result of the recession. In the public sector, on the other hand, employees reported more changes in workplaces that were less likely to have been weakened by recession. One possible interpretation is that the downturn may have permitted managers to push through changes to employees' terms and conditions which led to an improvement in the overall health of those public sector workplaces.

After controlling for the extent of the workplace's exposure to the recession, some other workplace characteristics remained informative about the employee's experience. Looking first at variations by industry, in the public sector it was employees in Public administration who reported the most changes to their working conditions after controlling for the other factors. Earlier models indicated that, in the private sector, employees in Construction reported the most changes to their working conditions but that effect disappeared after controlling for the other factors. Regional variations were also apparent, with employees in Wales reporting the fewest recession-induced changes in the private sector, while employees in the North East reported the fewest changes in the public sector. Working in a multi-site organisation was associated with more changes, but only in the private sector. Neither trade union recognition in the private sector nor union density in the public sector were associated with the number of changes that the employee experienced, perhaps indicating an inability of unions to block or limit managerial actions in response to recession.

In order to examine the importance of employee and job characteristics, the analysis switched to an approach in which the workplace characteristics were replaced with a single identifier for the workplace in which each employee was located. Employees from the same workplace necessarily have the same workplace identifier. Including these in the regression model isolates and removes any part of the employee experience which is determined by the workplace in which they are located (that is, the 'fixed' effect of the workplace which is common to all employees who work there). The regression model is then able to identify those employee and job characteristics which are associated, on average, with differences in experience between employees within the same workplace.[4] These fixed-effects models accounted for two fifths of the variability in employee responses (43 per cent in the private sector and 41 per cent in the public sector). These are higher than the equivalent figures for the standard models, further indicating that the workplace in which the employee is located accounts for a substantial part of their experience of the recession.

A number of employees' demographic characteristics were significantly associated with the extent to which their terms and conditions were subject to change as a result of the recession. These effects were broadly similar across the public and private sectors. Men reported more changes to their working conditions as a result of the recession than women after controlling for other factors. Employees aged between 30 and 39 years also bore the brunt of the changes, with younger and older employees less likely to report recession-induced changes to their jobs. The number of changes reported was also greater among those with higher academic qualifications. The only demographic characteristics that were not clearly associated with recession-induced changes to working conditions were disability, ethnicity and marital status.

Turning to job characteristics, the occupation in which the employee worked was important. In the public sector, those in managerial occupations stood out as reporting the largest number of enforced changes. In the private sector, it was Process, plant and machine operatives and employees in Elementary occupations who were most notable, but here it was because they experienced the fewest changes.

Another job characteristic that was associated with the number of changes was contract type, with employees on permanent contracts in both the public and private sectors more likely than those on fixed-term contracts to report having their employment conditions changed as a result of the recession.

Other job characteristics were included in the analysis but one must be cautious about interpreting any associations because of the possibility that they may partly indicate the effect of any recession-induced changes. For instance, the number of recession-induced changes to terms and conditions was higher among workers with lower job autonomy and among those with higher job demands. But this may at least partly indicate that recession led to a reduction in autonomy for some employees and an increase in workload for others. One therefore has to be cautious in inferring that those employees with lower-than-average autonomy or higher-than-average job demands *prior to the recession* were necessarily more likely to experience changes during the recession, although this is possible.

Similarly, while employees who gave their managers higher ratings on the supportive management index (used in Chapters 6 and 7) reported fewer changes to their job as a result of the recession, it is possible that the number of changes they experienced informed their rating to some extent. The alternative explanation – which is also plausible – is that workplaces in which managers had a more supportive management style were less likely to make changes to employees' terms and conditions, perhaps because they were able to find other ways of dealing with the recessionary shock.

In summary, managers made a number of changes to employees' terms and conditions as a result of the recession. The majority of employees reported experiencing at least one type of change, and many of those who were affected reported multiple changes to their working conditions. The extent to which employees were subject to these changes depended to a considerable extent on the particular workplace in which they were located. Part of this variability between workplaces was accounted for by the differential impact that the recession had on workplaces, but an additional component was explained by other attributes such as their industry sector and location. Looking within workplaces, part of the variation in experiences between different types of employees could be explained by the occupation they worked in, or other facets of their jobs. But employee characteristics were also found to be important, even after controlling for other factors, with the number of changes that employees experienced being higher among men, employees aged 30–39 years, employees with a disability and those with higher academic qualifications. It appears that the recession did not affect employees equally, even after accounting for the job they were doing and the workplace in which they were doing it.

WHICH WORKPLACES WERE WEAKENED BY THE RECESSION AND DID MANAGERS MAKE A DIFFERENCE?

At the time of the 2011 WERS, the economy had been in a depressed state for three to four years and there was little prospect of a return to sustained economic growth (see Chapter 1). Against this backdrop, managers were asked to reflect on how the workplace had weathered the storm by stating how much they agreed or disagreed with the statement, 'This workplace is now weaker as a result of its experience during the recent recession'. This second part of the chapter considers whether there were specific aspects of the approach to employment relations within a workplace that either improved or reduced its ability to cope with the recession.

The analysis uses the panel of workplaces that were surveyed in both 2004 and 2011 to explore the links between the workplace's characteristics and employment practices *prior to* the recession (that is, those observed in 2004), those actions that managers took *during* the recession (that is, over the period 2008–11), and the workplace's state of health at the end of this period (that is, whether it was considered in 2011 to have been weakened by its experience of recession).

Around one fifth (21 per cent) of workplace managers in the panel either strongly agreed or agreed in 2011 that the workplace was weaker as a result of its experience during the recession, whereas over half (56 per cent) either strongly disagreed or disagreed (Figure 9.1).

The workplace characteristics in 2004 did not prove to be particularly informative in Chapter 2 when attempting to discern which types of workplaces were most exposed to the effects of the recession (see p. 17). This also proved to be the case here when attempting to identify which types of workplaces coped best with recession in the public sector, as discussed later in this section. However, workplace characteristics did prove to be informative in determining how private sector workplaces coped with recession. In summary, private sector workplaces were less likely to have

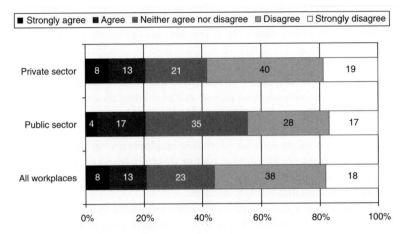

Figure 9.1 *Continuing workplaces: 'This workplace is now weaker as a result of its experience during the recent recession', 2011, row per cent*

Base: Workplaces with five or more employees that were surveyed in both 2004 and 2011. Figures are based on responses from 649 private sector and 334 public sector workplace managers.

been weakened by recession if there was already a good climate of employment relations and if they already used flexible working arrangements (either functional flexibility or numerical flexibility). They were also less likely to have been weakened by recession if they introduced performance-related pay or introduced new initiatives to involve employees in the workplace. Recognising a trade union did not affect private sector workplaces' chances of coping with the recession.

The more detailed results from the analysis are discussed further, taking the private and public sectors separately.

Which private sector workplaces were weakened by recession?

As outlined earlier, the analysis sought to assess whether it was possible to identify the extent to which a workplace would be weakened by recession by looking at its characteristics and employment practices *prior to* the recession (that is, those observed in 2004), and at the actions that managers took *during* the recession (that is, over the period 2008–11).

The analysis first focused on the influence of the workplace's characteristics and practices prior to the recession. A multivariate analysis was conducted in which a wide range of data items that had been collected on the workplace in the 2004 WERS were entered into a regression of whether the workplace was weaker as a result of the recession (see the first bar of Figure 9.1). Some of the variables entered into the regression sought to capture various basic characteristics of the workplace, namely its size (number of employees), the industry and region in which it was operating, whether it was part of a larger organisation, and whether it was foreign-owned. The remaining variables sought to capture various features of the workplace's approach to employment relations in 2004. Some captured the presence of specific arrangements, namely whether the workplace recognised trade unions, had arrangements for direct consultation with employees, had a strategic business plan with an employee focus, paid some employees by results, operated an employee share plan, had arrangements for numerical or functional flexibility, or provided off-the-job training to most of the experienced employees in the largest occupation at the workplace. Other variables sought to gauge the less explicit elements of a workplace's approach to employment relations by using the responses to evaluative questions asked of the workplace manager in 2004, namely whether managers had good relations with employees at the workplace, whether managers preferred direct consultation to consultation via a trade union, whether employees were led to expect long-term employment, whether managers made decisions without consulting employees, whether employees said they carried out tasks not required as part of their job, whether employees shared the values of the organisation, and whether managers reported that employees sometimes tried to take unfair advantage of them.

This full set of workplace characteristics and employment practices from 2004 accounted for around one third (31 per cent) of the variability in whether the workplace was weakened by its experience of the recession. The statistically significant associations are presented in Table 9.2, having also controlled for the workplace's

Table 9.2 Private sector workplaces weakened by recession, 2004–11, multivariate analysis

	Weakened by recession
Workplace characteristics in 2004	
Financial performance at or below industry average	+
Organisation size (ref: 5–50 employees)	
50–249 employees	–
250 or more employees	~
Largest occupational group (ref: Elementary occupations)	
Administrative and secretarial	–
Sales and customer service	–
Employment relations practices in 2004	
Workplace manager rates relationship with employees as 'Very good'	–
Workplace manager 'Strongly disagrees' that employees sometimes try to take unfair advantage of management	–
Workplace manager 'Strongly agrees' that changes are not introduced without first discussing with employees	+
Workplace has one or more types of numerical flexibility (excluding part-time work)	–
Functional flexibility: Some employees in largest occupation at the workplace are trained to do other jobs	–
Profit-related pay scheme for any employees	–
Merit pay for any employees	+
Proportion of variability in managers' responses accounted for by the model (R^2)	0.44

Notes: Ordinary least squares regression model where positive effects indicate stronger agreement with the statement, 'This workplace is now weaker as a result of its experience during the recent recession'. '~' is used to identify differences that are not statistically significant. Other control variables are discussed in the text.
Base: Private sector workplaces with five or more employees surveyed in both 2004 and 2011. Figures are based on responses from 561 workplace managers.

exposure to the recession so as to account for differences between workplaces in the strength of the recessionary shock. There was a strong positive link between exposure to the recession and being weakened by it that accounted for another 13 per cent of the variability. To simplify the presentation, '+' is used to indicate that workplaces with the specified characteristic or practice were more likely to be weakened by recession, '−' is used to indicate the reverse and '~' is used to identify differences that are not statistically significant.

Workplaces with financial performance at or below the average for their industry in 2004 were significantly more likely to say they had been weakened by the recession in 2011. This finding – that recessions can be particularly damaging for workplaces in a weaker financial position – is consistent with the common contention that recessions select the strong and winnow out the weak in a process akin to natural selection.

Workplaces belonging to small firms (those with fewer than 50 employees) were also significantly more likely to report being weakened by recession than workplaces belonging to medium-sized organisations (those with up to 249 employees). This indicates that smaller firms find it harder to cope with any given recessionary shock and is consistent with the idea that larger firms have more resources on which to draw in combating recessionary pressures, even if the managerial challenge can be more complex for larger employers.

Beyond this, few workplace characteristics were informative about the workplace's experience of recession, with the exception of some regional differences. In particular, there were no statistically significant variations between workplaces in different industry sectors once the workplace's exposure to the recession had been controlled for. However there were significant variations between workplaces with different types of core staff. Workplaces in which the largest occupation at the workplace comprised employees from Elementary occupations were more likely to be weakened by the recession than workplaces in which the largest occupation was of a higher skill level.

The same models were run for trading private sector workplaces, in which it was possible to incorporate additional variables capturing the product market conditions faced by the workplace in 2004. The only feature of the product market that was associated with whether the recession had weakened the workplace was the number of competitors faced by the workplace. After controlling for other factors, those workplaces that had many competitors in 2004 (that is, six or more) were significantly more likely to say they had been weakened by the recession than other workplaces. This is further evidence in support of the proposition that recessions have their biggest impact on the fortunes of those facing strong competitive pressures.

The lower part of Table 9.2 shows the significant associations with the workplace's employment practices in 2004. After controlling for other factors, managerial trust in employees in 2004 – as indicated by the workplace manager's opinion of whether employees tried to take unfair advantage of them – was associated with a lower likelihood of being weakened by recession. Similarly, workplaces in which the manager rated the relationship between management and employees as 'Very good' in 2004 were significantly less likely than other workplaces to say they were weakened by the recession. (The effect is not apparent in this model, but it is significant in the identical model controlling for workplace size as opposed to firm size). Together these findings suggest there is a business case for creating a good climate of employment relations. There also appears to be a good case for involving employees in workplace decisions, as those workplaces in which managers strongly agreed that any changes were first discussed with employees were less likely than other workplaces to be weakened by the recession.

Workplaces that deployed their employees in a flexible fashion in 2004 were less likely to be weakened by recession than other workplaces. Functional flexibility – also known as multi-skilling and indicated by training employees in the largest occupation at the workplace to do jobs other than their own – was strongly associated with a lower likelihood of being weakened by the recession. The same was true of a greater use of numerical flexibility – indicated by the number of flexible types of labour deployed at the workplace.[5]

Workplaces with flexible pay systems linking pay to performance could benefit if those systems incentivise workers to deliver greater productivity in spite of recession or if they permit managers to set pay in a more flexible way than might be possible under a fixed wage system. The effects of linking pay to performance varied according to the type of incentive scheme in place. The only payment method associated with a lower probability of being weakened by the recession was the use of a profit-related pay scheme. Perhaps surprisingly, workplaces using merit pay in 2004 (whereby employees' pay is partly determined by the managers' subjective assessment of employees' performance) were more likely to have been weakened by recession than those who had not used it. Neither share ownership schemes nor payments by results (linking employee pay to objectively determined performance) were statistically significant predictors of how the workplace coped with recession.

Having considered the characteristics and employment practices of the workplace prior to the recession, the discussion now moves on to consider actions that workplace managers took during recession. An important part of management is the ability to diagnose and tackle problems which threaten workplace performance and survival. The 2011 WERS distinguishes two types of actions taken by workplaces. The first set comprises those employment-related actions that were taken at the workplace as a direct response to the recession, such as freezing wages or making redundancies. The second set comprises changes that managers had introduced at the workplace in the two years prior to the 2011 survey, including taking initiatives to involve employees, to upgrade technology or to introduce performance-related pay.

The first set comprises actions that were prompted specifically by the recession and which arguably would not have been taken otherwise. The full list of actions taken by managers was presented in Table 2.3 but we first use a summary measure which counts the number of actions that were taken at the workplace. The mean number of actions undertaken by workplaces in the panel was 2.2 (from a possible 14). A simple cross-tabulation showed that private sector workplaces that took more actions towards the employment conditions of their workers were more likely to be weakened by the recession. This association remained after controlling in a regression analysis for the characteristics of the workplace in 2004 (discussed earlier). However, it was apparent in Chapter 2 that the number of actions taken by a workplace was also positively associated with its exposure to the recession, as one might expect. Once the analysis controlled for the extent to which the workplace was affected by the recession (refer to Figure 2.2), the number of actions was no longer associated with the extent to which the workplace was weakened by recession. The number of actions taken by the workplace manager was therefore heavily influenced by the workplace's exposure to the recession but it was not informative in predicting its ability to cope.

When we turn to indicators of specific actions, two were significantly associated with managers saying their workplace was weaker as a result of the recession. These were making compulsory redundancies and requiring employees to take unpaid leave. These are among the actions one would expect employers to resort to *in extremis* and, while we are looking here for actions that protected the workplace from being weakened by recession, neither of them is likely to offer a long-term solution to the problems posed by the downturn.

The second set of actions referred to previously comprise the kinds of changes that workplaces are typically engaged in throughout the economic cycle. Such actions are a response to business needs that arise periodically, such as the need to update equipment or products, or else they are decisions, often long in planning, which signal a change in direction or significant alteration to normal practices, such as a change to the payment system at the workplace. As such the changes are much more likely to have occurred regardless of the recession, although the recession may have had some influence over whether they happened and their timing. Two of the seven changes that workplace managers were asked about related to capital investment (introducing or upgrading new technology and product or service innovation), four were labour-related (changes in working time, work organisation, work techniques or procedures, and employee involvement) and the final one was a change to the compensation system (introduction of performance pay). Elsewhere they have been used as indicators of the innovativeness of the workplace (see Bryson et al., 2009a).

In the private sector, around three quarters (76 per cent) of the panel of workplaces surveyed in both 2004 and 2011 had made at least one of the changes and one fifth (18 per cent) had made at least four of them (Table 9.3). Half (50 per cent) of these workplaces had upgraded or introduced new technology and just under one third (30 per cent) had introduced or significantly improved products or services – a level of investment that underscores Geroski and Gregg's (1997: 90) finding that investment continues to take place even in the depths of recession. Changes in working time arrangements, work organisation and work techniques or procedures were also very common. But it is striking that almost one quarter (23 per cent) of workplaces had introduced initiatives to increase employee involvement. In contrast, the introduction of performance-related pay was uncommon, occurring in 4 per cent of workplaces.

In the private sector, the number of managerial changes was not significantly associated with the degree to which workplaces were adversely affected by recession, in contrast to the actions taken in response to the recession. A mean of 1.8 changes had been instituted in the last two years in workplaces that were adversely affected 'A great deal' by the recession, compared to a mean of 2.1 changes among those workplaces that experienced no adverse effect. This suggests that the actions

Table 9.3 *Management initiated change in the previous two years, 2011, column and cell per cent, respectively*

	Private sector	Public sector	All workplaces
Number of changes			
None	24	15	22
One	17	9	16
Two	22	22	22
Three	19	19	19
Four	9	14	10
Five or more	9	22	11
Type of change introduced			
Introduced performance related pay	4	5	4
Introduced/upgraded technology	50	52	51
Working time arrangements	22	36	24
Organisation of work	34	51	37
Work techniques or procedures	39	58	42
Initiatives to involve employees	23	34	25
New or significantly improved product or service	30	43	33
None of the above	24	15	22

Base: Workplaces with five or more employees that were surveyed in both 2004 and 2011. Figures are based on responses from 649 private sector and 332 public sector workplace managers.

listed in Table 9.3 were not responses to the recession per se but instead serve as indicators of managers' willingness to innovate, whether in good times or bad.

Private sector workplaces that had initiated more changes in the previous two years were less likely to have been weakened by recession and in regression analysis, the number of managerial changes remained negatively associated with being weaker, after controlling for other workplace characteristics. The association was unaffected when also controlling for the degree to which the workplace was adversely affected by the recession. In other words, innovating workplaces appeared to be better able to cope with the effects of the recession. But were specific types of workplace innovation more helpful than others?

Three of the changes listed in Table 9.3 were statistically significant when entered into a regression analysis which controlled for other workplace characteristics. Introducing performance-related pay and introducing initiatives to involve employees were both associated with a lower probability of being weakened by recession, whereas changes in working time arrangements were associated with a greater likelihood of being weakened by recession.[6] All three changes remained statistically significant having controlled for the degree to which the workplace was adversely affected by recession.[7]

The implication is that private sector workplaces that had introduced performance-related pay, and those that had taken steps to increase employee involvement, had protected themselves, to some degree, from the effects of recession. One might argue that only workplaces in a strong enough position to make these changes, and those who perceive them as potentially improving matters, will actually proceed with such changes. In that sense, it is hard to argue that there is a clear causal relationship between instituting such changes and improving the workplace's prospects. That said, the analysis does control for the financial performance of workplaces going into the recession, and it also accounts for the degree to which the manager thought the workplace had been adversely affected by the recession. It is therefore reasonable to suggest that introducing performance pay and initiatives to involve employees may have had some impact on what happened to private sector workplaces in recession, even though we cannot categorically claim that the link is causal.[8]

Weakened by Recession? Public Sector Workplaces

The analyses reported previously were repeated for workplaces in the public sector. The characteristics of public sector workplaces in 2004 and the actions that public sector managers took since the onset of recession were not as influential as they were in the private sector in determining which workplaces were weakened by recession. However, some specific characteristics and actions did emerge as important.

First considering the characteristics of public sector workplaces in 2004, there were some variations between industry sectors and regions, in contrast to the results for the private sector. Workplaces in Education and Transport and communications were significantly more likely than those in Health and social work to report being weakened by recession, while public sector workplaces in London were more likely to have been weakened than those in other regions, after controlling for other factors. Also, public sector workplaces in which the largest occupation at the workplace was comprised of Professional employees were more likely to have been weakened than those in which the largest occupation was Caring, leisure and personal service, or Sales and customer service.

The employment relations practices of the workplace in 2004 tended not to be associated with perceived weakness due to recession, the exception being the type of employment contracts used in the workplace.[9] Workplaces were less likely to have been weakened if managers in 2004 had strongly agreed that employees were led to expect long-term employment. On the other hand, managers were more likely to think the workplace had been weakened by recession if it used flexible employment contracts in 2004.

Chapter 2 showed that public sector workplaces experienced more employment-related changes in direct response to the recession than their private sector counterparts. After controlling for the characteristics of public sector workplaces in 2004, there was a positive association between the number of actions taken and the extent to which managers agreed that the workplace was weaker as a result of the recession. However, this association ceased to be statistically significant after controlling for the degree to which the workplace was adversely affected by recession. So as in the private sector, the number of actions taken by workplace managers was influenced by the workplace's exposure to the recession but it was not informative in predicting the workplace's ability to cope.

When examining the individual actions themselves, four were significantly associated with the extent to which public sector managers agreed that the workplace had been weakened by recession. Postponing plans to expand the workforce, reducing basic hours and reductions in training expenditures were all positively associated with the workplace being weakened by the recession.

Turning to those actions which managers took in the two years prior to the 2011 survey interview, public sector workplaces had again instituted more changes than their private sector counterparts (see Table 9.3). Here more changes were made in workplaces that had been more heavily exposed to the recession. But did these managerial actions and changes affect the fortunes of public sector workplaces as indicated by whether they had been weakened by the recession?

In contrast to the private sector, the introduction of performance-related pay was *positively* associated with a workplace being weakened by the recession. Changes in work organisation, on the other hand, were associated with a lower probability of being weakened by the recession.

Overall, then, the analyses were able to identify fewer specific characteristics or practices which linked to the subsequent fortunes of workplaces in the public sector. This may partly reflect the locus of decision-making in the public sector, whereby the fortunes of particular workplaces may – to a greater extent than in the private sector – be determined by decision-makers higher up in the organisation rather than by the specific characteristics of the workplace itself.

CONCLUSION

This chapter has focused exclusively on the recession as experienced by workplace managers and employees. It sought to extend the introductory analysis presented in Chapter 2 in two specific ways: first by seeking to identify the types of employees who were most likely to have their employment conditions altered when managers sought to respond to recessionary pressures, and second by investigating whether there were specific aspects of the approach to employment relations within a workplace that either improved or reduced its ability to cope with the recession.

The chapter began by investigating employees' experiences of the recession. Chapter 2 showed that the majority of employees had suffered from changes to their terms and conditions as a result of recession, with the effects being most acutely felt in the public sector. The analyses presented in the current chapter showed that the extent to which employees experienced changes to their working conditions could be explained to a large degree by the effects of recession on the workplace in which the employee was located. Nevertheless, differences in employee experiences were apparent within workplaces, and these related in part to employees' demographic characteristics. In particular, employees with a disability experienced more changes than non-disabled employees, after controlling for other factors. Men also experienced more changes than women – a finding which, as noted earlier, complements other evidence that men have found it more difficult than women to find employment through the recession.

Chapter 2 had shown that it was difficult to predict which workplaces would be most exposed to the recession, especially in the private sector. This is consistent with the idea that recessionary shocks have a sizeable random component, as analysts before us have suggested (Geroski and Gregg, 1997). In the present chapter, however, it proved easier to predict which workplaces were weakened by recession. The employment relations characteristics of workplaces in 2004 were significant predictors of whether workplaces were emerging weaker from recession, though which structures and practices mattered varied across the public and private sectors. The actions taken by workplace managers in direct response to recession were not associated with the workplace's subsequent fortunes, after controlling for the extent to which the workplace was exposed to the recession. However, there were strong and independent associations between management's introduction of change during the recession and whether the workplace had been weakened by the recession. In the private sector the introduction of employee involvement initiatives and the introduction of performance-related pay were both associated with a lower likelihood of being weakened by the recession. In the public sector the introduction of performance-related pay was positively associated with a workplace being weakened by the recession whereas changes in work organisation were associated with a lower probability of being weakened by the recession.

10 Conclusion

Britain enjoyed over a decade of sustained economic growth from the mid-1990s. Employment and real earnings were at record highs, skill levels were rising, and working hours were falling. There was evidence of growing wage inequality at the top of the income distribution, but there were indications of a gradual improvement in many aspects of working life.

Following the 2008 financial crisis, however, the British economy endured a sustained period of contraction unparalleled since the depression of the 1930s. Five years on, although employment was above pre-recessionary levels, the timing of any sustained recovery remained uncertain. The challenges posed for employers and management extended to all types of workplaces, and were increasingly intense in the public sector as the Coalition Government sought cuts in public expenditure.

The timing of the 2011 WERS was therefore fortunate as it coincided with the challenges posed by the recession and the actions taken to meet them. The previous survey, in 2004, provides a benchmark by which we can judge how the course of employment relations changed, what role the recession played, and what other factors were important.

Casting one's mind back to 2004, employment relations was characterised by a continuation of the decline in union influence – albeit at a slower pace than in the 1990s – with no great compensation for this through other forms of collective representation. Direct communication with workers was growing, but at the same time there was no consistent trend towards a universal adoption of practices associated with human resources or high involvement management (Wood and Bryson, 2009). Managers' and employees' perceptions of the quality of employment relations were stable and positive, and strikes were extremely rare (Dix et al., 2009; Guest and Bryson, 2009). Differences between the public and private sector remained, especially in the extent and scope of collective bargaining which were considerably higher in the public sector.

During their three terms, the Labour governments did little to reverse the earlier government legislation aimed at reducing the power of the trade unions, but instead instituted measures that focused more on creating fairness and equality for individual workers. Evaluations of the key elements – the minimum wage, equal opportunity provisions, family-friendly practices and statutory union recognition procedures – suggested that the provisions had been successful but the impact on employment relations outcomes was limited. The exception was the minimum wage – fears it would reduce employment or increase inflation were largely allayed, though some profit margins may have been adversely affected (Wood, 2005). Labour market policy concerns centred on increasing participation in the labour market, addressing skills deficiencies, and enhancing the quality and productivity of the workforce.

Virtually no one was offering predictions of the future of employment relations in the mid-2000s, perhaps reflecting a belief that 'more of the same' was the most likely outcome as further substantial changes in legislation were not anticipated. Within the limited speculation that did exist, the Information and Consultation of Employees (ICE) regulations were seen, in some quarters, as a potential source of change when they were first introduced in 2005. In considering the prospects for reversing the decline in unionism, Kelly (2005: 81) suggested the reduced majority of the Labour government in 2005 might give unions more opportunities for political influence. Moreover, tensions between the public sector unions and the government were beginning to surface as public sector reform was identified as a priority of the government.

However, these factors proved to be minor compared to the financial crisis that emerged in 2008. As it transpired, the recession precipitated by this crisis was arguably the most significant event in the period between the 2004 and 2011 WERS surveys. Indeed, the scale and duration of the economic decline experienced from 2008 was unprecedented since the 1930s.

A priority of this book, as with others in the WERS series, is to map the evolution of employment relations in Britain. An underlying theme of the series has always been the continuity and change in institutions and practices of employment relations. This theme is interlocked with the second theme of the book which has been the impact of this recession on workplaces and employees.

The role of the government and government policy also needs to be assessed. Indeed, in the case of the public sector, the government's austerity programme has provided a vital element of the recessionary context. A core aspect of government policy from the 1980s onwards has been to create the conditions in which management has choice over how it conducts its employment relations. The Labour governments of 1997–2010 framed many of their policies in terms of encouraging management to ensure fairness and equality, embrace best practice, and promote employee involvement. But to what extent have these objectives been achieved or have they been thrown off course by the need to respond to the recession?

In this chapter we draw out the main findings reported in this book and their implications for our understanding of developments in employment relations. First, we explore the broader trends in employment relations institutions and practice; we then examine what we have learnt about the role of government policy and the impact of the recession in these broader trends. We then discuss the implications these developments have had on employees' working lives and finally conclude on the role of employment relations in workplaces that have operated in the shadow of an economic recession.

CONTINUITY AND CHANGE IN EMPLOYMENT RELATIONS INSTITUTIONS AND PRACTICE

Most workplaces were adversely affected by the recession in one way or another but, in spite of this, there was no fundamental change in the nature of employment relations institutions or in the way employers deployed labour. The rate of redundancies in 2011 was higher than that seen in 2004, but not substantially so. The rate of workplace closure remained unchanged, and as many as 40 per cent of workplaces that continued in existence between 2004 and 2011 experienced employment growth. There was no marked change in either the private or public sectors in the proportion of workplaces that used part-time workers, or agency workers between 2004 and 2011. There was some increase in the proportion of workplaces using zero hour contracts and annualised hours in the private sector, but their use still remained relatively low. Furthermore, there was no significant increase in the use of functional flexibility (that is, multi-skilling) or widespread extension of flexible family-friendly practices.

Similarly there was continuity in the basic institutions of employee representation. The proportion of all workplaces that recognised a union for negotiating pay and conditions has remained around one fifth. All but a few public sector workplaces still have a recognised union and, as a whole, under half of all employees are in a unionised workplace, as was the case in 2004.

There has been change in collective bargaining, however. In the private sector, the number of items over which managers bargained with unions declined, continuing a trend first noted in the 1998 WERS (Millward et al., 2000; Kersley et al., 2006: 126). In the public sector, the overall scope of bargaining has remained largely unchanged; though there was a decline in bargaining directly with unions. Less than half of public sector employees had their pay determined by collective bargaining, with some of the decline attributable to the increasing prevalence of Pay Review Bodies. Overall, the proportion of employees covered by any form of representation (union or non-union) has remained relatively stable.

Consultation with unions has not filled the space created by the decline of bargaining. And structures for non-union representation have failed to materialise. Although Joint Consultative Committees remain rare in the private sector, the decline noted between 1998 and 2004 (Kersley et al., 2006: 126) appears to have ceased. Nonetheless, it appears more managers were content to directly inform staff, rather than representatives, about change.

The growth in the use of direct communication methods has continued and is now almost ubiquitous. The increasing preference managers have for communicating directly with employees is manifest in the widespread use of briefing methods, either at the workplace or team level. But the use of two-way communication methods which may give employees more of a voice, such as staff surveys and suggestion schemes, has not increased.

One notable change in management practice that was observed was an increase in the use of appraisal. The extent to which appraisal is an opportunity for employees to voice their concerns and increase their involvement in the workplace depends on its purpose and how it is conducted. The range of purposes it can serve, even in the same workplace, include clarifying roles, connecting individuals' goals to the wider organisation's, monitoring performance and identifying training needs. But the significant increase in the linking of pay to appraisal outcomes may reflect that the more dominant purpose is the evaluation of employees rather than their involvement in workplace decisions. This is further supported by the finding that there was an increase in disciplinary sanctions for poor performance in the workplaces using appraisals.

In summary it would seem that, overall, employment relations institutions and practices are not very different in 2011 than they were in 2004. Employment relations continue to be characterised by a low presence of unions in the private sector, increasing direct communication, and limited employee consultation and involvement. Differences between the public and private sectors remain strong although there has been some convergence, with the public sector moving towards the private sector in the form of a reduction in pay bargaining and an increase in direct communication.

GOVERNMENT POLICY AND LEGISLATION

Recent changes in legislation have had limited effects on management practices. After an initial spur for employers to sign voluntary agreements, the statutory union recognition procedure has not had a telling effect on collective bargaining coverage, and certainly not on union membership. Recent union recognition applications have involved public sector unions reapplying for bargaining rights as workplaces have changed ownership as a consequence of contracting out (Moore and McKay, 2013; Wood and Moore, 2004). The ICE regulations appear to have had no real effect on the spread of formal consultation arrangements. This is perhaps attributable to the UK's interpretation of the EU Directive, including the fact that the onus of the legislation is on employees to initiate the development of consultation arrangements (Lorber, 2006; Hall and Purcell, 2012). Equally, following the Labour governments' lead on family-friendly practices, there has not been a widespread increase in flexible working arrangements to help employees balance their work and non-work life. The equality legislation seems though to have encouraged workplaces to have put equality policies in place – with three quarters having them by 2011 – and most of these included the more recent additions to the discrimination legislation of age, religion or belief and sexual orientation. But the prevalence of practices for monitoring equality had changed little since 2004.

Of the Labour government's measures, the minimum wage has probably had the strongest effect. One third of private sector workplaces had regard to the National Minimum Wage in their last pay review, as did one in seven public sector workplaces. The emphasis on improvement in the information and guidance available to employers, particularly through Acas, is perhaps apparent in the increase in dispute procedures. While the effects of pre-1997 legislation remains significant in limiting trade union activity (Pissarides, 2013), the underlying policy emphasis on individual voice has become increasingly pronounced. This is most apparent in the Coalition government's review of employment law in 2013 when it stated, 'In a fair labour market, people have the confidence to ask for changes to their work, or seek new opportunities or even a radical career change' (Department for Business Innovation and Skills, 2013: 15). But there has been no increase in the use of organisational involvement methods aimed at harnessing employees' ideas such as quality circles and suggestions schemes. Although the fastest growing practice, appraisals, may offer individual voice in so far as they are not totally confined to monitoring performance, there is as yet little evidence that they are being used in this fashion. If we take organisational involvement methods as core 'best practice' then on this basis we might conclude that the quality of management has not improved greatly. Nevertheless, there has been an improvement in employee perceptions of management's ability to listen to workers which may reflect an improvement in the quality of management. It may be that it is this aspect of leadership behaviour, which the government and others (such as Acas, and MacLeod and Clarke, 2009) have been attempting to nurture at all levels of organisations, that is improving most. Such behaviours are less readily measurable in large-scale surveys like WERS.

Modern Management in the Public Sector

Government employment relations policies also seem to have had limited direct impact on managerial practices in the public sector. For instance, exhortations and provisions to encourage adoption of flexible family-friendly practices beyond those mandated by the law have not resulted in significantly greater usage in the public sector, although provision has always tended to be more extensive than in the private sector. In spite of greater union presence in the sector and more turbulent employment relations, including a spike in strike action, unions remain constrained by legislation in the same way as they are in the private sector. In the public sector they must also deal with Pay Review Bodies which now sit between them and their members' pay determination.

From the 1980s onwards the marketisation, privatisation and contracting out of public services have been continually on the agenda of public sector policy. These features are a key part of what has sometimes been referred to as the new public sector management. Initially this precipitated speculation that the combined effects of these, coupled with the intensified concern for efficiency in the public sector, would lead to a convergence in employment practice between the public and private sector. The evidence of the 2004 WERS was that the two sectors still had distinct approaches (Kersley et al., 2006: 316). However, according to Bach (2009: 307) some convergence was taking place due to 'the diminished regulatory influence of industry-level collective bargaining, increased responsibility delegated to managers for local employment relations practice and the spread of human resource management techniques'. These forces may have been given added impetus through the increasing pressure on public expenditure which has resulted in austerity measures that are unprecedented in modern times, measures that have sparked strike action in the public sector and increased job insecurity among employees.

One might argue that the austerity programme was embedded in approaches to modernisation that emerged before the recession. A fundamental element of these has been performance management of which appraisals and target setting are the fulcrum. Its development was particularly crucial to the public sector modernisation programme of the second term of the Labour government (2002–07). Seen in this light, appraisals are central to the public sector performance management system. While we cannot identify within WERS the precise form appraisals are taking, in so far as they are increasingly linked to pay and target setting, we may speculate that they are as much about monitoring as anything else. This type of appraisal may have contributed, along with the wage freezes, reorganisations and increased insecurity, to the lower levels of well-being and job satisfaction in the public than the private sector.

THE RECESSION

Most managers said their workplaces had been adversely affected by the recession and for some there were more lasting effects – around one in five workplaces were deemed to be weaker as a result of their experience during the recession. Despite this, some longer-term trends in management practices, such as the increase in direct communication and the use of appraisals did not appear to be affected by these recessionary experiences.

The most immediate and palpable effect of the recession on management practice was through the direct actions taken in response to the recession. Among the three quarters of workplaces that did act, the most common employment relations responses were wage freezes, hiring embargos and changes to work organisation. The prevalence of pay freezes is pronounced, and these have undoubtedly contributed to a decline in real wage growth which was unprecedented in recent British history. There was a private–public sector difference as public sector workplaces were most likely to have taken one or more actions.

The actions taken by managers appear to be primarily aimed at reducing costs. This is consistent with the other evidence from past and current recessions (Geroski and Gregg, 1997; Roche and Teague, 2013). The specific responses to the recession made by employers also seem similar to those reported in the early phase of the Irish recession in that they were pragmatic and 'unlikely to shift the centre of gravity in work and employment practices' (Roche and Teague, 2013: 18).

The employment relations climate and practices prior to the recession both played an important role in how workplaces fared during the recession. Workplaces that had a good employment relations climate and a high trust relationship between managers and employees were less likely than other similar workplaces to be weakened by the recession. Greater use of both numerical and functional flexibility, and profit-sharing – a form of financial flexibility – had similar beneficial effects.

Regardless of the wider economic environment, managers continue to make changes to their employment relations practices, their workforce, and invest in capital and labour. Workplaces that had made such changes in the two years prior to the survey had a greater likelihood of not being weakened by the recession: while these changes were unprompted by the recession itself they did prove beneficial in terms of combating the recession. In the private sector these benefits accrued to those introducing performance-related pay and initiatives to involve employees. In the public sector, on the other hand, the introduction of performance-related pay was associated with a greater likelihood of being weakened by the recession. So clearly, no one type of action was a panacea for all workplaces.

While our analysis has shown that the recession has not fundamentally shifted the employment relations system, we have also been able to test whether the employment relations system is critical to a workplace's ability to weather the storm of the recession. Judged by its impact on whether the workplace was weakened by recession, employment relations – both its climate and specific practices such as employee involvement initiatives – proves to be an important contributor.

There is complementary evidence showing that employment relations matter to how the recession affected workplaces. Among trading workplaces in the private sector, those recognising unions for pay bargaining were significantly less likely than non-unionised workplaces to be adversely affected by the recession. This finding is consistent with other evidence suggesting that unionised workplaces have become more competitive in recent years relative to their non-union counterparts (Blanchflower and Bryson, 2009; Bryson et al., 2013c).

The results may help explain, in part, the unusual shape of the recession, that is, the decline in output not being matched by a decline in employment. The pay freezes observed mean that real pay has been falling, so employers have not been faced with the kind of cost pressures they confronted in previous recessions. Conversely, although we did not ask directly whether managers were hoarding labour, there was little direct evidence that short-time working was a major factor in the recession or that compulsory training or leave during slack periods was widespread.

EMPLOYEES' EXPERIENCE

Despite the recession, there are a number of respects in which employees' welfare appears to have improved since 2004. The proportions of employees that are satisfied in their jobs, including their involvement in workplace decision-making, has increased slightly, while those experiencing job anxiety has fallen. Despite pay freezes, a greater number of employees are reporting pay satisfaction. Several aspects of job quality showed some improvement. These developments are mirrored by the increase in employees who think management is sincere about understanding their views and conscious of their responsibilities outside work. Employees' organisational commitment has also risen and their perceptions of the employment relations climate have also improved slightly.

However, the picture of employees' experiences at work, across the whole economy, masks differences in the public and private sectors. One point of departure was employee satisfaction. A key aspect of satisfaction – that with job security – declined greatly in the public sector between 2004 and 2011. Average levels of satisfaction with pay and the scope to use initiative increased slightly. But, unlike in the private sector, where levels of the other dimensions of job satisfaction rose, these remained unchanged in the public sector. In contrast, changes in well-being, as measured by job-related contentment, were similar in both sectors. It was increasing job insecurity in the public sector that accounted for overall lower levels of job satisfaction and well-being. While job demands increased to a greater extent in the private sector, job demands remained higher in the public sector. These we can take to be manifestations of the recession and austerity measures, and may have contributed to the increase in strikes and ballots for industrial action in the public sector.

Perceptions of managerial quality and support also differed across the two sectors. While positive perceptions of management behaviour were still common-place in the private sector, the proportion of employees with such views was lower in the public sector. Furthermore, the rise in the average perception of supportive management was limited to the private sector.

One might have expected the recession to play a larger role in determining how employees felt about their jobs and working environment than it has. Although overall job satisfaction was not different between workplaces that were more or less adversely affected, satisfaction with pay and job security and well-being levels were nonetheless lower in workplaces most strongly affected by the recession.

THE ROLE OF EMPLOYMENT RELATIONS

The decade before 2004 could be characterised as one in which the economy grew steadily, yet the employment relations landscape was transformed. Since 2004 there has been a reversal: the economy has experienced a great deal of turbulence while the system of employment relations has settled down. What we have seen is a maturation of the employment relations system that evolved from the Conservative government's programme of reform in the 1980s and 1990s. That is, a setting that is largely non-union, which legitimises managers' right to manage, and encourages managers to directly engage with employees. The public sector remains different, of course, in that it remains strongly unionised, but even here there are signs of convergence towards some managerial practices that are well-established in the private sector.

Whether this largely non-union system characterised by direct communication and low-level employee involvement is sustainable in the long-run depends, in part, on whether it satisfies the demands and needs of both employers and employees. This remains to be seen, but the early signs are that, at least in the private sector, employees are more positive about their jobs and their working environment than they were in the early 2000s, a time when the economy was growing. In the public sector, employees' outlooks are dominated by perceptions of job insecurity. Perhaps the true test for this emergent system will be the extent to which it can meet the challenges of economic recovery, for example, the challenges posed by employees seeking to make up for some of the real wage losses they have endured.

Prior to the 1980s, one aim of public policy was to establish the mechanisms for joint regulation by employers and trade unions, under which the economic outcomes were the result of bargaining (Kahn-Freund, 1972). Since the late

1980s, the responsibility for delivering satisfactory economic outcomes through employment relations has fallen on 'the law, governmental policy and administration' (Davies and Freedland, 2007: 249). This is reflected in both the Labour and Coalition governments' 'light touch' approach to employment-related responses to the recession, instead putting their faith in Britain's flexible labour market to minimise the impact of the recession and increase the speed of recovery.

While we have shown that reactions to the recession do not appear to have altered the course of the evolution of employment relations, the specific actions managers took in response have been extensive and had some positive effect on reducing the potential further weakening of workplaces. Rather than helping us to predict the future, the greatest value of our analysis of the recession has been to show that employment relations has played a part in ensuring that many workplaces survived it.

Technical Appendix

INTRODUCTION

The 2011 WERS was the sixth in a series of studies which has mapped the contours of employment relations in Britain over the last 30 years. Previous studies were conducted in 1980, 1984, 1990, 1998 and 2004. The 2011 WERS was sponsored by the Department for Business, Innovation & Skills, the Advisory, Conciliation and Arbitration Service, the Economic and Social Research Council, the UK Commission for Employment and Skills and the National Institute of Economic and Social Research (NIESR). NIESR's involvement was made possible through funding from the Nuffield Foundation. The main objectives of WERS are as follows:

1. To map workplace employment relations in Britain and changes over time.
2. To inform policy development and stimulate and inform debate and practice.
3. To provide a comprehensive and statistically reliable dataset on British workplace employment relations that is made publicly available and easily accessible.

This technical appendix describes the design and conduct of the 2011 WERS. It aims to set out the key features of the 2011 study and to highlight the steps taken to quality assure the stages of data collection and processing. This appendix will begin with an overview of the design of the study, followed by more detailed sections on sample design, questionnaire development, fieldwork procedures, survey response, data coding, editing and quality assurance, weighting and sampling errors. Further technical details on the 2011 WERS are provided in the paper on the design and administration of the study (Forth, 2013).

OVERVIEW OF THE STUDY DESIGN

The survey population for the 2011 WERS was all workplaces in Britain that had five or more employees and were operating in Sections C-S of the Standard Industrial Classification 2007 at the time of the survey (Office for National Statistics, 2009). At the time of the study, this population accounted for 35 per cent of all workplaces and 90 per cent of all employees in Britain. A workplace is defined in WERS as comprising 'the activities of a single employer at a single set of premises'. A branch of a high street bank, a factory, the head office of a large firm and a local council's town hall, for example, are all considered to be workplaces in their own right.

The 2011 WERS had three components:

- Survey of Managers;
- Survey of Worker Representatives; and
- Survey of Employees.

At each participating workplace, the study commenced with an interview with the most senior manager with responsibility for employment relations, human resources or personnel. The manager was asked to provide a demographic profile of the workforce prior to the interview and, if the workplace was in the private sector or a trading public sector corporation, the manager was also asked after the interview to provide financial performance information about the workplace. Permission was also sought from the manager to distribute a self-completion questionnaire to a maximum of 25 employees at the workplace. If a union or non-union employee representative was present, an interview with that representative was sought. If a workplace had both union and non-union representatives, an interview with each was sought. Workplace managers and employee representatives were asked to act primarily as informants about their workplaces, and so the vast majority of the data collected in those interviews related to the features of the sampled workplace rather than to the particular characteristics of the individual respondent. In contrast, the Survey of Employees focused primarily on employees' own characteristics, experiences and attitudes.

The 2011 WERS saw the introduction of a major sample design innovation. The 1984, 1990, 1998 and 2004 WERS had two entirely separate samples. The first was a fresh cross-section sample of workplaces that were surveyed to provide representative results for the population of workplaces in existence at the time of the study. The second was a panel sample which consisted of all participating workplaces from the previous cross-section who remained in existence at the time of the new WERS (for example, surviving workplaces from the 1998 cross-section sample in the case of the 2004 study). The panel sample was used in the primary analyses to assess the extent to which individual workplaces changed their behaviour over time and workplaces in the panel sample were asked to take part in an abridged version of the Survey of Managers only. The samples were always analysed separately. A summary of the design of the two samples of the 2004 WERS is provided in the technical appendix of Kersley et al. (2006).

The sample design innovation of the 2011 WERS was the integration of the fresh cross-section and the panel samples. For the first time in the WERS series, the workplaces in the 2011 panel sample were eligible for all of the three component surveys. This means that many of the 2004–11 panel workplaces have management, employee and worker representative data for both waves (although responses obtained in 2004 and in 2011 were not necessarily from the same individual, nor can individual respondents be matched across waves). In addition, weights have been devised that enable the panel sample to be combined with the fresh sample to form a combined sample that is cross-sectionally representative of all workplaces in 2011. This more than compensates for the smaller size of the fresh sample in 2011 and creates a cross-sectionally representative combined sample that is larger than the cross-section sample that was available in 2004.

THE SAMPLE

The design of the sample of the 2011 WERS had two overarching aims:

1. to obtain interviews at 900 of the 2,295 workplaces that participated in the 2004 Cross-Section Survey; and
2. to obtain interviews at a further 1,800 workplaces from a new (and independent) refreshment sample, which could then be combined with the 900 panel workplaces to form a cross-sectionally representative combined sample of 2,700 workplaces.

The Panel Sample

The sampling process in 2011 differed to that undertaken in 2004 (for the WERS 1998–2004 panel) in that almost all (2,286) of the available panel sample of 2,295 workplaces was issued to the field in 2011. (Nine workplaces were not issued to the field because they were in ineligible SIC 2007 categories.) The issued sample needed to be larger in 2011 than in 2004 for two reasons. First, the 2004–11 panel sample was to cover continuing workplaces with five or more employees, rather than ten or more as in the 1998–2004 panel, and so a higher proportion of the sample was expected to become ineligible due to closure. Second, response rates were lower in 2011 than in 2004 and that further depressed the yield.

The Refreshment Sample

The 2011 refreshment sample was selected as a stratified random sample from the Inter Departmental Business Register (IDBR) which is maintained by the Office for National Statistics.[1] The IDBR is acknowledged to be the highest-quality sampling frame for workplace surveys in Britain. The sampling unit was the IDBR 'local unit' which, in most instances, corresponded with the WERS definition of a workplace.[2] A sample of 4,848 local units was selected from the IDBR in July 2010.

The sample was drawn from the population of local units with five or more employees, operating in Sections C–S of the Standard Industrial Classification 2007 and located within Great Britain. To avoid duplication between the 2011 refreshment and panel samples, local units meeting the aforementioned criteria were exempt from selection if they could be identified as having formed part of the issued sample for the WERS 2004 Cross-Section Survey. Once the exempted local units had been removed, the population of local units meeting the criteria for selection contained 734,078 eligible local units.

The eligible local units were categorised into 153 strata composed of the nine workplace size bands disaggregated into 17 SIC sectors. A simple random sample was drawn within each stratum. Sampling fractions varied across the strata so that larger workplaces and small industries were over-sampled – with the rationale for doing so explained subsequently. The sampling fraction to be applied within each stratum was determined by the desired size and industry profile of the combined sample, and after taking into account the expected outturn from the panel.

The Combined Sample

The first columns of Tables A.1 and A.2 show the number of interviews that the study aimed to achieve in different workplace size bands and industry categories within the full combined sample. The second columns of Tables A.1 and A.2 show the size and profile of the combined issued sample formed by adding together the local units selected for the refreshment sample and the 2,286 workplaces in the panel sample issued for interview in 2011. The tables also indicate the effective sampling fraction, that is, the combined issued sample as a proportion of the total available population indicated on the IDBR in July 2010. These sampling fractions indicate the extent of over-sampling among larger workplaces and within smaller industry sectors.

In the 2011 WERS, as in previous studies in the series, larger workplaces were over-sampled to obtain a minimum number of interviews so that they could be separated from smaller workplaces in cross-tabular analysis. Larger

Table A.1 *Number of interviews to be achieved, size of the combined issued sample and effective sampling fraction by size of the workplace*

Workplace size	Number of interviews to be achieved	Size of the combined issued sample[a]	Effective sampling fraction
5–9 employees	365	1334	1 in 245
10–24 employees	365	1055	1 in 222
25–49 employees	365	969	1 in 95
50–99 employees	365	885	1 in 54
100–249 employees	365	836	1 in 25
250–499 employees	365	859	1 in 13
500–999 employees	210	478	1 in 6
1,000–1,999 employees	150	318	1 in 2
2,000 or more employees	150	345	1 in 2
All workplaces	2700	7079[b]	1 in 104

Notes: Workplace size is as observed on the sampling frame, rather than at interview.
[a]Includes panel and refreshment samples. In order to combine these samples for the purposes of the table, panel cases were allocated to strata based on their estimated IDBR size and SIC in 2010. In many cases, this was estimated by tracing the workplace on the IDBR in 2010.
[b]Some 55 panel workplaces in the issued sample are excluded from this table because their estimated IDBR size in 2010 was one to four employees (in fact 6 of these 55 workplaces responded to WERS 2011, indicating the IDBR measure was incorrect and the case actually in scope; the remaining cases were non-contacts or ineligible). As explained in the note to Table A.3, nine workplaces were not issued to the field because they were in ineligible SIC 2007 categories. Those nine workplaces together with the 55 workplaces mentioned here and the 7,079 in column two of the table formed the total issued sample of 7,143 workplaces.

Table A.2 Number of interviews to be achieved, size of the combined issued sample and effective sampling fraction by Standard Industrial Classification 2007

SIC 2007 section	Number of interviews to be achieved	Size of the combined issued sample[a]	Effective sampling fraction
C	229	565	1 in 96
D	85	206	1 in 4
E	85	207	1 in 21
F	108	313	1 in 151
G	398	1107	1 in 152
H	116	300	1 in 82
I	155	450	1 in 173
J	85	210	1 in 102
K	104	256	1 in 95
L	85	258	1 in 70
M	157	407	1 in 136
N	199	500	1 in 96
O	157	403	1 in 44
P	248	601	1 in 70
Q	320	773	1 in 107
R	85	257	1 in 98
S	85	266	1 in 96
All workplaces	2700	7079[b]	1 in 104

Note: Industry is as observed on the sampling frame, rather than at interview.
[a]Includes panel and refreshment samples. In order to combine these samples for the purposes of the table, panel cases were allocated to strata based on their estimated IDBR size and SIC in 2010. In many cases, this was estimated by tracing the workplace on the IDBR in 2010.
[b]Some 55 panel workplaces are excluded from this table because their estimated IDBR size in 2010 was one to four employees (in fact 6 of these 55 workplaces responded to WERS 2011, indicating the IDBR measure was incorrect and the case actually in scope; the remaining cases were non-contacts or ineligible). As explained in the note to Table A.3, nine workplaces were not issued to the field because they were in ineligible SIC 2007 categories. Those nine workplaces together with the 55 workplaces mentioned here and the 7,079 in column two of the table formed the total issued sample of 7,143 workplaces.

workplaces were also over-sampled because they employ a disproportionate share of all employees (Figure A.1) and so are of specific interest. Over-sampling large workplaces also enables the study to minimise the standard errors associated with any employee-based estimates derived from the workplace data (for example, the percentage of employees in workplaces with recognised unions) and to minimise the variance in the weights within the Survey of Employees (again with the aim of limiting standard errors). However, any actions to over-represent larger employers have the simultaneous effect of raising the standard errors associated with workplace-level estimates (for example, the percentage of workplaces with recognised unions). Since workplace level analysis has always been the mainstay of WERS analysis, the sample was designed so that

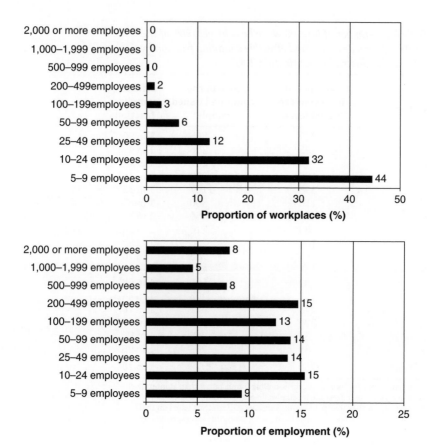

Figure A.1 *IDBR population of workplaces and employment coverage by workplace size, 2010, column per cent*

Base: Local units in Britain with five or more employees, operating in SIC 2007 Sections C–S.

Source: Inter Departmental Business Register, March 2010.

the benefits derived from over-sampling large workplaces on employee-based estimates are not outweighed by the negative impacts on workplace-based findings.

In addition to over-sampling large workplaces, WERS has also always over-sampled the industry sectors that account for relatively small numbers of workplaces in the population at large. Those sectors were over-sampled on the 2011 WERS to achieve a minimum number of interviews in each of the sections of the 2007 Standard Industrial Classification. The degree of industry level over-sampling in 2011 was much smaller than in the case for workplace size.

QUESTIONNAIRE DEVELOPMENT

Draft questionnaires were developed following a broad consultation among Government Departments, organisations outside government and the academic community (see McConaghy et al., 2010). The draft questionnaires included new or revised questions on topics such as the employment of migrant workers, work–life balance, religion, sexual orientation and the impact of the recession.

To ensure that respondents could understand and answer the new or revised questions with ease, the National Centre for Social Research (NatCen), the agency commissioned to undertake fieldwork for the 2011 study, carried out a cognitive test on all the new and substantially revised questions in May 2010. The main aim of the cognitive test was to assess respondents' comprehension of the questions and to examine the judgement, recall and response processes respondents used to formulate their answers.

The questionnaires and fieldwork procedures underwent further testing in a pilot survey in September 2010 and in a dress rehearsal in November 2010. The pilot survey tested the questionnaires and some elements of the fieldwork procedures. It took place at 28 workplaces in five locations, including London. The dress rehearsal assessed the questionnaires revised after the pilot and the full suite of fieldwork procedures, including tests of the online versions of the paper questionnaires (see the next section for details) and the telephone mode of the Survey of Worker Representatives. A total of 45 Survey of Managers interviews and seven Survey of Worker Representatives interviews were conducted in the dress rehearsal. Five Financial Performance Questionnaires (a component of the Survey of Managers applicable to the trading sector workplaces) and 107 Survey of Employees questionnaires were returned within the time allowed.

THE QUESTIONNAIRES

Five questionnaires were used on the 2011 WERS:

1. Employee Profile Questionnaire
2. Management Questionnaire
3. Financial Performance Questionnaire
4. Worker Representatives Questionnaire
5. Survey of Employees Questionnaire.

Their contents and process of administration are described in the following sections. Copies of the questionnaires are available from the GOV.UK website.[3]

The Employee Profile Questionnaire (EPQ)

The Employee Profile Questionnaire (EPQ), together with the Management Questionnaire and Financial Performance Questionnaire made up the Survey of Managers. It collected key information about the size and structure of the workforce at the workplace and was provided to the management contact prior to the management interview.

WERS 2011 was the first in the series to offer an online option alongside the paper version and 382 workplaces (14 per cent) completed the EPQ online.

Where an online EPQ was completed, the information was fed into the computerised interview program before interviewers went to the workplace to carry out the management interview. In all other cases, the information was inputted from the paper form by the interviewer at the start of the management interview.

The Management Questionnaire (MQ)

The Management Questionnaire (MQ) was the core of WERS. Along with Question 1 on the EPQ, it was the one required element for a workplace to count as having participated in the WERS. The MQ was administered in a face-to-face interview with the most senior manager responsible for employment relations at the workplace. The MQ consisted mostly of 'closed questions' that involved the interviewer coding the answer provided by the manager respondents to one of a number of pre-specified answer options. There were, however, a number of questions where the interviewers recorded the answers verbatim for coding afterwards. The MQ included these 'open-ended' questions because it was not always possible to pre-specify all the answer options or, in the case of the questions on the activities of the workplace or the largest occupational group, coding the answers at the interview would be too time consuming. Show cards printed with the answer options were shown to the respondent at questions which had a large number of possible answer categories to reduce respondent burden or to prompt the respondent to consider all the options.

Where management interviews were successfully achieved, they averaged 87 minutes in length. The duration of the interviews rose with the size of the establishment. Some interviews were conducted off-site with managers who did not work at the sampled workplace. This occurred in cases where the only person with a good overview of employment relations issues at the workplace was located in a regional or head office. In total, 386 (14 per cent) of the management interviews were conducted with an off-site manager. The corresponding figure in 2004 was 16 per cent.

The Financial Performance Questionnaire (FPQ)

The Financial Performance Questionnaire (FPQ) gathered financial detail about workplaces in the trading sector. It was given to management respondents at the end of the MQ interview, either for them to complete or for passing on to someone else who would be able to provide the necessary detail. The FPQ could be completed as a paper questionnaire or online; 105 workplaces (19 per cent of those that responded to the FPQ) completed the form online. Non-respondents received two reminders, both of which included a blank FPQ in case the original had been misplaced. Findings from the FPQ are not reported in this book.

The Worker Representative Questionnaire (WRQ)

Up to two worker representatives were eligible for the Worker Representative Questionnaire (WRQ) at each workplace:

1. The most senior representative of the largest recognised union (in terms of members at the workplace) or where there was no recognised union, the most senior representative of the largest non-recognised union.
2. The most senior non-union representative sitting on the Joint Consultative Committee (JCC) that covered the widest range of issues or, if there was no JCC, a stand-alone non-union representative who acted on behalf of employees at the workplace.

The 2011 WERS was the first in the series to allow interviewers to carry out WRQ interviews via telephone as well as face-to-face. This telephone option was introduced in an attempt to improve the efficiency of the assignment of interviews. This is because interviewers were often unable to interview the WRQ contacts on the same day as the MQ. To enable the implementation of the dual-mode approach, all WRQ respondents interviewed on the telephone were sent the show cards in advance of the interview. In addition, the number of show cards was minimised and some questions which were asked using show cards in earlier WERS were converted to be read out.

Employee representative interviews in 2011 averaged 30 minutes in length. In total, 26 per cent of WRQ interviews were carried out via telephone.

The Survey of Employees Questionnaire (SEQ)

The Survey of Employees Questionnaire (SEQ) was administered to up to 25 staff members at each workplace. With the managers' agreement, 25 employees were selected at random by the interviewer from a list of all employees at the workplace, provided by the management respondent. If the workplace had 25 or fewer employees, all were selected to participate. Paper questionnaires were left for distribution to each selected employee. For the first time, the 2011 SEQ was also made available, on request, in six languages other than English.[4] Freepost envelopes were provided for respondents to return their questionnaire. Login details were printed on the personally addressed paper questionnaire so that employees could choose to complete the questionnaire online (2,709 employees, 12 per cent of the SEQ respondents did so).

The SEQ had a three-stage reminder process. Where no responses were received from a workplace after three weeks, it was assumed that the questionnaires had not been distributed by the workplace contact, and a reminder pack containing further copies of questionnaires for all selected employees was sent to the contact. Subsequent to this, two reminders were sent to individual employees, including via email if the email address of the selected employee had been provided at the point of sampling.

FIELDWORK AND RESPONSE

Fieldwork for the study was conducted between March 2011 and June 2012. The first stage of fieldwork involved contacting the sampled workplaces in order to seek an appointment to conduct the management interview. The 2011 study followed the practice adopted at the later stage of the 2004 study so the responsibility for making the first contact with workplaces and making appointments was assigned to a Central Contacting Team (CCT) of dedicated, experienced telephone interviewers. Once appointments had been made, these were then allocated to a team of 120 field interviewers. Refusals and cases where workplaces proved to be ineligible were recorded within the CCT. Extensive efforts were made to contact workplaces. The CCT contacted individual workplaces numerous times and on different days and times to make contact. In cases where the CCT was unable to contact the workplace after many attempts, the case was released to field interviewers who would make further contact attempts.

As in previous studies, the sample of workplaces was divided into two types, known within the fieldwork team as 'waves', each containing addresses from the panel and refreshment samples. 'Wave One' workplaces were either independent establishments that were not part of a larger organisation or establishment for which gaining consent for participation in the study was considered to be possible, in the view of the research team, without the workplace manager referring the decision to a higher level in the organisation. These addresses were issued directly to the CCT.

Establishments that were part of larger organisations in which experience suggested that there was little prospect of an interviewer obtaining an interview without prior approval from the Head Office, were classified as 'Wave Two' workplaces. These were typically workplaces belonging to: central government departments; police, fire and ambulance services; utilities; transport, telecommunications and postal services; and large organisations in financial services and retail. Overall 28 per cent of workplaces in the issued sample were classified to Wave Two. For these cases, an approach was first made to the senior human resources or personnel director at the head office of each organisation to outline the purpose and features of the study. This person was asked to provide contact details for a local manager at each of the workplaces in their organisation that had been selected to take part in WERS. Wave Two workplaces where no head office contact could be established were eventually moved into Wave One so that a direct approach to the workplace could be attempted.

Fieldwork Outcomes

Response to the Survey of Managers

From the issued sample of 7,143 workplaces, a total of 2,680 workplaces generated productive management interviews. A further 404 workplaces (176 panel and 228 refreshment workplaces) were confirmed to have closed down and 947 workplaces proved to be ineligible or out-of-scope for other reasons. In addition, 3,112 eligible workplaces chose not to participate in the study (Table A.3). The overall response rate for the combined sample was therefore 46 per cent of the 5,792 eligible workplaces (2,680 / (7,143 − 1,351)).

MQ interviews were achieved in steady numbers throughout the fieldwork period. Overall 64 per cent had been conducted before the end of December 2011 (that is, within the 2011 calendar year) and 73 per cent had been conducted by

Table A.3 *Fieldwork outcomes for the Survey of Managers, 2011*

	Combined sample		Panel sample		Refreshment sample	
	Number	Per cent	Number	Per cent	Number	Per cent
Initial sample	7,143	100.0	2,295[a]	100.0	4,848	100.0
Ineligible/out of scope (workplace closed down)	404	5.7	176	7.7	228	4.7
Ineligible/out of scope (for other reasons)	947	13.2	228	9.9	719	14.8
Unproductive	3,112	43.6	902	39.3	2,210	45.6
Survey of Managers achieved	2,680	37.5	989	43.1	1,691	34.9
Response rate		46.3		52.3		43.3

Notes: [a]Includes the nine workplaces not issued to the field because they were in ineligible SIC 2007 categories.

the end of January 2012 (that is, within 12 months of the start of fieldwork). The median interview date was 30 September 2011.

Productive interviews were obtained from 989 workplaces in the panel sample and from 1,691 workplaces in the refreshment sample. The yield, defined as the number of productive units divided by the number of units in the issued sample, was higher within the panel sample (43 per cent) than within the refreshment sample (35 per cent), primarily because of a higher response rate among panel workplaces (52 per cent compared with 43 per cent).

Response rates for the Survey of Managers were notably lower in 2011 than they had been in 2004. A direct comparison can be made between fieldwork outcomes in the 2011 refreshment sample and those obtained in the 2004 Cross-Section Survey, since the latter was conducted on a wholly fresh sample drawn from the IDBR. (As noted earlier, the panel survey in 2004 was an entirely separate exercise.) In 2004, 53 per cent of the initial sample of 4,293 cases yielded productive EPQs and MQs (compared with 35 per cent in 2011), 16 per cent were out-of-scope (20 per cent in 2011) and 30 per cent were eligible but unproductive (46 per cent in 2011); this gave a response rate of 64 per cent in 2004, compared with a response rate of 43 per cent in 2011. A similar comparison for the panel survey is complicated by the fact that the 1998–2004 panel survey was conducted only among workplaces with ten or more employees, but if one looks at this subset of the 2004–11 panel the principal difference is a higher response rate in 2004 (77 per cent, compared with 52 per cent in 2011) rather than an increase in the proportion of ineligible workplaces.

The decline in response rates between 2004 and 2011 continues the decline between the 1998 and 2004 studies. This trend is not unique to WERS and declines have been seen in surveys of many different populations and those using various approaches to data collection. It is not possible to be definitive about the reasons for the decline, but factors that affect many social surveys, such as a reduced sense of obligation to participate in government-sponsored research, greater reluctance to provide potentially sensitive data, and research saturation may all be relevant.

There may also be some factors that are more specific to the 2011 WERS. A number of those contacted to take part indicated that participation in the study would be impossible or inappropriate in a time of economic uncertainty, particularly where the workplace had experienced redundancies or restructuring. Any consequent response biases that could be detected were addressed in the derivation of the survey weights, described later in this chapter.

Response to the Survey of Worker Representatives

Eligible employee representatives were present at 1,339 of the 2,680 workplaces that generated productive management interviews. Some 1,153 workplaces had eligible union representatives and 415 had eligible non-union representatives; 229 workplaces had eligible representatives of both types.

Among the 1,153 workplaces that had an eligible union representative, 797 workplaces generated a productive interview, giving a response rate of 69 per cent. Among the 415 workplaces with an eligible non-union representative, 205 generated a productive interview, giving a response rate of 49 per cent among non-union representatives. Among the 229 workplaces with eligible union and non-union representatives, interviews were obtained with both types of representatives in 82 workplaces (36 per cent). The total number of productive interviews was 1,002.

In 2004 the response rates were 84 per cent for union representatives and 77 per cent for non-union representatives. As in 2004, the most common single reason for failing to obtain employee representative interviews in 2011 was the refusal by management to agree to interviewers approaching the employee representative. However, there were also a substantial number of cases in 2011 where the representative was either never available or could not be contacted, including some cases where managers reported that a representative structure was present but no individual could be identified at the time of the survey who had responsibility for taking on that representative role at the workplace.

A total of 432 worker representative interviews were conducted in panel workplaces in 2011 (comprising interviews with 337 union representatives and 95 non-union representatives). In the refreshment sample, a total of 570 worker representative interviews were conducted (comprising interviews with 460 union representatives and 110 non-union representatives).

Of the panel workplaces with at least one productive worker representative interview in 2011, 281 had productive worker representative interviews in 2004 as well as in 2011.

Response to the Survey of Employees

Managers gave permission for interviewers to select a sample for the Survey of Employees in 2,170 workplaces (81 per cent). Interviewers then placed a total of 44,371 questionnaires in these workplaces. A total of 21,981 were returned, 19,272 by post and 2,709 (12 per cent) online, giving a response rate of 50 per cent among all sampled employees. No questionnaires were returned from 247 workplaces. It is possible that the 3,858 questionnaires that interviewers left for distribution at these workplaces did not reach the sampled employees. If one assumes that these questionnaires were not distributed, then the response rate among employees who are assumed to have received a questionnaire is 54 per cent.

Another way of expressing the response to the SEQ is to calculate an 'effective response rate' which is the number of productive questionnaires returned as a percentage of all the employees who would have received an SEQ if all the 2,680 responding workplaces had agreed to take part in the Survey of Employees and had successfully distributed an SEQ to all the selected employees. In 2011, 57,067 employees would have been sent an SEQ had all the responding workplaces had agreed to and had successfully distributed an SEQ to all selected employees. Consequently, the 'effective response rate' is 39 per cent.

In 2004, managers gave permission for interviewers to select an SEQ sample at 86 per cent of workplaces. The response rate among all issued questionnaires was 54 per cent and, among those questionnaires that were issued in workplaces where at least one SEQ was returned, the response rate was 61 per cent. The 'effective response rate' was 46 per cent in 2004. The response rate was therefore lower in 2011 than in 2004, but it did not fall as sharply as for the Survey of Managers and Worker Representatives.

A total of 8,821 SEQs were returned from panel workplaces and the remaining 13,160 were returned from workplaces in the refreshment sample. In the combined sample, a total of 1,755 workplaces generated three or more SEQ returns, 1,109 workplaces generated SEQ response rates of over 50 per cent and 1,150 workplaces generated SEQs from more than 10 per cent of the total workforce.[5]

Of the 989 panel workplaces, 600 had at least one SEQ returned in both 2004 and 2011.

Questionnaires Available for Analysis

The number of MQs, WRQs and SEQs available for analysis in 2011 and 2004 are summarised in Table A.4. Information on how to access the data is presented at the end of this appendix.

Table A.4 *Productive interviews achieved by sector of ownership, 2004 and 2011*

	Private sector	Public sector	All workplaces
Survey of Managers			
2004	1,706	589	2,295
2011	1,858	822	2,680
Survey of Worker Representatives			
2004	552	432	984
2011	471	531	1,002
Survey of Employees			
2004	15,327	7,124	22,451
2011	13,657	8,324	21,981

DATA CODING, EDITING AND QUALITY ASSURANCE

Coding and editing of the data consisted of three stages. The first involved coding the responses to all open-ended questions – for example, those that asked the manager to describe the industrial activity of the workplace. The coders also assigned numeric codes to the responses given to questions that gave the respondent the opportunity to provide a verbatim answer rather than simply one of a set of pre-specified response options.

The second stage of editing involved the resolution of a series of checks which sought to identify internal inconsistencies in the survey data (for example, an EPQ in which the sum of all full-time and part-time staff cited at Question 2 did not equal the total number of employees recorded at Question 1). The main tasks of the editors were to check that any information on the paper EPQ had been entered accurately into the interviewer's laptop and to look for any interviewer notes that might explain why some answers may be internally inconsistent. Issues which could not be resolved by the Stage 2 editing team were referred to Stage 3.

The third stage of editing was carried out by researchers from NatCen and the sponsoring Research Team. This stage involved the resolution of the outstanding queries from Stage 2 and queries arising from an additional series of 57 checks that sought to identify unusual patterns of data in the EPQ, MQ, WRQ and FPQ. An example was a check that identified large discrepancies between the number of employees recorded for the workplace on the IDBR and the number reported by the management respondent on the EPQ; that discrepancy might indicate a mistake in identifying the correct workplace for interview.

Detailed rules were developed for resolving the Stage 3 checks, which sometimes led researchers to edit the interview data in cases where the nature of the error was clear. In other cases, it was necessary to try to re-contact the respondent in order to clarify some details. The most difficult cases were referred to the sponsoring Research Team to attempt a resolution. After the Stage 3 edit, a small number of interviews were deleted in instances where it was determined that the interview had been undertaken at the wrong workplace or with an ineligible respondent.[6] In addition, flags known as 'overcodes' were added to a small number of cases at the end of Stage 3 edit because the editors could not determine with certainty whether a set of data items were valid. These cases are flagged using 'overcodes' so that analysts can consider whether they should include those cases in their analyses. A complete list of the edit checks is provided in the editing codebooks (NatCen, 2011b, 2011c, 2011d).

WEIGHTING

When drawing a simple random sample, each member of the population has the same probability of selection and so, in the absence of non-response biases, the achieved sample will be expected to resemble the population from which it was drawn. However, as noted earlier, the WERS sample design purposefully gives an above-average probability of selection to larger workplaces and those from less populated industries. Consequently, large workplaces and those from small indus-tries are proportionately over-represented and so the profile of the issued sample of workplaces does not mirror the population at large.

In the case of the Survey of Employees, once an employee's workplace has been selected to participate in WERS, a member of staff in a small workplace has a higher probability of receiving an SEQ than an employee in a large workplace. This is because questionnaires were distributed to all employees in workplaces with between five and 25 employees and to only 25 employees in larger workplaces. Employees from small workplaces are therefore over-represented in the employee sample.

On top of biases introduced purposefully as part of sampling, variable rates of non-response can also cause the achieved sample to depart from the population that it is intended to represent. To remove the known biases introduced by the sample selection and non-response, weights broadly equal to 1/(probability of selec-tion and response) were devised to bring the profiles of the achieved samples of workplaces and employees into line with the profiles of the respective populations. A series of forward stepwise logistic regression models were fitted to identify the variables that were significantly related to non-response to the MQ, WRQ, SEQ and FPQ. The variables that were significantly related to non-response to the various questionnaires are detailed in Forth (2013) but included: for the Survey of Managers – workplace size, organisation size, industry and region; and for the Survey of Employees – workplace size, industry, region, ethnicity of the workforce and the climate of employment relations.

In the 2011 WERS, weights were devised for each of the instruments (the EPQ/ MQ, the WRQ, the FPQ and the SEQ). Separate sets of weights were devised for the panel sample and the combined sample. The process for deriving the weights for analysing the 2011 WERS data is detailed in Forth (2013). Weights were applied to all analyses presented in this book to ensure that the estimates are representative of the survey population. Small improvements were made to the non-response adjust-ment between the earlier editions of the First Findings (van Wanrooy et al., 2013) and the completion of the book and so some 2011 estimates may differ slightly between the two publications.

In order to optimise the validity of the 2004–11 comparisons presented in this book, a revised set of 2004 weights was also derived using the same approach to non-response adjustment as was adopted for the 2011 data. The use of revised 2004 weights means that some 2004 estimates cited in this book will differ from those previously published elsewhere, although the impact of the revised weights is generally small. Comparisons carried out indicate that using the revised weights will only alter the value of a small number of 2004 MQ estimates by between one and two percent-age points. The derivation of the revised 2004 weights is detailed in Forth (2013).

SAMPLING ERRORS

In common with any other sample survey, the figures obtained from WERS are *estimates* of the true population parameters, since any survey estimate can be expected to vary under repeated sampling. Statistical theory allows us to quantify the degree of likely variation – labelled the 'standard error of the esti-mate' – and thus to construct confidence intervals around any estimate from the specific sample that has been drawn. The standard errors of survey esti-mates are affected by the sample design, particularly by the effect of sampling weights, clustering and stratification, and these factors have to be taken into account when calculating standard errors (and, as a consequence, p-values and confidence intervals).

To help identify the precision of estimates from the 2011 WERS, the true standard errors for a range of estimates have been approximated using the statistical software package Stata. These standard errors are listed individually in Forth (2013). To ascertain the precision of any particular estimate presented in this book the reader is advised, where possible, to identify its standard error from those tables. However, from each of those standard errors it is possible to identify the degree of inflation in the sampling error that has been introduced by

Table A.5 *Approximate standard errors for MQ estimates derived from the 2011 WERS combined sample*

Estimate (%)	Number of observation (unweighted)					
	100	500	1,000	1,500	2,000	2,500
10	4.7	2.1	1.5	1.2	1.0	0.9
20	6.2	2.8	2.0	1.6	1.4	1.2
30	7.1	3.2	2.2	1.8	1.6	1.4
40	7.6	3.4	2.4	2.0	1.7	1.5
50	7.8	3.5	2.5	2.0	1.7	1.6
60	7.6	3.4	2.4	2.0	1.7	1.5
70	7.1	3.2	2.2	1.8	1.6	1.4
80	6.2	2.8	2.0	1.6	1.4	1.2
90	4.7	2.1	1.5	1.2	1.0	0.9

Notes: Median design factor – 1.55.

Table A.6 *Approximate standard errors for WRQ estimates derived from the 2011 WERS combined sample*

Estimate (%)	Number of observation (unweighted)				
	100	250	500	750	1,000
10	7.4	4.7	3.3	2.7	2.3
20	9.9	6.2	4.4	3.6	3.1
30	11.3	7.2	5.1	4.1	3.6
40	12.1	7.7	5.4	4.4	3.8
50	12.4	7.8	5.5	4.5	3.9
60	12.1	7.7	5.4	4.4	3.8
70	11.3	7.2	5.1	4.1	3.6
80	9.9	6.2	4.4	3.6	3.1
90	7.4	4.7	3.3	2.7	2.3

Notes: Median design factor – 2.47.

Table A.7 *Approximate standard errors for SEQ estimates derived from the 2011 WERS combined sample*

Estimate (%)	Number of observation (unweighted)				
	1,000	**5,000**	**10,000**	**15,000**	**20,000**
10	1.7	0.8	0.5	0.4	0.4
20	2.3	1.0	0.7	0.6	0.5
30	2.6	1.2	0.8	0.7	0.6
40	2.8	1.2	0.9	0.7	0.6
50	2.8	1.3	0.9	0.7	0.6
60	2.8	1.2	0.9	0.7	0.6
70	2.6	1.2	0.8	0.7	0.6
80	2.3	1.0	0.7	0.6	0.5
90	1.7	0.8	0.5	0.4	0.4

Notes: Median design factor – 1.79.

the sample design when compared with a simple random sample of the same size (the design factor). The median design factor for estimates from the MQ is 1.55, for the SEQ is 1.79 and for the WRQ is 2.47 (all for the combined sample). These figures suggest that the sample design features of the 2011 WERS will typically increase the standard errors of the EPQ/MQ estimates from the combined sample by 55 per cent, the SEQ estimates from the combined sample by 80 per cent and the WRQ estimates from the combined sample by 150 per cent, when compared with simple random samples of the same size. To illustrate what this implies for estimates based on different sub-samples of the WERS combined sample datasets, Tables A.5, A.6 and A.7 present approximate standard errors for estimates derived from each sample.

ACCESSING THE DATA AND FURTHER INFORMATION

The survey data from WERS 2011 can be accessed with full documentation from the UK Data Service: http://discover.ukdataservice.ac.uk/catalogue/?sn=7226&type=Data%20catalogue.

The deposited data have been anonymised to protect the identity of individual respondents and participating establishments. Survey variables that would significantly increase the chance of a user being able to identify a participating workplace have also been withheld from this 'general purpose' dataset. These variables comprise the region in which the workplace was located, the detailed industry classification (beyond SIC Section level), and all data from the FPQ. These data items are available in the secure access version of the dataset released through the Secure Access facility of the UK Data Service: http://ukdataservice.ac.uk/get-data/secure-access/about.aspx#/tab-what-is-secure-access.

Among the 2,680 management respondents who completed an MQ in 2011, 2,477 gave their consent for authorised researchers to link the data collected from their workplaces to those collected in other surveys and datasets. The IDBR local unit reference numbers of the workplaces that have consented to data linking are included in the secure access version of the data to enable data linking.

The full 2011 WERS Technical Report (Deepchand et al., 2013) is available on request from wers@bis.gsi.gov.uk. Further information about the 2011 survey, including full questionnaires, the First Findings report and key tables are provided on the GOV.UK website: https://www.gov.uk/government/publications/the-2011-workplace-employment-relations-study-wers.

Notes

1 Introduction

1. Trading public sector workplaces include those belonging to a government-owned limited company, nationalised industry or a Trading Public Corporation. The data from the Financial Performance Questionnaire – for which 545 questionnaires were completed resulting in a response rate of 32 per cent – is not used in analysis for this book.
2. Where the workplace had 25 or fewer employees, the questionnaire was distributed to the entire workforce.
3. In common with the 2011 WERS, the 2004 survey covered workplaces with five or more employees. The 1998 WERS only surveyed workplaces with ten or more employees. The first survey conducted in 1980 included workplaces with 25 or more employees and throughout the series workplace coverage has gradually increased.

2 In the Shadow of Recession

1. The analysis focuses on private sector workplaces that trade beyond the boundaries of their own organisation (that is, those which sell goods or services either to the general public or to other organisations). The analysis thus excludes the small number of private sector workplaces that do not trade externally (that is, administrative offices and those providing goods or services only to other workplaces in their organisation). It also excludes public sector workplaces. Private sector trading workplaces accounted 85 per cent of all workplaces and 72 per cent of employment in 2011. The figures were unchanged from 2004. The analysis is based on 1,604 workplaces in 2004 and 1,753 in 2011.
2. Respondents in some 14 per cent of workplaces in 2011 responded that they 'Did not know' their market share; it was 15 per cent in 2004. These workplaces are excluded from the base for the estimates cited in the text. The substantive finding is unaltered if they are included.
3. The one exception was that the proportion of panel workplaces facing competition from overseas suppliers increased from 18 per cent in 2004 to 24 per cent in 2011.
4. In other words, each of these sectors would each have registered statistically significant net changes in the first two columns of Table 2.1. Precise figures are not given as the underlying estimates are based on fewer than 50 observations in each of Construction, Education and Other business services.
5. Office for National Statistics: Index of Production, Index of Services, and All in Employment by Industry Sector (2008Q1 to 2012Q2).
6. We ran survey-weighted OLS models for the ordered responses to the question regarding the adverse effects of recession. Results were robust to the use of ordinal regressions.
7. The proportion of workplaces making compulsory redundancies was also higher in the private sector than in the public sector but here the difference was not statistically significant.

3 Employment and Flexible Working

1. The closure rate was the number of workplaces with ten or more employees that participated in the 2004 management survey that had closed by 2011 divided by

the total number of workplaces with ten or more employees that participated in the 2004 management survey. Where a workplace dropped below the survey size threshold between 2004 and 2011, the workplace was regarded as continuing. The closure rate was derived in a similar way for the period from 1998 to 2004.

2. Data from the Insolvency Service (2012) also shows that company liquidations in the private sector were lower in the period between 2004 and 2011 than in the period 1998 to 2004, although changes brought in by the Enterprise Act 2002 introduced a discontinuity into the time series.

3. In addition to the characteristics listed in Table 3.1 the analysis also controlled for: managers' views of relations with employees (the climate); legal status; whether the workplace traded externally; whether the workplace was part of a larger organisation; family ownership; foreign ownership; financial performance; whether the workplace concentrated on a single product or service; the number of competitors; the degree of competition in the market; whether the workplace faced any overseas competition; whether it operated in a local or international market; whether it faced a growing, stable, declining or turbulent market; the proportion of the workforce who were female, aged 50 or more, disabled, non-white, on fixed-term contracts and in higher-skilled occupations; the number of employees in the organisation; industry; and region. All of these variables were measured at the time of the 2004 survey. Aside from those items shown in Table 3.1 the only statistically significant associations were with the proportion of the workforce who were disabled and the legal status of the workplace. The analysis was based on 1,410 observations.

4. This analysis used a similar set of control variables to those used in Bryson (2004). The finding that private sector workplaces which recognised unions were more likely to have closed by 2011 was also evident in a version of the model which used a reduced set of control variables.

5. This analysis controlled for the variables listed in note 3, with the exception of the age of the workplace. All of these variables were measured at the time of the 2011 survey. Aside from those items noted in the text, the only statistically significant associations were with legal status, organisation size and region. The analysis was based on 1,589 observations.

6. The analysis controlled for the set of variables listed in note 3, with the addition of whether the workplace was adversely affected by the recession in 2011. With the exception of this item, all variables were measured at the time of the 2004 survey. The analysis was based on 533 observations.

7. This analysis controlled for the variables listed in note 3, with the addition of whether the workplace was adversely affected by the recession in 2011, the substitution of union density for union recognition and the exclusion of financial performance. With the exception of the impact of the recession, all variables were measured at the time of the 2004 survey. Aside from those items noted in the text the only statistically significant associations were with the proportion of employees who were female, disabled or non-white; workplace size; and region. The analysis was based on 248 observations.

8. For private sector workplaces, the analysis controlled for the variables listed in note 3, with the addition of whether the workplace was adversely affected by the recession and the exclusion of whether any redundancies were made in the year prior to survey. For public sector workplaces, the analysis controlled for the variables listed in note 7. All of these variables were measured at the time of the 2011 survey. For private sector workplaces, aside from those items noted in the text, the only statistically significant associations were with the proportion

of female or disabled employees, organisation size and region. For public sector workplaces, aside from those items noted in the text, the only statistically significant association was with whether the workplace was part of a larger organisation.

9. This is consistent with earlier evidence that job-leavers who are union members are less likely to leave a job because of redundancy than non-union members (Theodossiou, 1996).

10. This analysis controlled for the measures listed in note 3, measured at the time of the 2004 survey (with the exception of the impact of the recession). Aside from those items noted in the text, the only statistically significant associations were with the proportion of employees who were female or non-white, financial performance, legal status, organisation size and region.

11. For private sector workplaces, this analysis controlled for the variables described in note 3, with the exception of the proportion of employees who were on temporary or fixed-term contracts. For public sector workplaces, the analysis controlled for the variables described in note 7, with the exception of the proportion of employees on temporary or fixed-term contracts. All variables were measured at the time of the 2011 survey. For private sector workplaces, aside from those items noted in the text, the only statistically significant associations were with exposure to overseas competition, legal status, organisation size and region. For public sector workplaces, aside from those items noted in the text, the only statistically significant associations were with union density, organisation size, region and whether the workplace was part of a larger organisation.

12. This analysis controlled for the variables listed in note 3 and the different types of numerical and functional flexibility. All of these variables were measured at the time of the 2011 survey.

4   The Involvement of Employees in Workplace Change

1. Trade unions have a legal right to be recognised for negotiating specified terms and conditions if they can demonstrate sufficient support within the workforce. Employers are legally required to consult employees or their representatives over health and safety issues, collective redundancies, business transfers, changes to occupational pensions and other decisions likely to lead to substantial changes in work organisation or contractual relations.

2. Paragraph 20(c) of The Information and Consultation of Employees Regulations 2004 (Statutory Instrument 2004 No. 3426).

3. Unless otherwise stated, the discussion in this section focuses on those workplaces in which the main management interview was conducted with an on-site manager. There were 1,943 such workplaces in 2004 and 2,294 in 2011 (accounting for 85 per cent of all management interviews in 2004 and 86 per cent in 2011). The remaining management interviews were conducted with someone at a regional or head office. This was most common for small branch sites and many of those instances indicate that all substantive employment relations matters are dealt with by a regional or head office manager, who is then the most informed person to complete the survey interview. These cases are omitted from most of the analysis in this section so as not to bias the picture of workplace managers' perceptions.

4. The figures cited by Kochan for the HR profession in the United States (2003: 12) suggest that this is not only happening in Britain.

5. The aggregate figure fell because it became less common in small organisations, and such organisations accounted for a growing share of all private sector workplaces.

6. Alongside those characteristics cited in the text, the OLS model also included indicators for: job title, proportion of time spent on ER issues, whether the manager held any ER-related qualifications, the degree of autonomy of the workplace manager and the presence of an ER specialist on the Board of Directors – none of these were statistically significant. The regression controlled for workplace size (positively associated with 'consultation'), organisation size (negatively associated), sector of ownership (more positive attitudes in the public sector), year and industry sector. The model was based on 4,047 managers who worked at the sampled workplace with an R^2 of 0.07.

7. Membership density appeared to fall in Education (from 56 per cent to 52 per cent) and in Health (from 42 per cent to 37 per cent), but the declines were not statistically significant in these sectors.

8. See Kersley et al. (2006: 110) on the positive relationship between workplace size and union membership density.

9. These estimates of the level of density within individual workplaces rely on reports of union membership provided by the workplace manager. Managers typically underestimate union membership density at their workplace (see Kersley et al., 2006: 111). However, even if we allow for some under-counting, the number of workplaces with majority density must still be very small.

10. The difference of 3.6 hours reduces to around one hour after controlling for the number of employees at the workplace who belong to the representatives' union and whether that union is recognised.

11. These figures include European Works Councils. The EWC Regulations – which were implemented in the UK in 1999 – apply only to multinational firms with at least 1,000 employees in the European Economic Area, and with 150 employees in each of at least two Member States. It is not possible to identify such firms precisely in WERS but, in branch sites that belonged to multinational corporations, the workplace manager was asked whether the organisation operated an EWC. A substantial minority of managers did not know (24 per cent in 2004; 13 per cent in 2011) but a further 17 per cent in 2004 and 15 per cent in 2011 said that an EWC did operate. The change was not statistically significant.

12. It did so in instances where there was an on-site JCC that covered multiple issues, but not where the only on-site JCC(s) covered a single topic such as health and safety. In 2011, some 96 per cent of those workplaces with an on-site JCC had at least one that covered multiple issues (90 per cent in 2004).

13. When considering written forms, the discussion focuses on arrangements that allow for at least some flow of communication upwards from employees to managers. We do not discuss arrangements that are typically designed to allow only for downward communication, such as workplace intranets or newsletters.

14. Social media are also increasingly popular and are likely to be used increasingly by managers as a means of sharing information with, and consulting, employees (Smith and Harwood, 2011). However, the use of social media for such purposes is still very much in its infancy in most organisations and is not covered in the 2011 WERS.

15. The constituent components of the measure are described in the note to Table 4.7. We ignore representative structures which are not accompanied by on-site

representatives (for example, higher-level JCCs), because of the inevitable distance from the employees of the sampled workplace. In respect of direct arrangements, we ignore face-to-face meetings at which less than one quarter of the time is made available for employees, and we ignore all written forms of consultation, because of the limited opportunities these offer for substantive dialogue.

16. The outcomes from redundancy consultation are discussed to some extent in Chapter 3, while readers interested in the outcomes of consultation over organisational change may refer to existing WERS-based research (e.g. Bryson et al., 2009a) which has examined this issue in more detail.

17. The ONS (series RED02) estimates that 6.1 employees per thousand were made redundant over the six quarters from 2011Q1 to 2012Q2. This compares with a rate of 10.3 employees during the period 2008Q4 to 2009Q3 and 5.4 per thousand during the period 2004Q1 to 2008Q3.

18. In the 7 per cent of workplaces that consulted via a JCC in 2011, 73 per cent used an existing committee and the rest used a new committee.

19. The legislation covering redundancy consultation only requires the employer to consult with employee representatives when at least 20 employees are expected to be laid off in a single 90-day period.

20. As with much of the analysis in the earlier part of this chapter, this analysis is confined to those workplaces in which the management respondent was located at the sampled workplace (that is, excluding those based at a head office or regional office).

21. If we exclude workplaces in which the introduction of new technology or computers was the most important change, we find that managers consulted or negotiated with employees in 68 per cent of all workplaces. Again this was not statistically significant from the equivalent proportion in 2004, indicating that changes in the questionnaire are not affecting our view of change over time.

22. The regression was conducted by ordinary least squares and based on 36,689 responses from employees with an R^2 of 0.04.

5 Pay and Rewards

1. The estimates presented here are time-consistent estimates which rely exclusively on information on pay determination methods that was collected from managerial respondents for each of the nine occupational groups that were present at the workplace (labelled 'FSOC' in the Management Questionnaire). They are lower bound estimates. An upper bound estimate, which draws additionally on questions about the most recent pay settlement for the largest occupational group of employees at the workplace and the manager's banded estimate of coverage, indicates collective bargaining employee coverage in the private sector was 25 per cent in 2004 and 27 per cent in 2011. In the public sector it was 91 per cent in 2004 and 88 per cent in 2011. The lower bound estimates are preferred for two reasons. First, we are unable to edit the 'FSOC' data to account for instances in which managers in the public sector mistake collective bargaining for pay setting by an Independent Pay Review Body, and vice versa. Second, we can relate the estimates derived from FSOC to detailed occupation-level information on other forms of pay determination discussed later.

2. WERS excludes employees in workplaces with fewer than five employees and those in agriculture and mining. The QLFS is a survey of employees, whereas WERS collects information on pay determination from the workplace manager. The survey questions also differ in a number of respects. A third data source, the employer-focused Annual Survey of Hours and Earnings estimated coverage in 2011 to be considerably higher at just over one quarter (27 per cent) of private sector employees. We are grateful to Ivan Bishop at the Department for Business, Innovation and Skills, for calculating this figure.

3. A similar question is asked if there are non-union representatives at the workplace but these are excluded from the analysis reported here.

4. In 2011 a single item covered 'grievance and disciplinary procedures' whereas in 2004 managers were asked about grievance procedures and disciplinary procedures separately. The table presents figures confined to grievance procedures in 2004. If one includes interactions with unions over grievances or disciplinary procedures in 2004, the figures are virtually identical.

5. As in the case of the private sector, ASHE suggests higher collective bargaining coverage than WERS or the QLFS: according to ASHE, 92 per cent of public sector employees were covered by collective bargaining in 2011.

6. Agenda for Change was a systematic review of pay structures and job descriptions in the NHS which was negotiated with unions. If we had treated those covered by Agenda for Change as subject to a Pay Review Body in 2004, employee collective bargaining coverage among public sector employees in Health would have been 31 per cent instead of 75 per cent. This would result in a decline in public sector collective bargaining coverage of 10 percentage points (from 54 per cent in 2004 to 44 per cent in 2011) instead of the 24 percentage point drop presented (68 per cent in 2004 to 44 per cent in 2011).

7. The incidence of pay freezes was higher among public sector workplaces in these sectors. In 2011, 58 per cent of Education workplaces in the public sector had introduced a pay freeze or cut, as had 56 per cent of those in Health and 56 per cent of those in Other community services.

8. The comparison with 2004 should be treated with some caution because the National Minimum Wage was not included as one of the response options in 2004 and the 'other, please specify' option was not offered. The question was not therefore identical. However, we judge the impact on the proportion citing the cost of living in either year to be small.

9. The increase in sick pay entitlement for those in the largest occupational group and the decline in managers' entitlements to company vehicles or allowances are both on the margins of statistical significance. The change in question wording means it is not possible to compare the annual leave items in 2004 and 2011.

10. The tetrachoric correlation coefficients were 0.43, 0.40, 0.39 and 0.37, respectively.

11. OLS models were run separately for the private and public sectors. The private sector model is based on 1,788 workplaces with an R^2 of 0.05. The public sector model is based on 798 workplaces with an R^2 of 0.15.

12. In addition to the workplace identifier (or 'fixed effect') the models reported on here contain sex, age, ethnicity, academic qualifications, union membership, single digit occupation, wage, contracted hours, tenure and contract type (permanent, temporary or fixed). The private sector model is based on 9,705 employee observations and has an R^2 of 0.31. The public sector model is based on 6,605 employee observations and has an R^2 of 0.26.

13. The pre-coded responses to this question in 2004 were: 'Myself', 'Trade union', 'Employee representative (non-union)', 'Another employee' and 'Somebody else'.

In 2011 the 'Somebody else' response option was replaced with 'Line manager', so the responses are not identical across years. Many more respondents responded 'Line manager' in 2011 than 'Somebody else' in 2004 so that the estimates of the desire for union representation in 2011 are, if anything, a lower bound estimate relative to 2004.

6   The Quality of Jobs and Employment

1. Ordinary Least Squares (OLS) model controls for gender, age, ethnicity, marital status, dependent children, union membership, academic qualifications, tenure, contract type, workplace and organisation size, sector, union recognition, industry and region. The model is based on 21,660 employee observations with an R^2 of 0.04.
2. The largest occupation is the SOC 2000 Major Group that accounts for the largest number of non-managerial employees at the workplace.
3. Even so, Wood and Bryson (2009) had found an increase in job variety in the public sector between 1998 and 2004.
4. Among non-managerial employees not belonging to the largest occupation at the workplace, there was an increase in the percentage reporting 'A lot' of influence over both items (from 38 per cent to 42 per cent for the pace of work, and from 50 per cent to 54 per cent for how the work is done).
5. The estimate for Financial services is based on 46 workplaces.
6. Managers were asked about one additional arrangement in 2011: 'The ability to change set working hours (including changing shift pattern)'. Around half (49 per cent) of managers responded that they had this arrangement for at least some employees at the workplace.
7. Although here the apparent increase in working at home is not statistically significant at the 5 per cent level in the panel.
8. For the remaining arrangements asked about, the proportion of employees who did not know whether this would be available to them exceeded 10 per cent for: job sharing (15 per cent); the chance to reduce working hours (17 per cent); working the same number of hours per week across fewer days (16 per cent); and term-time working (14 per cent).
9. This figure is based on workplaces with ten or more employees, as the 1998 WERS did not include workplaces with between five and nine employees. If we calculate comparable figures for 2004 and 2011 based on workplaces with ten or more employees, the estimates are 66 per cent and 75 per cent, respectively.
10. The proportion of managers agreeing rose from 69 per cent to 74 per cent in this latter group. Comparison is based on the six flexible working arrangements that were asked about in both 2004 and 2011. An increase in provision was identified where workplaces provided at least one arrangement in 2011, compared with no arrangements in 2004, or had increased the number of arrangements provided between 2004 and 2011.
11. Where the level of risk varied between different occupational groups, the respondent was asked to rate the average across all groups.
12. The estimate for Financial services is based on 48 workplaces.
13. Managers were asked whether any employees had sustained any of the following types of injury during work hours: bone fracture; amputation; dislocated joint; loss of sight; chemical or hot metal burn to the eye; penetrating eye injury; acute illness requiring medical treatment; any other

injury leading to unconsciousness or requiring resuscitation or admittance to hospital for more than 24 hours.

14. Managers were asked whether any employees suffered from any of the following illnesses, disabilities or other physical problems that were caused or made worse by their work: bone, joint or muscle problems; breathing or lung problems; skin problems; hearing problems; stress, depression or anxiety; eye strain; heart disease/attack or other circulatory problem; infectious disease (virus, bacteria).

15. For example, for each of the two items within the job demands scale, employees were asked to respond on a five-point scale from 'Strongly agree' to 'Strongly disagree'. Responses were then scored from 0 for 'Strongly disagree' to 4 for 'Strongly agree', and summed so that the score for the total job demands scale ranges from 0 to 8.

16. Separate OLS regressions with workplace fixed effects were run for each of the four job quality indices: job demands (21,368 employee observations), job control (21,287 employee observations), job security (20,994 employee observations) and supportive management (20,705 employee observations).

7   Employee Well-being

1. Depression here is self-reported by employees and does not necessarily meet any clinical threshold.

2. The original anxiety–contentment and depression–enthusiasm scales (Warr, 2007) each comprise six items: three positives and three negatives. However, it was only possible to accommodate a total of six items in the 2011 Survey of Employees Questionnaire, due to space restrictions, and so three negative items were included from each scale.

3. Eight of the items were included on a single question. The item on involvement in decision-making was asked separately, in conjunction with questions about information and consultation.

4. The OLS regressions controlled for: employee characteristics – gender, age, ethnicity, marital status, dependent children, academic qualifications, union member; job characteristics – occupation, usual working hours, tenure, contract type; and job quality – work intensity, job autonomy, job security, job supports, pay (refer to Table 7.3); and workplace characteristics – industry, sector, workplace size, organisation size, union recognition, and region. The models were based on at least 20,596 observations with an R^2 of 0.32 (contentment), 0.33 (enthusiasm) and 0.60 (satisfaction).

5. The EQLS measure for the UK rises from a mean of 7.2 (on a ten-point scale) in 2003 and 7.1 in 2007 to 7.5 in 2009. We are grateful to the European Foundation for the Improvement of Living and Working Conditions for providing these figures.

6. Specifically, the replacement of three positive items from the anxiety–contentment scale with three negative items from the enthusiasm–depression scale could possibly have influenced the way employees responded to the three ever-present negative items from the anxiety–contentment scale, although it is impossible to test this hypothesis retrospectively.

7. The assumption throughout this section is that, if the questionnaire change referred to previously has played some part, the effect is homogenous for all types of employee. It may therefore affect levels of well-being in 2011, but does not impair attempts to identify other causes of change between 2004 and 2011. As

mentioned in note 6, it is impossible to determine whether there has been any impact at all from the change in the questionnaire.

8. The detailed decomposition reveals offsetting effects of changes in job quality with changes in pay and job demands militating against a rise in job contentment, whereas job control and management quality were associated with rising contentment.

9. The regression models explain much of the variation in employees' well-being. For example, the models account for 66 per cent of the variance in employees' ratings of non-pecuniary job satisfaction in both the public and private sectors.

8 The Quality of Employment Relations

1. ONS (2012), LABD01: Labour Disputes in Labour Market Statistics Data Tables, November 2012 release.

2. Multiple claims are those brought by a group of individuals on the same issue and against the same employer.

3. The second indicator is preceded in the questionnaire by that on formal grievances. In 2004 the question on formal grievances asked simply whether there were any or none, but in 2011 managers were asked the number of formal grievances. It is possible that this more specific focus on the number of formal grievances (and hence implicitly on specific incidents) may have framed managers' responses to the next question in such a way that informal grievance incidents were more easily overlooked.

4. The declines in the public sector and private manufacturing were of the same magnitude as in private services; therefore the lack of statistical significance is due to smaller sample sizes in those sectors. So it is not that the estimated fall in grievances is lower in those sectors, but rather that we cannot be as confident that the falls truly occurred in the population at large.

5. A comparative figure for 2004 is not available as the information was not collected.

6. The variables included in the model are industry (12 categories); presence of a recognised union; single establishment; region (11 categories); proportion of workforce that are female, from a non-white ethnic group, aged 16–21 years, aged 50 years or older, and in lower skilled occupations of Administrative and secretarial; Caring, leisure and other personal service; Sales and customer services; Process, plant and machines operatives and drivers; and Routine occupations. All significant factors were at the $p < 0.05$ level. The model was based on observations from 2,442 workplaces with an R^2 of 0.123.

7. This measure of representatives structures includes the presence of a recognised trade union, a trade union that is not recognised but has a representative present at the workplace, a Joint Consultative Committee (JCC) at the workplace or a higher level in the organisation, or a 'standalone' representative that does not represent a union and is not a member of a JCC.

8. The regressions controlled for workplace size, industry, region, whether the workplace was part of a larger organisation and the presence of a recognised union. For the analysis of grievances, the number of observations was 2,515, $R^2 = 0.106$. For the model on disciplinary sanctions, the number of observations was 2,516, $R^2 = 0.104$.

9. The results for non-union representatives are not reliable due to an error in the questionnaire in 2004, whereby 178 of the 248 non-union representatives were not asked the question.

10. Author's calculations from the publicly available dataset.
11. The models controlled for the employee's age, sex, marital status, ethnicity, disability, academic qualification, occupation, union membership, working hours, job tenure and employment contract. Workplace characteristics controlled for were workplace size, industry, presence of a recognised union, region and whether it was a single establishment or part of a larger organisation. Analysis was based on responses from at least 20,316 employees. R^2 = 0.069 (loyalty), 0.090 (values), 0.085 (pride).
12. The model specification was the same as that outlined in note 11. R^2 = 0.058.
13. The number of changes the employee experienced as a result of the recession was added to the previous regression model, thus the same variables were controlled for. However, the models only include employees who were at the workplace at the time of the recession. Analysis was based on responses from at least 17,705 employees. R^2 = 0.099 (loyalty), 0.112 (values), 0.129 (proud), 0.061 (initiative).
14. See note 11 for variables controlled for, and additional variables included were: employees' rating or relationship with managers (from 1 to 5), whether any industrial action took place, whether any grievances were raised by employees (either through a procedure or not) and whether any disciplinary sanctions were applied to employees at the workplace. Models are based on at least 19,831 responses from employees. R^2 = 0.274 (loyalty), 0.256 (values), 0.324 (proud), 0.068 (initiative).

9   The Impact of Recession

1. The full list is presented in Table 2.4.
2. Employees are deemed to have a disability where day-to-day activities are limited because of a health problem or disability which has lasted, or is expected to last, at least 12 months. The effect of disability on the number of changes employees experienced was significant in the standard models only. In the fixed-effects models, the effect of a disability ceased to be statistically significant once the effects of the other factors had been taken into account.
3. The private sector analysis is based on 15,647 employees and the public sector analysis is based on 15,784 employees.
4. When the workplace identifiers are introduced, all of the variables that identify workplace characteristics, such as workplace size and age, are dropped from the analysis since they do not vary across individuals in the same workplace. The introduction of the workplace identifiers makes very little difference to the coefficients on the demographic and job characteristics when compared with the standard model. The private sector analysis was based on 9,257 employees in 1,211 workplaces. The public sector analysis was based on 6,176 employees in 614 workplaces.
5. The numerical flexibility measure counts the number of the following types of arrangements used at the workplace in 2004: fixed-term contracts, temporary contracts, freelance, shift work, annualised hours, zero hours contracts and home workers.
6. The models already account for the presence of different types of incentive pay in 2004, so the benefits of linking pay to performance are not confined solely to those workplaces which had no incentive pay in 2004.

7. The models were estimated using ordinary least squares and were based on observations 561 workplaces. They accounted for 37 per cent of the variance in managerial perceptions of whether the workplace was weaker as a result of recession, and 49 per cent after adding the indicator of how adversely the workplace had been affected by recession.

8. Identifying causal relationships between managerial changes and workplace outcomes usually requires those changes to be randomly allocated across firms or within firms, either through an experimental evaluation, or through a natural experiment of some kind. Our setting is not like this, although the advent of recession – a macro-shock to the economy – creates market turbulence, as we have shown, in a way that uncovers relationships between what management does and how the workplace fares which might not ordinarily be apparent in more settled times.

9. In some estimates having a strategic plan with a focus on employees and trust (as indicated by managers strongly disagreeing that employees took unfair advantage of management) were associated with a lower likelihood of being weakened by recession, whereas a managerial belief that those at the top were best placed to make decisions was associated with an increased likelihood of being weakened by recession. However, these results were not as robust to changes in model specification.

Technical Appendix

1. Details about the Inter-Departmental Business Register can be found in this page of the website of the Office for National Statistics: http://www.ons.gov.uk/ons/about-ons/who-we-are/services/idbr/about-the-idbr/index.html.

2. The instances when an IDBR 'local unit' did not correspond to the WERS definition of a workplace were when the IDBR 'local unit' represented only a subsection of a workplace (a partial sampling unit) or when the 'local unit' represented two or more workplaces (an aggregate unit). In total there were 20 partial and 20 aggregate units in the 2011 sample.

3. The questionnaires can be found on this page on the GOV.UK website: https://www.gov.uk/government/publications/the-2011-workplace-employment-relations-study-wers.

4. The 2011 SEQ was made available in Polish, French, Welsh, Bengali, Urdu and Punjabi (Shahmukhi).

5. The threshold of 10 per cent is commonly acknowledged as the point at which the finite population correction begins to substantively reduce the standard error associated with any survey estimate.

6. These cases are treated as either out-of-scope or unproductive in the section on response.

Bibliography

Acas (2009) *Trade Union Representation in the Workplace: A Guide to Managing Time Off, Training and Facilities*, London: Acas.

Acas (2011) *Non-Union Representation in the Workplace: A Guide to Managing Time Off, Training and Facilities*, London: Acas.

Acas–CIPD (2009) *How to Manage Your Workforce in a Recession*, Joint Acas–CIPD Guidance Note, February, London: Chartered Institute for Personnel and Development.

Alpin, C., Shackleton, J. R. and Walsh, S. (1998) 'Over- and under-education in the UK graduate labour market', *Studies in Higher Education*, 23 (1), 17–34.

Bach, S., Kolins Givan R. and Forth J. (2009) 'The public sector in transition', pp. 307–331 in W. Brown, A. Bryson, J. Forth and K. Whitfield (eds) *The Evolution of the Modern Workplace*, Cambridge: Cambridge University of Press, pp. 307–331.

Bell, D. and Blanchflower, D. (2013) 'Underemployment in the UK revisited', *National Institute Economic Review*, 224 (1), F8–F22.

Bernard, A. B., Redding, S. J. and Schott, P. K. (2010) 'Multi-product firms and product switching', *American Economic Review*, 100 (1), 70–97.

Bewley, H., Bryson, A., Forth, J. and Stokes, L. (2010) *Review of the Workplace Employment Relations Survey (WERS) 2004: Survey of Employees Questionnaire*, London: Department for Business, Innovation and Skills.

Black, C. (2008) *Working for a Healthier Tomorrow: Dame Carol Black's Review of the Health of Britain's Working Age Population*, London: The Stationary Office.

Black, C. and Frost, D. (2011) *Health at Work: An Independent Review of Sickness Absence*, London: The Stationary Office.

Blanchflower, D. G. and Bryson, A. (2009) 'Trade union decline and the economics of the workplace', pp. 48–73 in W. Brown, A. Bryson, J. Forth and K. Whitfield (eds) *The Evolution of the Modern Workplace*, Cambridge: Cambridge University Press, pp. 48–73.

Blanchflower, D. and Oswald, A. (2011) 'International happiness: a new view on the measure of performance', *Academy of Management Perspectives*, 25 (1), 6–22.

Bloom, N., Genakos, C., Sadun, R. and van Reenan, J. (2011a) *Management Practices Across Firms and Countries*, NBER Working Paper No. 17850, Cambridge, MA: National Bureau of Economic Research, http://www.nber.org/papers/w17850, accessed 18 June 2013.

Bloom, N., Lemos, R., Qi, M., Sadun, R. and van Reenen, J. (2011b) *Constraints on Developing UK Management Practices*, Research Paper No. 58, London: Department for Business, Innovation and Skills.

Boeri, T. and Bruecker, H. (2011) 'Short-time work benefits revisited: some lessons from the Great Recession', *Economic Policy*, 26 (68), 697–765.

Bozio, A. and Disney, R. (2011) 'Public sector pay and pensions', in M. Brewer, C. Emmerson and H. Miller (eds) *The IFS Green Budget 2011*, London: Institute for Fiscal Studies, pp. 163–191.

Bovil, D. (2013) *Patterns of Pay: Results from the Annual Survey of Hours and Earnings, 1997 to 2012*, Newport: Office for National Statistics.

Brignall, M. (2009) 'Welcome to pay-cut Britain', *Guardian*, 18 April http://www.guardian.co.uk/money/2009/apr/18/pay-cut-workers-recession, accessed 18 June 2013.

Broadbent, B. (2012) *Productivity and the Allocation of Resources*, Speech given at Durham Business School, 12 September, http://www.bankofengland.co.uk/publications/Documents/speeches/2012/speech599.pdf, accessed 30 June 2013.

Brown, D. and Reilly, P. (2009) 'HR in recession: What are the prospects and priorities for HR management in 2009?', *IES Opinion*, London: Institute for Employment Studies.

Brown, W., Bryson, J., Forth, J. and Whitfield, K. (2009a) *The Evolution of the Modern Workplace*, Cambridge: Cambridge University of Press.

Brown, W., Bryson, A. and Forth, J. (2009b) 'Competition and the retreat from collective bargaining', W. Brown, A. Bryson, J. Forth and K. Whitfield (eds) *The Evolution of the Modern Workplace*, Cambridge: Cambridge University Press, pp. 22–47.

Brown, W., Bryson, A. and John Forth Whitfield (2009c) 'Conclusion: the evolutionary process', in W. Brown, A. Bryson, J. Forth and K. Whitfield (eds) *The Evolution of the Modern Workplace*, Cambridge: Cambridge University Press, pp. 353–356.

Brown, W. and Edwards, P (2009d) 'Researching the changing workplace', in W. Brown, A. Bryson, J. Forth and K. Whitfield (eds) *The Evolution of the Modern Workplace*, Cambridge: Cambridge University Press, pp. 1–21.

Brown, A., Charlwood, A., Forde, C. and Spencer, D. (2007) 'Job quality and the economics of new Labour: A critical appraisal using subjective survey data', *Cambridge Journal of Economics*, 31, 941–971.

Brownlie, N. (2012) *Trade Union Membership 2011*, London: Department of Business, Innovation and Skills.

Bryan, M. (2012) 'Job-related stress, working time and work schedules', in S. L. McFall (ed.) *Understanding Society: Findings 2012*, Colchester: Institute for Social and Economic Research, University of Essex.

Bryson, A. (2004) 'Unions and workplace closure in Britain 1990–1998', *British Journal of Industrial Relations*, 42 (2), 283–302.

Bryson, A. (2005) 'Union effects on employee relations in Britain', *Human Relations*, 58 (9), 1111–1139.

Bryson, A. and White, M. (2006) *Unions, Within-Workplace Job Cuts and Job Security Guarantees*, Centre for Economic Performance Discussion Paper No. 733, London: London School of Economics, Centre for Economic Performance.

Bryson, A. and Dale-Olsen, H. (2008) *A Tale of Two Countries: Unions, Closures and Growth in Britain and Norway*, Centre for Economic Performance Discussion Paper No. 867, London: London School of Economics, Centre for Economic Performance.

Bryson, A., Barth, E. and Dale-Olsen, H. (2009a) *How Does Innovation Affect Worker Well-being?*, National Institute of Economic and Social Research Discussion Paper No. 348, London: National Institute of Economic and Social Research.

Bryson, A., Cappellari, L. and Lucifora, C. (2009b) 'Workers' perceptions of job insecurity: Do job security guarantees work?', *Labour*, 23 (s1), 177–196.

Bryson, A. and Forth, J. (2010a) 'The evolution of the modern worker: Attitudes to work', in A. Park, J. Curtice, E. Clery and C. Bryson (eds) *British Social Attitudes 27th Report: Exploring Labour's Legacy*, London: Sage, pp. 103–130.

Bryson, A. and Forth, J. (2010b) *Trade union membership and influence 1999–2009*, National Institute of Economic and Social Research Discussion Paper No. 362, London: National Institute of Economic and Social Research.

Bryson, A. and Forth, J. (2011) 'Trade unions', in P. Gregg and J. Wadsworth (eds) *The Labour Market in Winter: The State of Working Britain*, Oxford: Oxford University Press, pp. 255–271.

Bryson, A., Barth, E. and Dale-Olsen, H. (2012) 'Do higher wages come at a price?', *Journal of Economic Psychology*, 33 (1): 251–263.

Bryson, A. and Freeman, R. B. (2013) 'Employee perceptions of working conditions and the desire for worker representation in Britain and the US', *Journal of Labor Research*, 34 (1), 1–29.

Bryson, A., Forth, J. and Stokes, L. (2013a) *What Happens to Performance-Related Pay in Recession?*, London: National Institute for Economic and Social Research, mimeo.

Bryson, A., Freeman, R., Lucifora, C., Pellizzari, M. and Perotin, V. (2013b) 'Paying for performance: Incentive pay schemes and employees' financial participation', in T. Boeri, C. Lucifora and K. J. Murphy (eds) *Executive Remuneration and Employee Performance-related Pay: A Transatlantic Perspective*, Oxford: Oxford University Press, pp. 123–278.

Bryson, A., Willman, P., Gomez, R. and Kretschmer, T. (2013c) 'The comparative advantage of non-union voice in Britain: 1980–2004', *Industrial Relations*, 52 (s1), 194–220.

Budd, J. (2004) *Employment with a Human Face: Balancing Efficiency, Equity and Voice*, Ithaca, NY: Cornell University Press.

Cabinet Office. (2012) *Consultation on Reform to Trade Union Facility Time and Facilities in the Civil Service*, London: Cabinet Office.

Caves, R. E. (1998) 'Industrial organisation and new findings on the turnover and mobility of firms', *Journal of Economic Literature*, 36 (4), 1947–1982.

Charlwood, A. and Forth, J. (2009) 'Employee representation', in W. Brown, A. Bryson, J. Forth and K. Whitfield (eds) *The Evolution of the Modern Workplace*, Cambridge: Cambridge University Press, pp. 74–96.

Chevalier, A. (2003) 'Measuring over-education', *Economica*, 70 (279), 509–531.

CIPD (2010) *Employee Outlook: Year Review*, London: Chartered Institute of Personnel and Development.

Clark, A. E. (2011) 'Worker wellbeing in booms and busts', in P. Gregg and J. Wadsworth (eds) *The Labour Market in Winter: The State of Working Britain*, Oxford: Oxford University Press, pp. 128–143.

Clark, A. E., Diener, E., Georgellis, Y. and Lucas, R. E. (2008) 'Lags and leads in life satisfaction: A test of the baseline hypothesis', *The Economic Journal*, 118, F222–F243.

Clark, A., Oswald, A. and Warr, P. (1996) 'Is job satisfaction u-shaped in age?', *Journal of Occupational and Organisational Psychology*, 69 (1), 57–81.

Commission on Social Determinants of Health (2008) *Closing the Gap in a Generation: Health Equity Through Action on the Social Determinants of Health*, Geneva: World Health Organization.

Crawford, R., Emmerson, C., Phillips, D. and Tetlow, G. (2011) 'Public spending cuts: Pain shared?', in *The IFS Green Budget: February 2011*, London: Institute for Fiscal Studies.

Cully, M., Woodland, S., O'Reilly, A. and Dix, G. (1999) *Britain at Work: As Depicted by the 1998 Workplace Employee Relations Survey*, London: Routledge.

Dale-Olsen, H. (2006) 'Wages, fringe benefits and worker turnover', *Labour Economics*, 13 (1), 87–105.

Davies, P. and Freedland, M. (2007) *Towards a Flexible Labour Market: Labour Legislation and Regulation Since the 1990s*, Oxford: Oxford University Press.

Deepchand, K., Drever, E., Gilby, N., Prestage, Y., Purdon, S., Tipping, S. and Wood, M. (2013) *Workplace Employment Relations Study (WERS) 2011/12: Technical Report*, London: National Centre for Social Research.

Department for Business, Innovation and Skills (2011a) *Flexible, Effective, Fair: Promoting Economic Growth through a Strong and Efficient Labour Market*, London: Department for Business, Innovation and Skills.

Department for Business, Innovation and Skills (2011b) *Resolving Workplace Disputes: A Consultation*, January, London: Department for Business, Innovation and Skills.

Department for Business Innovation and Skills (2013) *Employment Law 2013: Progress on Reform*, London: Department for Business Innovation and Skills.

Department for Communities and Local Government (2013) *Taxpayer Funding of Trade Unions: Delivering Sensible Savings in Local Government*, London: Department for Communities and Local Government.

Dex, S. and Forth, J. (2009) 'Equality and diversity at work', in W. Brown, A. Bryson, J. Forth and K. Whitfield (eds) *The Evolution of the Modern Workplace*, Cambridge: Cambridge University Press, pp. 230–255.

Dickerson, A. and Green, F. (2012) 'Fears and realisations of employment insecurity', *Labour Economics*, 19 (2), 198–210.

Dix, G., Sisson, K. and Forth, J. (2009) 'Conflict at work: The changing pattern of disputes', in W. Brown, J. Bryson, J. Forth and K. Whitfield (eds) *The Evolution of the Modern Workplace*, Cambridge: Cambridge University of Press, pp. 176–200.

Dustmann, C., Ludsteck, J. and Schonberg, U. (2009) 'Revisiting the German wage structure', *The Quarterly Journal of Economics*, 124 (2), 843–881.

Eigen, Z. J. and Litwin, A. S. (2011) *Ducks and Decoys: Revisiting the Exit-Voice-Loyalty Framework in Assessing the Impact of a Workplace Dispute Resolution System*, Faculty Working Paper No. 8, Chicago, IL: Northwestern University School of Law, http://scholarlycommons.law.northwestern.edu/facultyworkingpapers/8, accessed 18 June 2013.

Commission of the European Communities (2002) *The European Social Dialogue: A Force for Innovation and Change*, COM(2002) 341, Brussels: Commission of the European Communities.

Faggio, G., Gregg, P. and Wadsworth, J. (2011) 'Job tenure and job turnover', in P. Gregg and J. Wadsworth (eds) *The Labour Market in Winter: The State of Working Britain*, Oxford: Oxford University Press, pp. 97–107.

Fairbrother, P. (2000) *Trade Unions at the Crossroads*. London: Mansell.

Felstead, A., Gallie, D., Green, F. and Inanc, H. (2013) *Skills at Work in Britain: First Findings from the Skills and Employment Survey 2012*, London: Centre for Learning and Life Chances in Knowledge Economies and Societies, Institute of Education.

Felstead, A., Green, F. and Jewson, J. (2012) 'An analysis of the impact of the 2008–9 recession on the provision of training in the UK', *Work, Employment and Society*, 26 (6), 968–986.

Fevre, R., Lewis, D., Robinson, A. and Jones, T. (2012) *Trouble at Work*, London: Bloomsbury.

Fitzner, G. (2006) *How Have Employees Fared? Recent UK Trends*, Employment Relations Research Series No. 56, London: Department of Trade and Industry.

Forth, J. (2013) *The Design and Administration of the 2011 Workplace Employment Relations Study*, available from the UK Data Service, University of Essex and University of Manchester, http://discover.ukdataservice. ac.uk/catalogue/?sn=7226&type=Data%20catalogue, accessed 18 June 2013.

Freeman, R. B. (1980) 'The exit-voice tradeoff in the labour market: unionism, job tenure, quits and separations', *The Quarterly Journal of Economics*, 94 (4), 643–73.

Freeman, R. and Lazear, E. (1995) 'An economic analysis of works councils', in J. Rogers and W. Streeck (eds) *Works Councils: Consultation, Representation and Cooperation in Industrial Relations*, Chicago, IL: University of Chicago Press, pp. 27–52.

Freeman, R. B. and Medoff, J. L. (1984) *What Do Unions Do?*, New York: Basic Books.

Geroski, P. A. and Gregg, P. (1997) *Coping with Recession: UK Company Performance in Adversity*, Cambridge: Cambridge University Press.

Gibbons, M. (2007) *A Review of Employment Dispute Resolution in Great Britain*, London: Department of Trade and Industry.

Green, F. (2006) *Demanding Work: The Paradox of Job Quality in the Affluent Economy*, Princeton, NJ: Princeton University Press.

Green, F. (2011) 'Job quality in Britain under the Labour government', in P. Gregg and J. Wadsworth (eds) *The Labour Market in Winter: The State of Working Britain*, Oxford: Oxford University Press.

Green, F. (2013) *Is Britain Such a Bad Place to Work? The Level and Dispersion of Job Quality in Comparative European Perspective*, Centre for Learning and Life Chances in Knowledge Economies and Societies Research Paper No. 40, London: Centre for Learning and Life Chances in Knowledge Economies and Societies, Institute of Education.

Green F., Felstead, A., Gallie, D. and Inanc, H. (2013) *Job-Related Well-Being in Britain: First Findings from the Skills and Employment Survey 2012*, London: Centre for

Learning and Life Chances in Knowledge Economies and Societies, Institute of Education.

Green, F., McIntosh, S. and Vignoles, A. (2002) 'The utilisation of education and skills: Evidence from Britain', *The Manchester School*, 70 (6), 792–811.

Green, F. and Tsitsianis, N. (2005) 'An investigation of national trends in job satisfaction in Britain and Germany', *British Journal of Industrial Relations*, 43 (3), 401–429.

Green, F. and Whitfield, K. (2009) 'Employees' experience of work', in W. Brown, A. Bryson, J. Forth and K. Whitfield (eds) *The Evolution of the Modern Workplace*, Cambridge: Cambridge University Press, pp. 201–229.

Gregg, P. and Wadsworth, J. (2011) *The Labour Market in Winter: The State of Working Britain*, Oxford: Oxford University Press.

Gregg, P. and Machin, S. (2012) *What a Drag: The Chilling Impact of Unemployment on Real Wages*, London: The Resolution Foundation.

Grell, M. and Sisson, K. (2005) *Has Consultation's Time Come?*, Acas Policy Discussion Paper No. 5, London: Acas.

Guest, D., Brown, W., Peccei, R. and Huxley, K. (2007) 'The study of trust and workplace partnership', in K. Whitfield and K. Huxley (eds) *Innovations in the 2004 Workplace Employment Relations Survey*, Cardiff: Cardiff University, pp. 38–54.

Guest, D. and Bryson, A. (2009) 'From industrial relations to human resource management: The changing role of the personnel function', in W. Brown, A. Bryson, J. Forth and K. Whitfield (eds) *The Evolution of the Modern Workplace*, Cambridge: Cambridge University Press, pp. 120–150.

Hall, M., Hutchinson, S., Purcell, J., Terry, M. and Parker, J. (2011) 'Promoting effective consultation? Assessing the impact of the ICE regulations', *British Journal of Industrial Relations*, 51 (2), 355–381.

Hall, M. and Purcell, J. (2012) *Voice and Participation in the Modern Workplace: Challenges and Prospects'*, Acas Future of Workplace Relations Discussion Paper, March, London: Acas.

Hawes, W. R. (2000) 'Setting the pace or running alongside? ACAS and the changing employment relationship', in B. Towers and W. Brown (eds) *Employment Relations in Britain: 25 Years of the Advisory, Conciliation and Arbitration Service*, Oxford: Blackwell, pp. 1–30.

Heery, E. and Nash, D. (2011) 'Trade union officers and collective conciliation: A secondary analysis', Research Paper 10/11, London: Acas.

Hirschman, A. (1970) *Exit, Voice, and Loyalty: Responses to Decline in Firms, Organisations and States*, Cambridge, MA: Harvard University Press.

Inanc, H., Felstead, A., Gallie, D. and Green, F. (2013) *Job Control in Britain: First Findings from the Skills and Employment Survey 2012*, London: Centre for Learning and Life Chances in Knowledge Economies and Societies, Institute of Education.

Incomes Data Services. (2009) *IDS Focus on Recession*, London: Incomes Data Services.

Incomes Data Services. (2011) *Has a Blanket of Pay Freezes Suddenly Engulfed the UK?* London: Incomes Data Services, http://idseye.com/2011/08/03/has-a-blanket-of-pay-freezes-suddenly-engulfed-the-uk/#more-863, accessed 18 June 2013.

Insolvency Service. (2012) *Insolvencies in the Fourth Quarter 2011*, London: Department for Business, Innovation and Skills, http://www.insolvency direct. bis.gov.uk/otherinformation/statistics/201202/, accessed 18 June 2013.

Jann, B. (2008) 'The Blinder-Oaxaca decomposition for linear regression models', *The Stata Journal*, 8 (4), 453–479.

Kahn-Freund, O. (1972) *Labour and the Law*, London: Hamlyn Trust.

Karasek, R. A. (1979) 'Job demands, job decision latitude, and mental strain: Implications for job redesign', *Administrative Science Quarterly*, 24 (2), 285–308.

Kelly, J. (1998) *Rethinking Industrial Relations: Mobilisation, Collectivism and Long Waves*, London: Routledge, pp. 62–82.

Kelly, J. (2004) 'Social partnership agreements in Britain: Labour cooperation and compliance', *Industrial Relations*, 43 (1), 267–292.

Kelly, J. (2005) 'Social movement theory and union revitalization in Britain', in S. Fernie and D. Metcalf (eds) *Trade Unions: Resurgence or Demise?*, London and New York: Taylor & Francis, pp. 62–82.

Kersley, B., Alpin, C., Forth, J., Bryson, A., Bewley, H., Dix, G. and Oxenbridge, S. (2006) *Inside the Workplace: Findings from the 2004 Workplace Employment Relations Survey*, London: Routledge.

Knight, K. G. and Latreille, P. L. (2000). 'Discipline, dismissals and complaints to Employment Tribunals', *British Journal of Industrial Relations*, 38 (4), 533–555.

Kochan, T. (2003) *Restoring Trust in the Human Resource Management Profession*, Paper Presented at the Celebration of 50 Years of Industrial Relations Teaching and Research at the University of Sydney, November 2003, Cambridge, MA: MIT Sloan Institute for Work and Employment Research, *mimeo*.

Kruse, D., Freeman, R. B. and Blasi, J. (2010) *Shared Capitalism at Work: Employee Ownership, Profit and Gain Sharing, and Broad-based Stock Options*, Chicago, IL: University of Chicago Press.

Lambert, R. (2010) *The Labour Market and Employment Relations Beyond the Recession*, Warwick Papers in Industrial Relations No. 93, Coventry: Industrial Relations Research Unit, University of Warwick.

Layard, R. (2009) *Why Subjective Well-Being Should Be the Measure of Progress*, OECD World Forum on Statistics, Knowledge and Policy – Charting Progress, Building Visions, Improving Life, Busan, Korea, 27–30 October. http://cep.lse.ac.uk/textonly/_new/staff/layard/pdf//OECDBusan12Oct09.pdf, accessed 29 July 2013.

Layard, R. (2011) *Happiness: Lessons from a New Science*, 2nd edn, London and New York: Penguin Books.

Levy, S. (2013) 'Changes in real earnings in the UK and London, 2002 to 2012', London: Office for National Statistics, http://www.ons.gov.uk/ons/dcp171766_299377.pdf, accessed 18 June 2013.

Lorber, P. (2006) 'Implementing the Information and Consultation Directive in Great Britain: A new voice at work' *International Journal of Comparative Labour Law and Industrial Relations*, 22 (2), 231–258.

Machin, S. (1995) 'Plant closures and unionisation in British establishments', *British Journal of Industrial Relations*, 33 (1), 55–68.

Machin, S. (2003) 'New workplaces, new workers: Trade union decline in the new economy', in H. Gospel and S. Wood (eds) *Representing Workers: Union Recognition and Membership in Britain*, London: Routledge, pp. 15–28.

Machin, S. (2011) 'Changes in UK wage inequality over the last forty years', in P. Gregg and J. Wadsworth (eds) *The Labour Market in Winter: The State of Working Britain*, Oxford: Oxford University Press, pp. 155–169.

MacLeod, D. and Clarke, N. (2009) *Engaging for Success: Enhancing Performance Through Employee Engagement*, London: Department of Business Innovation and Skills.

McConaghy, M., van Wanrooy, B. and Wood, S. (2010) *Report for the Consultation for the Workplace Employment Relations Survey (WERS6)*, London: Department for Business, Innovation and Skills.

McManus, S. and Perry, J. (2012) 'Hard work? Employment, work–life balance and wellbeing in a changing economy', in A. Park, E. Clery, J. Curtice, M. Phillips and D. Utting (eds) *British Social Attitudes: The 29th Report*, London: NatCen, pp. 99–115.

Millward, N., Bryson, A. and Forth, J. (2000) *All Change at Work?*, London: Routledge.

Milner, S. (1995) 'The coverage of collective pay-setting institutions in Britain, 1895–1990', *British Journal of Industrial Relations*, 33 (1), 69–91.

Ministry of Justice. (2012) 'Employment Tribunal statistical tables', London: Ministry of Justice. Published online at: https://www.gov.uk/government/publications/employment-tribunal-and-employment-appeal-tribunal-statistics-gb, accessed 21 May 2012.

Mishel, L. (2013) *Vast Majority of Wage Earners Are Working Harder, and Not for Much More: Trends in US Work Hours and Wages Over 1979–2007*, Briefing No. 348, Washington, DC: Economic Policy Institute.

Mishel, L., Bivens, J., Gould, E. and Shierholz, H. (2012) *The State of Working America*, Washington, DC: Economic Policy Institute and Ithaca, NY: Cornell University.

Moore, S. (2013) 'Ten years of statutory recognition: A changed landscape for UK industrial relations?', *Centre for Employment Studies Review*, Bristol: Centre for Employment Studies University of the West of England, January.

Moore, S. and McKay, S. with Veale, S. (2013) *Statutory Regulation and Employment Relations: The Impact of Statutory Trade Union Recognition*, Basingstoke: Palgrave Macmillan.

Mullholland, H. and Gabbatt, A. (2010) 'Boris Johnson calls for new laws to curb strikes', *Guardian*, 4 October.

NatCen (2011a) *Workplace Employment Relations Study 2011 (WERS6) Editors' Codebook: Main Stage*, http://discover.ukdataservice.ac.uk/catalogue/?sn=7226&type=Data%20 catalogue, accessed 18 June 2013.

NatCen (2011b) *Workplace Employment Relations Study 2011 (WERS6) Stage 2: Editing Instructions for the Office Edit*, http://discover.ukdataservice.ac.uk/catalogue/?sn=7226&type=Data%20catalogue, accessed 18 June 2013.

NatCen (2011c) *Workplace Employment Relations Study 2011 (WERS6) Stage 3: Researcher Checks*, http://discover.ukdataservice.ac.uk/catalogue/?sn=7226&type=Data%20 catalogue, accessed 18 June 2013.

Office for National Statistics (2009) *UK Standard Industrial Classification of Economic Activities 2007 (SIC 2007)*, Basingstoke: Palgrave Macmillan.

Office for National Statistics (2011a) *Hours Worked in the Labour Market, 2011*, Newport: Office for National Statistics, December.

Office for National Statistics (2011b) *The Inter-Departmental Business Register*, http://www.ons.gov.uk/ons/about-ons/who-we-are/services/idbr/about-the-idbr/index.html, accessed 18 June 2013.

Office for National Statistics (2012a) *Real Wages up 62% on Average Over the Past 25 Years*, Newport: Office for National Statistics, http://www.ons.gov.uk/ons/dcp171776_286266.pdf, accessed 18 June 2013.

Office for National Statistics (2012b) *LABD01: Labour Disputes in Labour Market Statistics Data Tables*, Newport: Office for National Statistics.

Office for National Statistics (2013) *Redundancies: Level and Rates, Statistical Bulletin*, Newport: Office for National Statistics.

Park, A., Clery, E., Curtice, J., Phillips, M. and Utting, D. (2012) *British Social Attitudes: The 29th Report*, London: NatCen.

Patterson, P. (2012) *The Productivity Conundrum, Explanations and Preliminary Analysis*, Newport: Office for National Statistics, 16 October.

Payne, R. L. (1979) 'Demands, supports, constraints and psychological health', in C. J. Mackay and T. Cox (eds) *In Response to Stress: Occupational Aspects*, London: IPC Business Press, pp. 85–105.

Pendleton, A., Whitfield, K. and Bryson, A. (2009) 'The changing use of contingent pay in the modern British workplace', in W. Brown, A. Bryson, J. Forth and K. Whitfield (eds) *The Evolution of the Modern Workplace*, Cambridge: Cambridge University Press, pp. 256–284.

Pensions Commission. (2011) *Independent Public Service Pensions Commission Final Report*, London: Pensions Commission.

Pessoa, J. P. and Van Reenen, J. (2013) *The UK Productivity and Jobs Puzzle: Does the Answer Lie in Labour Market Flexibility?*, Centre for Economic Performance Special Paper No. 31, June, London: London School of Economics, Centre for Economic Performance.

Philpott, J. (2012) 'Age, gender and the jobs recession', *CIPD Work Audit*, April, Issue 43, London: CIPD

Pissarides, C. A. (2013) *Unemployment in the Great Recession*, Centre for Economic Performance Paper Discussion Paper 1210, London: London School of Economics, Centre for Economic Performance.

Podro, S. (2010) *Riding Out the Storm: Managing Conflict in a Recession and Beyond*, Policy Discussion Paper, March, London: Acas.

Rahim, N., Brown, A., Graham, J. (2011) *Evaluation of the Acas Code of Practice on Disciplinary and Grievance Procedures*, Research Paper Ref 06/11, London: Acas.

Ranieri, N. (2011) *Collective Consultation on Redundancies*, Policy Discussion Paper, London: Acas.

Rayton, B., Dodge, T. and D'Analeze, G. (2012) *The Evidence: Engagement Task Force 'Nailing the Evidence' Workgroup*, London: Engaging for Success.

Roche, W. K. and Teague, P. (forthcoming 2013) 'Do recessions transform work and employment? Evidence from Ireland', *British Journal of Industrial Relations*.

Rosen, S. (1986) 'The theory of equalizing differences', in O. Ashenfelter and R. Layard (eds) *Handbook of Labor Economics, Vol. 1*, Amsterdam: Elsevier, pp. 641–692.

Russell, H. and McGinnity, F. (forthcoming 2013) 'Under pressure: The impact of recession on employees in Ireland', *British Journal of Industrial Relations*.

Saundry, R. and Dix, G. (forthcoming 2014) 'Conflict management in the United Kingdom', in W. K. Roche, P. Teague and A. Colvin (eds) *Oxford Handbook of Conflict Management in Organizations*, Oxford: Oxford University Press.

Scott, A. and Woodman, P. (2009) 'Honda workers return after four-month shutdown', *The Independent*, 1 June, http://www.independent.co.uk/news/business/news/honda-workers-return-after-fourmonth-shut-down-1694047.html, accessed 25 June 2013.

Smith, S. and Harwood, P. (2011) 'Social media and its impact on employers and trade unions', *Employment Relations Comment*, London: Acas.

Stiglitz, J., Sen, A. and Fitoussi, J. P. (2009) 'Report by the Commission on the Measurement of Economic Performance and Social Progress', http://www.stiglitz-sen-fitoussi.fr/documents/rapport_anglais.pdf, accessed 18 June 2013.

Theodossiou, I. (1996) *A Model of the Causes of Leaving Employment: Or Who Experiences the Highest Risk of Job Termination?*, Department of Economics Discussion Paper 96–20, Aberdeen: Department of Economics, University of Aberdeen.

Towers, B. (1997) *The Representation Gap: Change and Reform in the British and American Workplace*, Oxford: Oxford University Press.

UK Data Service (2011a) *About Secure Access: What You Need to Know Before Joining Our Community of Trusted Researchers*, http://ukdataservice.ac.uk/get-data/secure-access/about.aspx#/tab-what-is-secure-access, accessed 18 June 2013.

UK Data Service (2011b) *WERS 2011*, http://discover.ukdataservice.ac.uk/catalogue/?sn=7226&type=Data%20catalogue, accessed 18 June 2013.

Unionlearn with the TUC (2010) *Learning for Life: Annual Conference Report 2010*, London: Unionlearn.

van Wanrooy, B., Bewley, H., Bryson, A., Forth, J., Freeth, S., Stokes, L. and Wood, S. (2013) *The 2011 Workplace Employment Relations Study: First Findings*, London: Department for Business, Innovation and Skills.

Wakeling, A. (2010) 'Representation: Finding its voice', *Employment Relations Comment*, December, London: Acas.

Warr, P. (2007) *Work, Happiness, and Unhappiness*, London: Taylor & Francis.

Warr, P., Bindl, U. K., Parker, S. K. and Inceoglu, I. (forthcoming 2013) 'Four-Quadrant Investigation of Job-Related Affects and Behaviours', *European Journal of Work and Organizational Psychology*.

Webb, T. (2009) 'Part-time, part-pay: How firms are cutting workers' hours', *The Guardian*, 13 March.

White, M., Hills, S., Mills, C. and Smeaton, D. (2004) *Managing to Change? British Workplaces and the Future of Work*, Basingstoke: Palgrave Macmillan.

Whitener, E., Brodt, S., Korsgaard, M. and Werner, J. (1998) 'Managers as initiators of trust: An exchange relationship framework for understanding managerial trustworthy behaviour', *Academy of Management Review*, 23 (3), 513–530.

Willman, P., Gomez, R. and Bryson, A. (2009) 'Voice at work', in W. Brown, A. Bryson, J. Forth and K. Whitfield (eds) *The Evolution of the Modern Workplace*, Cambridge: Cambridge University Press, pp. 120–150.

Wood, S. (2005) 'Overview of the impact of employment relations law: Post-1997', in L. Dickens, M. Hall and S. Wood, *Review of research into the impact of employment relations legislation, Employment Relations Research Series No. 45*, London: Department of Trade and Industry, pp. 73–127.

Wood, S. (2008) 'Job characteristics, employee voice and well-being in Britain', *Industrial Relations Journal*, 39 (2), 153–168.

Wood, S. and Bryson, A. (2009) 'High involvement management', in W. Brown, A. Bryson, J. Forth and K. Whitfield (eds) *The Evolution of the Modern Workplace*, Cambridge: Cambridge University Press, pp. 151–175.

Wood, S. and Moore, S. (2004) 'Crafting a statutory union recognition procedure that works for the UK', in A. Verma and T. A. Kochan (eds) *Unions in the 21st Century: An International Perspective*, Basingstoke, UK: Palgrave Macmillan, pp. 75–90.

Wood, S., van Veldoven, M., Croon, M. and De Menezes, L. M. (2012) 'Enriched job design, high involvement management and organizational performance: The mediating roles of job satisfaction and well-being', *Human Relations*, 65 (4), 419–446.

Index